REA's Test Prep Books

(a sample of the <u>hundreds of letters</u> REA receives each year)

" The [REA *AP Psychology* test prep] is great for independent study for the exam. I gained test confidence and a positive attitude from this book. "

AP Psychology Student, Jackson, MS

" I'd buy it if I were you. "

AP Psychology Student, North Hollywood, CA

" My students report your chapters of review as the most valuable single resource they used for review and preparation. "

Teacher, American Fork, UT

" Your book was such a better value and was so much more complete than anything your competition has produced — and I have them all! "

Teacher, Virginia Beach, VA

" Your book was responsible for my success on the exam, which helped me get into the college of my choice... I will look for REA the next time I need help. "

Student, Chesterfield, MO

" Just a short note to say thanks for the great support your book gave me in helping me pass the test... I'm on my way to a B.S. degree because of you! "

Student, Orlando, FL

(more on next page)

(continued from front page)

" I just wanted to thank you for helping me get a great score on the AP U.S. History exam... Thank you for making great test preps! "
Student, Los Angeles, CA

" Your *Fundamentals of Engineering Exam* book was the absolute best preparation I could have had for the exam, and it is one of the major reasons I did so well and passed the FE on my first try. "
Student, Sweetwater, TN

" I used your book to prepare for the test and found that the advice and the sample tests were highly relevant... Without using any other material, I earned very high scores and will be going to the graduate school of my choice. "
Student, New Orleans, LA

" What I found in your book was a wealth of information sufficient to shore up my basic skills in math and verbal... The section on analytical ability was excellent. The practice tests were challenging and the answer explanations most helpful. It certainly is the *Best Test Prep for the GRE!* "
Student, Pullman, WA

" I really appreciate the help from your excellent book. Please keep up the great work. "
Student, Albuquerque, NM

" I am writing to thank you for your test preparation... your book helped me immeasurably and I have nothing but praise for your *GRE* preparation."
Student, Benton Harbor, MI

(more on back page)

THE BEST TEST PREPARATION FOR THE

ADVANCED PLACEMENT
EXAMINATION

PSYCHOLOGY

Staff of Research & Education Association
Dr. M. Fogiel, Director

Research & Education Association
61 Ethel Road West • Piscataway, New Jersey 08854

The Best Test Preparation for the
ADVANCED PLACEMENT EXAMINATION
IN PSYCHOLOGY

Printed in the United States of America

Library of Congress Control Number 00-130647

International Standard Book Number 0-87891-883-3

Research & Education Association
61 Ethel Road West
Piscataway, New Jersey 08854

REA supports the effort to conserve and
protect environmental resources by
printing on recycled papers.

CONTENTS

About Research & Education Association

Research & Education Association (REA) is an organization of educators, scientists, and engineers specializing in various academic fields. Founded in 1959 with the purpose of disseminating the most recently developed scientific information to groups in industry, government, and universities, REA has since become a successful and highly respected publisher of study aids, test preps, handbooks, and reference works.

REA's test preparation series includes study guides for all academic levels in almost all disciplines. Research & Education Association publishes test preps for students who have not yet completed high school, as well as high school students preparing to enter college. Students from countries around the world seeking to attend college in the United States will find the assistance they need in REA's publications. For college students seeking advanced degrees, REA publishes test preps for many major graduate school admission examinations in a wide variety of disciplines, including engineering, law, and medicine. Students at every level, in every field, with every ambition can find what they are looking for among REA's publications.

Whereas most test preparation books present only a few practice tests which bear little resemblance to the actual exams, REA's series presents tests which accurately depict the official exams in both degree of difficulty and types of questions. REA's practice tests are always based upon the format of the most recently administered exams, and include every type of question that can be expected on the actual exams.

REA's publications and educational materials are highly regarded and continually receive an unprecedented amount of praise from professionals, instructors, librarians, parents, and students. Our authors are as diverse as the subjects represented in the books we publish. They are well-known in their respective disciplines and serve on the faculties of prestigious high schools, colleges, and universities throughout the United States and Canada.

Acknowledgments

We would like to thank Dr. Max Fogiel, President, for his overall guidance, which brought this publication to completion; Larry B. Kling, Quality Control Manager of Books in Print, for supervision of revisions; Margaret Muckenhoupt for her research and compilation of the Advanced Placement course review material; Kristin Rutkowski, Project Manager, and Jennifer Payulert, Editorial Assistant, for their editorial contributions; Angela Nelson and Scott Miller for ensuring the book's conformity with DSM IV; and Wende Solano for typesetting the book.

Introduction

ABOUT THE BOOK

This book provides an accurate and complete representation of the Advanced Placement Examination in Psychology. The three practice exams and comprehensive review are based on the actual AP Psychology exam. Each exam takes two hours to complete and includes every type of question that may appear on the actual exam. Following each exam is an answer key complete with detailed explanations designed to clarify the material to the student.

By studying the review section, completing all three exams, and studying the answer explanations, students can discover their strengths and weaknesses, and prepare themselves for the AP Psychology examination.

ABOUT THE TEST

The Advanced Placement program is designed to allow high school students to pursue college-level studies while attending high school. The exam will be administered to high school students who have completed a year of study in a college-level psychology course. The results are then used for determining course credit and/or placement in college.

The Advanced Placement Psychology course is designed to represent college-level psychology studies. Students are expected to leave the course with a college-level understanding of various approaches to psychology, types of research in psychology, the facets of human behavior and cognition, and the treatment of various disorders. This course is intended for highly motivated students with an interest in psychology.

The exam is divided into two sections:

1. Multiple-choice:

This section is composed of 100 multiple-choice questions designed to measure the student's knowledge of psychology. The questions cover a wide variety of topics studied in the course. The student has 70 minutes to complete this section of the exam, which counts for two-thirds of the final grade.

2. Free response:

This section is composed of two essay questions designed to measure the student's analytical, organizational, and writing skills, as well as his or her background in psychology. The student has 50 minutes to complete this section. This section counts for one-third of the final grade.

ABOUT THE REVIEW SECTIONS

This book begins with a comprehensive review of psychology which is designed to give the student an idea of what type of information can be found on the AP exam. The review discusses the following psychological concepts and definitions in depth:

1. **Introduction**
   Including: history, approaches, methods, and careers in psychology

2. **Biological Bases of Behavior**
   Including: studies of the brain, the nervous system, the endocrine system, genetics, and nature vs. nurture

3. **Sensation and Perception**

4. **Cognition**
   Including: studies of memory, thinking, and language

5. **States of Consciousness**
   Including: sleep and dreaming, hypnosis, meditation, and psychoactive drugs

6. **Learning**

   Including: examples of classical and operant conditioning

7. **Intelligence**

   Including: the heredity vs. environment argument and measure of intelligence

8. **Motivation and Emotion**

   Including: drives and instincts, incentives, social learning, arousal, romantic love, and stress

9. **Developmental Psychology**

   Including: infancy and childhood through adolescence, to adulthood and later life, and sex roles and differences

10. **Personality**

    Including: psychoanalytic theory, trait theory, humanistic approaches, behavioral theories, biological studies, and personality assessments

11. **Social Psychology**

    Including: studies on conformity, compliance and obedience, group dynamics, aggression, and organizational behavior

12. **Abnormal Psychology**

    Including: history and definition, types of disorders and an introduction to the Diagnostic Statistical Manual (DSM)

13. **Treatment of Psychological Disorders**

    Including: psychodynamics, behavioral, cognitive, biological, and humanistic approaches and types of therapy

SCORING THE EXAM

The multiple-choice section of the exam is scored by crediting each incorrect answer with one point and deducting one-fourth of a point for each incorrect answer. Unanswered questions receive neither a credit nor a deduction.

The free-response essays are evaluated by psychology instructors and professors. The two essays are weighted equally and the total weight of the free-response section accounts for one-third of the total score. The multiple-choice section constitutes two-thirds of the total score.

Your score on the multiple-choice section and your grade on the free-response section are combined and converted to the program's five-point scale:

5—extremely well-qualified
4—well-qualified
3—qualified
2—possibly qualified
1—no recommendation

Colleges participating in the Advanced Placement Program usually recognize grades of 3 or higher.

Rule of Thumb: Examinees who perform acceptably on the free-response section of the test generally need to answer correctly between 50 and 60 percent of the multiple-choice questions to get a total grade of 3.

AP Psychology Study Schedule

It is important for you to discover the time and place for studying that works best for you. Some students may set aside a certain number of hours every morning to study, while others may choose to study at night before going to sleep. Other students may study during the day, while still others may study while waiting in a line. Only you will be able to know when and where your studying is most effective. The most important factor to keep in mind is consistency. Use your time wisely. Work out a study routine and stick to it.

You will find below a suggested six week study schedule. You may want to follow a schedule similar to this one. (Depending on how long before the exam you begin to study, you may want to add to this schedule, condense it, or reorganize it.)

Week	Activity
1	Study chapters 1 through 4. As you study, notice that the bolded words are defined in the text. Because there are so many of them, you may want to design a flashcard study system. Write the word on one side and the definition on the other. You can test yourself or study with a friend. This will help you to remember key terms and will refresh your memory as you learn more and more terms throughout later chapters. Be sure to also practice the mini-exercises at the end of each chapter. These will help you to evaluate your comprehension.

Week	Activity
2	Study chapters 5 through 9 in the same manner. Draw up flash cards to test your retention of key definitions and concepts. Take the quiz at the end of each chapter.
3	Study chapters 10-13 continuing again in the same manner. Draw up flash cards to test your retention of key definitions and concepts. Take the quiz at the end of each chapter.
4	Take Practice Test 1. Study the explanations. Do you notice that you incorrectly answer questions on a specific topic, such as personality or abnormal psychology? If so, make note of this and restudy those topics.
5	Take Practice Test 2. Compare your score to your score in Test 1. Has your score improved? Concentrate on studying those areas in which you need strengthening. Re-read the appropriate chapters .
6	Take Practice Test 3. Re-read any material about which you still feel unsure; refer to your flashcards as needed. By now, you should feel confident in your ability to do well on your AP Psychology exam. You may want to retake one or two tests if your time schedule permits.

ADVANCED PLACEMENT EXAMINATION IN
PSYCHOLOGY

Course Review

Chapter 1

Introduction to Psychology

WHAT IS PSYCHOLOGY?

Psychology is the scientific discipline devoted to the study of mental processes and behavior. Its goal is to measure, predict, and explain behavior. Some psychologists also describe psychology as the study of experience, or an organism's "internal" activities. Other psychologists believe that "experience" cannot be systematically studied. There are many varied approaches to the study of behavior, making psychology a rich and complex field.

Over time, psychology has acquired many definitions. Psychology was once considered to be the study of the mind. Researchers have come to agree that the mind is neither entirely open to study, nor very well defined. The mind can only be observed through the behavior it causes, but what this "mind" is and how it "causes" behavior has never been clearly defined.

Behavior refers to any action or reaction of a living organism which can be observed. Psychologists study all levels of behavior. Some psychologists focus on the biology of behavior, such as the actions of nerve cells, genetics, or sweat glands. Other psychologists study higher level behaviors, such as aggression, prejudice, or problem solving.

The key to the definition of behavior is that behavior is observable. Behavior refers to overt movement, activity, or action. Some behaviors are more observable than others. For instance, any bystander can see aggressive behavior on a city street. However, more subtle behavior, such as the change in brain waves when a person takes LSD, may require special equipment to be observed.

Psychologists do not want merely to describe behavior: they wish to predict and understand it. To do this, they have set forth four fundamental factors of behavior: the organism, motivation, knowledge, and competence.

The **organism** refers to the biological characteristics of a living biological entity, including the creature's nervous system, endocrine system, biological history, and heredity. **Motivation** entails the states which cause behavior. These are the immediate forces that act to energize, direct, sustain, and stop a behavior. The term is vague, but motivation generally includes the organism's internal state, e.g., tired, confused, and the behavior related to this state, e.g., searching for a warm den. Some psychologists include the goal of a behavior (e.g., rest) in their descriptions of motivation, though others deny that behavior has a goal. The term **cognition** refers to "knowledge," that is, what and how the organism thinks, knows, and remembers. For example, a contestant on a television game show who must choose which of three boxes she wants for a prize may base her decision on how big each box is, how much she trusts the game show host, and so on. Her guesses at the location of the prize, her reasoning about the estimation of the size of the boxes, and her memory of the host's past performance all make up her cognition. She does not know what is actually in the boxes. The contents of the boxes are not part of her cognition. **Competence** means the skills and abilities of an organism. How well can it perform a certain task? Does a rat have the physical ability to jump to the top of its cage? Does the college sophomore have the skill at fast writing and the physical stamina to finish her term paper on time? These are questions of competence.

Psychology is not as simple as it may first appear. Psychologists today study many other scientific fields such as biology, physics, chemistry, and linguistics, as well as other social sciences like sociology, anthropology, economics, and political science. To evaluate behavior, a psychologist should be familiar with all of these areas.

HISTORY OF PSYCHOLOGY

Since the beginning of thought, humans have asked psychological questions, such as, How do we experience the world around us? What is the relationship between the way we experience the world and how our bodies function, like the way food loses its taste when we are sick? How do we learn and what accounts for differences in behavior and temperament among people?

The science of psychology, like physics, chemistry, and biology, began in philosophy. Ancient Greek philosophers first observed and interpreted their environment, and organized their findings. Aristotle, in his *Poetics,* discussed the nature of sensory perception; in *The Republic,* Socrates and Plato explored the way government can influence individual behavior.

These philosophers were the first Europeans to reason that human beings have, in addition to a physical body, some kind of apparatus used for thinking. They called this thinking apparatus the **psyche.** Over the centuries, this word has meant such things as "soul," "form," and "function." The most popular equivalent evolved into "mind." The suffix "-ology" means "the study of." Thus, for many centuries psychology was considered to be the study of the mind.

The mind was an entity or structure with no physical substance. What, they asked, is the relationship between the mind and body? The French philosopher Rene Descartes (1596–1650) was very interested in this "mind-body" problem. He firmly believed in dualism, which states that humans have a dual nature — one part mental and the other physical. This is in contrast to "monism," which holds that only one type of nature exists.

In the eighteenth century, philosophers described the various functions of the mind as independent faculties. Every mental activity, such as loving, reading, or long division, was viewed as the work of a particular area of the mind. Any behavior could be explained by attributing it to the function of its respective faculty. This approach led to many explanations of behavior. It is easy to attribute a friend's hot temper to her "aggression faculty," but calling your friend's behavior a name does not explain it.

Certain scientists in the early nineteenth century tried to analyze the mind by examining the shape of the skull, a study called phrenology. (By this time, scientists commonly agreed that the mind was inside the head, as opposed to the heart or liver, two other popular spots.) Lumps in the skull were linked to faculties. For example, if a generous person had a very large lump on her head, that region of the skull would be labelled the "generosity" region of the mind.

By 1850, European laboratories were systematically experimenting with questions of perception, neural conduction, and other aspects of physiological psychology. Gustav Fechner (1801–1887) published a book titled *Elemente der Psychophysik* (Elements of Psychophysics), which detailed the measurement of sensory experiences. In 1879, Wilhelm Wundt (1832–1920) established the first laboratory solely devoted to psychology in Leipzig, Germany; the Johns Hopkins University started the first U.S. psychology lab in 1883.

Major Schools of Thought

By the late 1800s, psychology had become empirical and left the realm of mere fanciful philosophy forever. In organizing and explaining their observations, psychologists created eight major schools of thought: structuralism, functionalism, gestalt, and biological, cognitive, humanistic, and psychodynamic theories. There are many other branches of psychological study: social, educational, developmental, and so on. These are merely the theories which have had the greatest impact on psychology as a whole.

Structuralism, the first theoretical school in psychology, derived from Wundt's work. Wundt believed that the science of psychology should study the conscious mind. Influenced by the physical scientists of his time, Wundt embraced the atomic theory of matter. This theory stated that all complex substances could be separated and analyzed into component elements. Wundt wished to divide the mind into mental elements. This approach came to be called structuralism.

To analyze mental elements, Wundt used an experimental method called introspection. Subjects reported the contents of their own minds as objectively as possible, usually in connection with stimuli such as light, sound, or odors. The subjects verbal reports were analyzed to see the number and types of "mental elements" they contained. Subjects were specially trained to give elaborate reports.

The major drawback of structuralism was that it focused on the internal structure and activity of the mind, rather than overt, objectively observable behavior. Subjective reports of the mind's activities are easily manipulated by both the subject and the experimenter, and they are unreliable. Psychologists today are still concerned with internal activities, but are primarily interested in how these activities influence behavior.

While structuralist psychologists were busy asking their subjects to describe mental images, **functionalists** examined behavior from a different point of view. While structuralists were concerned with what the mind is, functionalists were asking what the mind does, and why. Functionalists were inspired by Darwin's theory of evolution; they believed that all behavior and mental processes help organisms to adapt to a changing environment. They expanded their studies beyond perception to include questions of learning, motivation, and problem solving. Functionalist William James (1842–1910) coined the phrase "stream of consciousness" to describe the way the mind experiences perception and thought as a constant flow of sensation.

Functionalists did not reject the structuralists' introspection, but they preferred to observe both the stream of consciousness and behavior. The functionalists' most important contribution to psychology was the introduction of the concept of learning, and thus adaptation to the environment, to psychological study. The most influential proponents of functionalism were William James and educational psychologist John Dewey (1859–1952).

Soon, psychologists tired of introspection's dainty ways. **Behaviorism,** as developed by John B. Watson (1878–1958), swept the United States at the turn of the century. Watson rejected the idea of the "mind," stating that this structure not only could not be objectively studied, but did not even exist! Instead, Watson presented behavior as consisting of the stimulus, a "black box" which processed the stimuli, and the response the "black box" produced. Nothing could be said about the "black box" apart from the behavior it regulated. Watson also disregarded introspection, asserting that only observations of outward behavior could provide valid psychological data. He stated that the major component of psychological study should be the identification of relationships between stimuli (environment) and responses (behavior).

While structuralists believed that the mind could be divided into mental/experiential elements, behaviorists believed that all behavior could be broken down into a collection of conditioned responses. These conditioned responses (CRs) were simple learned responses to stimuli. All human behavior was supposed to be the result of learning. According to this theory, everyone could become lawyers, murderers, or trapeze artists, if only they were given the correct training.

Behaviorists have also studied animal behavior extensively. Many held that there was no difference between human and animal behavior, and several tried to formulate general theories of behavior based on animal experiments. Leaders of this school, prominent in the late 1930s and 1940s, include Edward C. Tolman (1886–1959), Clark L. Hull (1884–1952), and Edwin R. Guthrie (1886–1949).

Behaviorism is still an active, vibrant branch of psychology. Its rigorous experimentation and emphasis on actual behavior has proved useful, especially in treating difficult groups such as institutionalized and mentally retarded patients.

Gestalt psychology, though, survives only as a name for a collection of theories. Like functionalism and behaviorism, gestalt psychology was a reaction to structuralism. It was founded in Germany in 1912 by Max Wertheimer (1880–1943). The word "gestalt" has no exact equivalent in English, but its meaning is similar to "form," or "organization." Gestalt psychologists emphasized the organizational processes in behavior, rather than the content of behavior. Like the structuralists, gestalt psychologists mainly focused on problems of perception.

Unlike the reductionist structuralists and functionalists, gestaltists believed that behavior and experiences consisted of patterns and organized sets. Like many physical scientists, gestalt psychologists believed the whole is more than the sum of its parts. A series of lines shows a picture, jumbled notes become a song; the mind constantly organizes perception into unified wholes.

Gestalt psychologists stressed **phenomenology,** or the study of natural, unanalyzed perception, as the basis for behavior. They instructed untrained subjects to introspect without structuralist elaboration on their experience. However, they studied other problems as well, particularly those involving learning, thought, and problem solving. W. Kohler (1887–1967) argued that learning and problem solving were organizational processes like perception. He described the "moment of insight" for an individual as when the solution to a problem suddenly crystallizes as a whole gestalt out of reasoning, intuition, etc.

Many of the gestaltists' observations about perception are still being explored. Current cognitive psychologists draw heavily on their ideas, particularly when dealing with questions of vision and information processing. How much information does a person need before she can figure out what she is seeing? What are the most important, salient parts of an object which let a person identify the whole? What kinds of information does a robot need to tell the difference between a rubber ball and an orange? These sorts of questions keep gestalt concerns alive.

Biological, cognitive, humanistic, and psychoanalytic psychologists are most active today. **Biological psychologists** explore the effect that changes in an organism's physical body or environment have on behavior, and the interaction between behavior and the brain. They do not study the mind, the soul, or most "internal" experiences. Biological psychologists concentrate on physical techniques and, hence, find physical results.

The term biological psychology covers a wide range of study. Its topics include genetics, the nervous system, and the endocrine system. Biological psychologists' research may involve dissecting the brain of a human or animal who suffered a behavior disorder, experimenting with drug treatments for mental illness, measuring brain waves during sleep, or investigating the effects of biological factors on eating and drinking, sexual behavior, aggression, speech disorders, dyslexia, or learning.

Major contributors to biological psychology include Ivan Pavlov (1849–1936), who conditioned dogs to salivate when they heard a bell ring; Eric Kandel, who pioneered the use of the sea slug Aplysia to study motor neurons; and

Norman Geschwind, who revolutionized studies of the neural basis of dyslexia.

Cognitive psychology is heir to the early experiential psychologists. It is concerned with the processes of thinking and memory, as well as attention, imagery, creativity, problem solving, and language use. In contrast to the behaviorists, cognitive psychologists discuss the mental processes which determine what humans can perceive, or communicate, as well as how they think. Cognitive psychologists also use animals, particularly in memory research.

In the 1950s, several events led to the rise of interest in the mind, after decades of neglect. Psychologists realized that behaviorism, while a useful approach, had taught them nothing about the "black box" of mental processing. Scientists like Norbert Wiener (1894–1964) began work on cybernetics, the study of automatic control systems like thermostats and computers, asking, "How does a thinking machine process information?" Noam Chomsky published his theories on language as a system with infinite, non-learned possibilities generated by rules. New technology and logic gave psychologists the power to explore realms that were considered too subjective by the dominant behaviorists. Many cognitive psychologists use computers to simulate human memory, language use, and visual perception.

Humanistic psychology also arose in the 1950s, with a completely different focus. According to the humanistic psychologists, behaviorism concentrated on scientific fact, to the exclusion of human experience, and psychoanalysis (described below) concentrated too much on human frailty. Humanistic psychologists sought to begin a psychology of mental health, not illness, by studying healthy, creative people.

Humanistic psychology grew out of two main influences: phenomenology, the idea that behavior is based on subjective perception, and **existentialism,** which states that humans' basic existential anxiety is fear of death. Both approaches concentrated on the individual's point of view. Humanistic psychologists had little use for statistics; the focus was to understand each person's struggle to exist.

Psychoanalytic theories have an important place in psychology. Sigmund Freud (1856–1939), the founder of psychoanalysis, is perhaps the most famous physician in the world, and his theories are perhaps the most often challenged. Though current psychodynamic theories of personality originated in his work, subsequent psychoanalysts have moved far beyond the scope of his theories.

In the nineteenth century, psychiatry did not offer either explanations of or treatment for mental illness. Freud developed his method of treatment and a theory of personality through empirical (observational) and experimental techniques. Freud developed a treatment called **psychoanalysis,** in which patients work with a therapist to explore their past to discover the sources of their illness by stressing early experience and unconscious, "repressed" memories. Freud's primary tool for investigation was the **case study,** which included both his commentary and a patient's autobiographical material, dream analysis, and free association.

Neo-Freudians revised Freud's theories to provide for more cogent views of women's development, learning throughout life, interpersonal influences on personality, and social interaction. Important writers included Eric Erikson (1902-1994), Karen Horney (1885–1952), C.G. Jung (1875–1961), and Alfred Adler (1870–1937).

Though psychoanalytic theory has its limitations, particularly with regard to biologically-based illnesses like schizophrenia, it is the most influential of psychological fields to date. Without it, clinical psychology as we know it would not exist.

METHODS OF STUDY

Types of Studies

Psychology is a science, and many different research methods are used to study the behavior of **subjects**—the humans or animals who are observed.

Naturalistic observation is the systematic observation of an event or phenomenon in the environment as it occurs naturally. The researcher does not manipulate the phenomenon. Laboratory investigation often interferes with the natural occurrence of a phenomenon. Therefore, psychologists may prefer to witness it in its natural environment. For example, social behavior in monkeys may differ in a safe laboratory from that exhibited in the more perilous wild world.

When psychologists wish to manipulate conditions, they perform experiments. Some event, treatment, or condition, is changed, controlled, or recorded by the psychologist: this factor is called the independent variable. The change in the organism—behavioral or biological—is recorded by the psychologist. This change is the dependent variable. By observing the change in the organism correlated with the change in conditions, the psychologist can infer the change in environment changed the organism's behavior. However, correlation is not causation. A social scientist must beware that the change in the dependent variable, behavior, is truly due to a change in the independent variable and not some other factor. Generally, psychologists perform their experiments in laboratories or other controlled settings, such as schools, prisons, or hospitals, where conditions are much the same for all subjects.

Surveys are another method of psychological investigation. Individuals are asked to reply to a series of questions or to rate items. The purpose is not to test abilities, but to discover beliefs, opinions, and attitudes. Psychologists may take answers to survey questions and see how they match with respondents' characteristics—age, gender, social class, and so on.

Three types of studies are typically used to examine human subjects: **longitudinal, cross-sectional,** and **case studies.** In longitudinal studies, psychologists study their subjects over a long period of time to observe changes in their behavior. Cross-sectional studies take a group of subjects and examine their behavior at one point in time. Case studies, or case histories, are commonly used in clinical psychology and medical research. A single individual is studied intensely to examine a problem or issue relevant to that person. Freud favored case studies in his research.

Reliability and Validity

To be applicable to the general population, any test a psychologist administers must be standardized. The results must be reproducible and must measure what the psychologist wishes to measure. These concerns are termed **reliability** and **validity.**

In psychology, reliability refers to how consistently individuals score on a test. Reliability measures the extent to which differences between individuals' scores show true difference in characteristics, and not "error variance," or the proportion of the score due to errors in test construction. With a reliability value for a test, a psychologist can predict the range of error in a single individual's score. For example, Scholastic Assessment Tests generally have an error variance of 10 points: your score may vary 10 points in either direction from your "true score."

The question of validity is whether a test measures what the examiner wants it to measure. Specifically, **construct validity** is the extent to which a test measures something—a theoretical construct. **Criterion-related validity** refers to how effective a test is in predicting an individual's behavior in other, specified situations. For example, if a student does well on the SAT, does that student also have high grades now? Will that student do well in college? If that student's teacher hears that she did poorly on the math SAT, the teacher may expect that the student will do badly in math in school, and grade her more harshly. This is known as **criterion contamination,** when results on a test bias an individual's score on another test.

Ethics in Psychological Research

Since psychological research involves live, fragile humans and animals, psychologists must consider the ethical implications of their research. A careless experimenter can wreak havoc in a trusting subject's life. The United States government requires that every institution receiving federal support establish review boards to decide the ethical implications of all research, and many other professional organizations have also created ethical guidelines.

In general, experimenters must be honest, practice **informed consent** (telling subjects all features of the experiment prior to the study), allow subjects to leave the experiment at any time, protect subjects from physical and mental harm, and protect all subjects' confidentiality.

Statistical Methods

Behavior is unbelievably complex. To scientifically study behavior, psychologists use statistics. Three terms psychologists use to refer to a set of scores are **population, sample,** and **distribution.** The population is the total set of possible scores, say, the weight of every person in the United States. Most statistics use a **sample** of a total population—the weights of one thousand U.S. citizens, for example. A distribution is simply any set of scores taken from a population or population sample.

Inferential statistics, such as T-tests, chi-squares, and analyses of variance, test the differences between groups. They are used to measure sampling error, draw conclusions from data, and test hypotheses. They answer the question, "What does this data show?"

Descriptive statistics answer the question, "What is the data?" They include measures of **central tendency** (mean, median, and mode), or whether or not the data is clumped in the middle of a graph. Descriptive statistics also include measures of **variability,** or how the data spreads across a graph (i.e., standard deviation, range, and Z-scores), and measures of **correlation,** or the relationship between two sets of scores.

The **mean** is the average of a set of scores. The **median** is the score in the exact middle of the distribution: half the scores fall above the median, half fall below it. The **mode** is the most frequently occurring score. For example, in the series 3, 4, 4, 5, 6, 8, 100, the mode is 4—the number which occurs twice. The median is 5. The mean, though, is 18.6.

Variability is commonly measured by the **range,** or the distance between the highest and lowest score. In the example above, the range is (100–3), or 97. The

standard deviation is an index of how much data generally varies from the mean. To find the standard deviation,

   (i)   Find the mean of the distribution.
  (ii)   Subtract each score from the mean.
 (iii)   Square each result - the "deviations."
 (iv)   Add the squared deviations from the mean.
  (v)   Divide by the total number of scores; this result is called the **variance.**
 (vi)   Find the square root of the variance; this is the standard deviation.

Many descriptive statistics involve the **normal distribution.** A distribution is a set of scores. A normal distribution is a bell-shaped curve which can be described completely by the mean and standard deviation. In a normal distribution, about 68% of the scores fall within plus or minus one standard deviation from the mean. Ninety-five percent of the scores fall within plus or minus two standard deviations from the mean. Ninety-nine point five percent of the scores fall within plus or minus three deviations from the mean.

Z-scores, or **standard scores,** are a way of expressing a score's distance from the mean in terms of the standard deviation. To find a Z-score for a number in a distribution, subtract the mean from that number, and divide the result by the standard deviation. A positive Z-score shows that the number is higher than the mean; a negative Z-score, lower. Z-scores allow psychologists to compare distributions with different means and standard deviations.

Correlations show how closely related two set of scores are to each other. Possible correlations range between +1.00 and −1.00. When a correlation is +1.00, high scores on one set are associated with high scores on the second set; in a correlation of −1.00, low scores are associated with high scores. There is a high positive correlation between children's age and height; there is a high negative correlation between driving competence and amount of alcohol drunk. A correlation of 0.00 shows that the two sets are not associated.

These statistics are all usually calculated on **samples,** not total populations. Using the sample, a psychologist can predict the intervals in which the mean and variance of the total population is likely to fall. To make this statement, the psychologist must know something about the populations of sample means and variances, i.e., their distributions.

Careers in Psychology

In addition to being a science, psychology is also a profession. Psychologists can be either researchers or practitioners. They may work for colleges and universities, elementary or secondary schools, clinics, industry, government, or in private practice. Psychologists are generally employed in one of nine areas of psychology: experimental, biological, social, developmental, educational, personality, clinical, counseling, or industrial/organizational psychology.

Experimental psychologists conduct experiments in various areas of psychology, such as cognition or sensory perception, to further knowledge of the subject. **Biological** psychologists study the influence of biological factors on human and animal behavior. These factors include genetics, the nervous system, or the endocrine system. For example, they may study the effect of environmental lead contamination on intelligence in rats. **Social** psychologists use scientific research methods to study the behavior of individuals in groups; they are concerned with an organism's interaction with others. One topic social psychologists have studied is the effects of racial integration on school children. **Developmental** psychologists study individuals' behavioral development from conception through adulthood. They observe the acquisition of skills through the development of cognition, perception, language, motor abilities, and social behavior. A developmental psychologist might work with a dyslexic child, or a child who is unusually shy. **Educational** psychologists are concerned with the process of education. They engage in research to develop new ways of teaching and learning. They also implement new systems of education. Educational psychologists developed most of the "workbooks" American children use in school. **Personality** psychologists study individuals to discover the development of basic underlying dimensions of personality and how these dimensions or traits affect behavior. For example, personality psychologists could study what effect the trait of introversion might have on an individual's behavior in situations requiring confidence. **Clinical** psychologists assess abnormal behavior to diagnose and change it. They treat both patients whose disorders are so severe that they cannot cope with reality, and clients who may have less severe problems. Psychosis, substance abuse, and reactive depression (say, in response to a death) can be treated by clinical psychologists, though the line between medical and psychological illness grows more blurred each day. Other personnel working in clinical psychology include behavior analysts, psychological nurses, and music therapists. **Counseling** psychologists usually treat people whose disorders are not so serious. They offer advice on personal, educational, or vocational problems. Marriage counselors and school guidance counselors fall into this category.

Finally, **industrial/organizational** psychologists generally work for public and private businesses or the government. They apply psychological principles to areas such as personnel policies, consumerism, working conditions, production efficiency, and decision making. Two basic fields of industrial psychology are personnel psychology and consumer psychology.

Most researchers and college teachers of psychology have a Ph.D. (Doctor of Philosophy) degree, which requires four to five years of graduate study. Many of the other professions demand a master's degree, which requires one to two years of graduate study. Psychology offers endless possibilities to a person who is fascinated by human and animal behavior.

REVIEW QUESTIONS

Remember, studies show it is much more effective to write out your answers rather than to say or think them to yourself. Good luck.

1. Fill in the blank.

    (a) Psychology is the _____ of behavior.
    (b) Psychologists study _____ behavior.
    (c) Greek philosophers called the _____ the _____ .
    (d) The four fundamental factors of behavior are _____ , _____ , _____ , and _____ .

2. Match the major schools of thought with the psychologist involved.

    (a) Structuralism   (1)   Abraham Maslow
    (b) Functionalism   (2)   William James
    (c) Gestalt   (3)   Max Wertheimer
    (d) Behaviorism   (4)   Paul Broca
    (e) Biological Psychology   (5)   Karen Horney
    (f) Cognitive Psychology   (6)   Wilhelm Wundt
    (g) Humanistic   (7)   Noam Chomsky
    (h) Psychoanalytic   (8)   John B. Watson
                                 (9)   Pierre Flourens
                                 (10) Sigmund Freud

3. Which of the major schools of psychology

    (a) emphasized studying perception?
    (b) believed all behavior is caused?

(c) believed that behavior could be reduced to a few key elements?

(d) involved studying "healthy" people?

(e) emphasized case studies?

(f) are still active?

(g) began after 1940?

4. What type of study would you use to observe

(a) the courtship rituals of penguins?

(b) the effect of high salt intake on rats' drinking habits?

(c) if lower-income women support your candidate for Congress?

(d) whether your little brother touched the fresh paint?

5. To ensure that human subjects are treated ethically, all psychological investigators must insure that their volunteers have given _____ prior to the start of the study.

6. (a) If a test is consistent, it's _____ .

(b) If a test measures what it's supposed to measure, it is _____ .

7. Which is larger: the population or the sample?

8. Name three measures of central tendency.

9. How are Z-scores related to the standard deviation of a distribution?

10. You are driving to a date at Pizza-Face, your favorite restaurant. You know that there is a +0.50 correlation between your driving speed and the probability of being stopped by a police officer. There is a +0.25 correlation between your driving speed and the probability of getting to your date on time. There is a −.05 correlation between your driving speed and keeping your body intact.

(a) If you go faster, does the chance of your being caught for speeding increase?

(b) Which probability is more likely to increase with your speed: the chance of dying in a car accident or the chance of getting to the date on time?

(c) Should you speed up or slow down?

ANSWERS

1. (a) science
    (b) observable
    (c) mind, psyche
    (d) knowledge, motivation, competence, organism

2. (a) 6
    (b) 2
    (c) 3
    (d) 8
    (e) 4
    (f) 7
    (g) 1
    (h) 5, 10

3. (a) Gestalt, Structuralism
    (b) Behaviorism, Psychoanalytic
    (c) Behaviorism, Structuralism
    (d) Humanistic
    (e) Psychoanalytic (Humanistic)
    (f) All except gestalt, functionalist, structuralist
    (g) Humanist, cognitive

4. (a) Naturalistic observation
    (b) Experiment
    (c) Survey
    (d) Outcome

5. informed consent

6. (a) reliable
    (b) valid (construct validity)

7. Population

8. Mean, median, mode

9. Z-scores are an index of how far a given score falls from the distribution's mean.

10. (a) Yes
    (b) In this example, the chance of getting to the date on time is more highly correlated with speed than dying in an auto accident, though a correlation of +0.25 is not very high.
    (c) This is a value judgment. I have not met the reader's date; thus, I cannot say.

Chapter 2

Biological Bases of Behavior

THE BRAIN

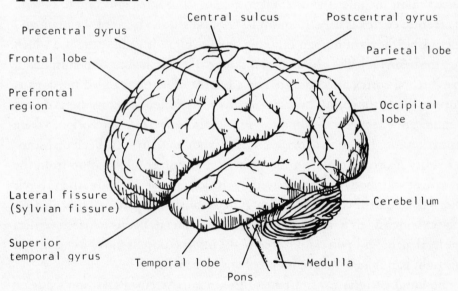

Precentral gyrus

Central sulcus

Postcentral gyrus

Frontal lobe

Parietal lobe

Prefrontal region

Occipital lobe

Lateral fissure (Sylvian fissure)

Cerebellum

Superior temporal gyrus

Temporal lobe

Pons

Medulla

Interior portion of one side of the human brain.

The human brain consists of three major divisions: the hindbrain, the midbrain, and the forebrain. The brains of rats, pigeons, and other animals differ substantially from human brains, but all share the structure of the **hindbrain.** The hindbrain lies at the base of the brain, over the back of the neck. Often called the "primitive" part of the brain, the hindbrain coordinates basic bodily functions involving movement. It is composed of three structures: the cerebellum and the pons, which make up the metencephalon, and the medulla, or myelencephalon.

The **cerebellum** coordinates smooth motor movements. It integrates information from auditory, balance, and skin senses, as well as feedback from individual muscles. If the cerebellum is damaged, a person will move jerkily, and perhaps not be able to stand.

The **pons** helps regulate sleep and arousal. It also connects the two hemispheres of the cerebellum, to coordinate movements on both sides of the body. The **medulla** regulates the cardiovascular system, respiration, and skeletal muscles.

Located above the hindbrain, the **midbrain,** or mesencephalon, consists of the tectum and the tegmentum. The **tectum** conveys auditory and visual information to other parts of the brain, and is involved in visual reflexes. The **tegmentum** controls sequences of movements, including eye movements.

The **forebrain** is the "highest" part of the human brain. The forebrain is divided into two sets of structures: the telencephalon and the diencephalon. The **telencephalon** includes the cerebral cortex, basal ganglia, and limbic system. The **cerebral cortex** is the outermost layer of cells at the front of the brain and is responsible for most human thinking and learning. It is the structure which makes the brain look like a head of cauliflower. The two halves, or hemispheres, of the cerebral cortex are connected by a bundle of neurons called the **corpus callosum.** When the corpus callosum is cut, the two cerebral hemispheres do not communicate effectively, leading to "split-brain" effects in perception, where information entering one half of the brain does not travel to the other half. Motor and sensory neurons "cross" in the brain. For example, information from the right side of your body is first received by the left side of the brain, then travels to the right across the corpus callosum. A male split-brain patient who only feels an object with his left hand may not be able to name it, because speech centers in the left half of his brain cannot receive the information. If the object is placed in his right hand, he will have no problems identifying it.

The **basal ganglia** control part of the motor system. Parkinson's disease attacks the basal ganglia, destroying basal ganglia motor neurons' ability to manufacture neurotransmitters. Patients have jerky, spasmodic movements, or simply cannot move at will. The **limbic system** contains many different interconnecting structures, like the hippocampus and amygdala. It is involved in emotions, motivation, and learning.

The **diencephalon** refers to the thalamus and hypothalamus. The **thalamus** sends the cerebral cortex most of its information. It receives information from lower sensory and motor areas and transmits it to the appropriate part of the cortex. The **hypothalamus** is a small structure at the base of the brain. It controls parts of the autonomic nervous system (described below), the endocrine system, and is involved in certain reactions: "fight" and "flight" impulses, foraging, and mating.

The Reticular Activating System

The reticular activating system (RAS), or reticular formation, relays information to the cerebral cortex. However, where the thalamus transmits specific sensory information to selected targets in the cerebral cortex, the RAS treats all sensory information as one input. The RAS activates wide regions of the cortex, not just sensory areas. It produces arousal; it alerts the cortex to something interesting or dangerous.

The RAS also receives output from the cortex. When the cortex receives arousal messages from the RAS, it may send excitatory messages right back to the RAS. The RAS, which is now excited by both sensory information and cortical messages, then sends a stronger message back to the cortex, which sends a message back to the RAS, and so on. This "feedback loop" can make the organism "feed" off its own emotional state, creating an emotional frenzy. If you have ever felt stage fright, then made yourself more nervous by thinking about stage fright, you have experienced the RAS-cerebral cortex feedback loop. Similarly, calm signals from the cerebral cortex—for example, "biting the bullet" in response to pain—can keep the RAS from spreading more arousal messages throughout the cerebral cortex.

Study of the Brain

Psychologists use four main techniques to study the brain's functions: ablation, direct stimulation, electroencephalograms, and brain scans. In **ablation,** a researcher removes part of an organism's brain, then tests that organism to see what behavior has changed. Though modern researchers typically operate on rats, cats, and monkeys, many important findings have been discovered through observing wounded soldiers, accident and stroke victims, and early participants in psychosurgery. Ablation is brutal, but it has helped scientists localize brain regions important in memory, learning, speech, and other functions.

Direct stimulation is the opposite of ablation. Instead of removing a portion of the brain, researchers electrically stimulate the surface of the brain. Gustav

Fritsch and Eduard Hitzig first mapped the primary motor cortex by weakly shocking a dog's exposed cerebral cortex. They recorded which muscles contracted when they shocked certain parts of the brain. W. Penfield stimulated the brains of patients undergoing surgery for temporal-lobe epilepsy and produced complex hallucinations, which inspired much memory research. This technique is no longer widely used, having been thoroughly explored by previous research.

Electroencephalograms (EEGs) are much less invasive. A researcher will apply electrodes to certain parts of the scalp, and measure the pattern of electrical activity in different parts of the brain. EEGs are used in biofeedback, where subjects watch the pattern of brain waves on an oscilloscope and try to change them. Researchers often study **evoked potentials,** or event-related potentials, the pattern of electrical activity in response to a specific stimulus or event. For example, a researcher would record the patterns in an infant's auditory cortex in the seconds after a loud noise. Clinical psychologists often use the EEG to teach patients to relax by producing different brain-wave patterns, or to diagnose brain abnormalities.

Various brain scans include CAT scans, PET scans, and NMR or MRI scans. Each creates a picture of brain activity instead of a wave on an oscilloscope. Unlike the EEG, which only finds patterns, these scans can pinpoint the sources of brain activity. They are expensive and difficult to conduct, though, and not as commonly used in research. Computerized axial tomography, or **CAT,** X-rays the brain in horizontal slices and is used to find lesions and blood clots. **PET** (positron emission tomography) scans show metabolic activity in the brain. Nucleo magnetic resonance imaging, termed either NMR or **MRI,** does not use radiation like CAT and PET scans, but shows differences between tissues, like the CAT. Strong magnetic fields cause different molecules to vibrate at different frequencies. Since diverse brain tissue has varying concentrations of these molecules, the various tissues resonate at different frequencies. The MRI uses these frequencies to produce images of slices of brain tissue.

THE NERVOUS SYSTEM

Neurons

Neurons are cells which process and transmit information in the nervous system. They have four structures: the cell body, or soma, dendrites, terminal buttons, and axons. The **soma** contains the cell nucleus, and other organelles which maintain the cell. Two types of arms or **processes** extend from the soma, called dendrites and axons. Axons electrically communicate messages within the cell. Axons typically look like a long stem, while dendrites resemble branches. **Receptor sites** receive chemical messages from other cells' terminal buttons and may be located on the axon, dendrite, or cell body. **Terminal buttons** release chemicals, which travel across the **synapse,** the gap between the dendritic spine and terminal button, to communicate with other neurons. There is no physical contact between neurons.

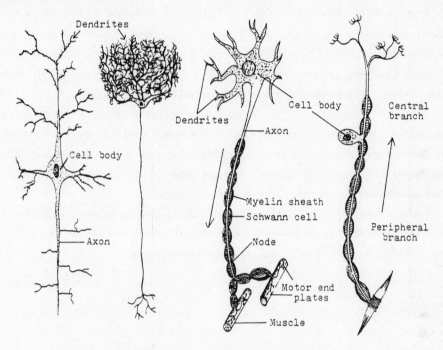

A variety of neuron types in human beings.

Neurons are not the only cells in the nervous system. The central nervous system (CNS), or brain and spinal cord, also contains **glial cells.** Glial cells wrap around neural cells, like a pancake wrapping a rope, holding them in place and supplying some of their chemical needs. More importantly, they isolate the neuron from surrounding chemicals, keeping messages straight. They guide the regrowth of damaged axons and destroy and remove old, damaged neurons. These cells make up the **myelin sheath** which colors the "white matter" of the brain; the "grey matter" is unmyelinated.

Neurotransmitters

A **Neurotransmitter,** or transmitter substance, is a chemical which produces a change in a neuron's potential. These chemicals are generally stored in terminal buttons' **synaptic vesicles,** or tiny bags of membrane. However, neurotransmitters are rather common bodily chemicals, also used in the gastrointestinal tract, heart, sweat and salivary glands among other places. This fact helps explain the side effects of some psychoactive drugs, such as nausea and dry mouth. The neurotransmitters which transport messages from neuron to neuron are the same chemicals as the hormones used in the rest of the body to control various processes. For example, Parkinson's disease is caused by a deficiency of the neurotransmitter dopamine. Yet if a Parkinson's disease victim is given an injection of dopamine, that drug will stimulate the blood flow to his kidneys and increase his heart rate. These side effects can be very dangerous to elderly patients. Parkinson's disease is currently treated with a form of dopamine which is broken down very rapidly in the body but remains stable in the brain.

Neurotransmitters are sent from the presynaptic terminal button to the postsynaptic dendrite. Dendrites contain **receptor sites** for neurotransmitters. Only certain molecules fit these receptors, the way a key fits a lock. These receptors control ion channels, which admit certain molecules into the cell, and produce changes in the neuron's electrical charge.

Once a neurotransmitter has been released, it must be removed from the synapse, or **deactivated.** It can be reabsorbed by the presynaptic neuron—a process called reuptake—or broken down by enzymes.

Neural Transmission; the Action Potential

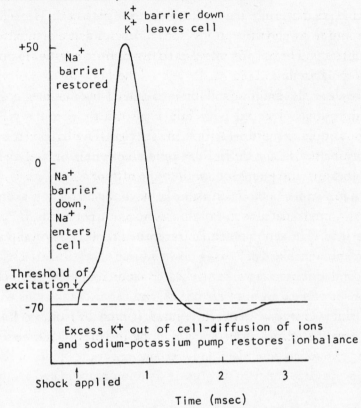

The ionic fluxes during the action potential.

Neurons are surrounded by fluid. The fluid inside a neuron contains different charged particles, or ions, from the fluid outside the neuron. The neural membrane only allows certain ions through its semipermeable membrane. The neurons usually contain (proportionally) more negatively charged ions than the fluid around them. Positive ions will tend to flow into the neuron if they are not stopped by the membrane, or "pumped" out. This state is called an **electrical potential.** The electrical potential is measured in volts, which tells how much of a difference there is between the concentrations of ions, or the charge. The neuron's usual charge is called the **resting potential,** about −70 millivolts. The neuron achieves this state by pumping out positive sodium ions while retaining a few excess positive potassium ions.

When a neuron is stimulated by receiving chemical messages from a terminal button, that neuron's charge changes. If the membrane admits more positive ions, this new potential is called an excitatory post-synaptic potential, or **EPSP;** more negative ions produce an inhibitory post-synaptic potential, or **IPSP.**

Once the resting potential has changed enough, about +10 millivolts, the membrane changes drastically and creates an **action potential.** The cell stops "pumping" sodium out, and these positive ions rush in until the potential reaches about +50 millivolts. The cell's potential has changed from negative to positive; it has been **depolarized.**

Then, the channels admitting sodium ions close. The cell is now positively charged, and positively charged potassium ions rush to leave the cell. The potential drops until it is more negative than the original resting potential. The potassium channels close, and the **sodium-potassium pump** once again begins to retrieve potassium and pump sodium into the surrounding fluid.

The action potential's electrical message is conducted along axons two different ways. Unmyelinated axons communicate action potentials via **"passive cable properties."** The action potential is recreated at every physical point on the axon's membrane, like dye flowing down a piece of fabric. It is a relatively slow way of conducting messages. In myelinated axons, only a few sites along the axon are not surrounded by a myelin sheath and can exchange ions with the surrounding fluid. These gaps in the covering are termed the **Nodes of Ranvier.** The action potential jumps from node to node in what is called **saltatory conduction.** The action potential is only regenerated at the Nodes of Ranvier; the signal is propagated much more quickly than in unmyelinated axons.

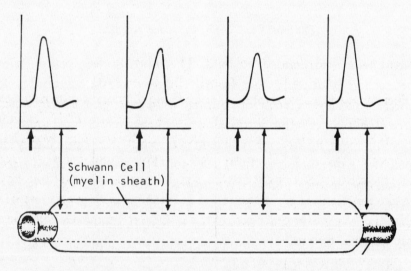

Schwann Cell
(myelin sheath)

Propagation of an action potential down a myelinated axon.

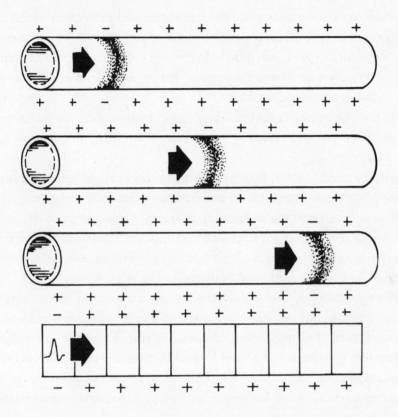

Propagation of an action potential down a unmyelinated axon.

Central and Peripheral Nervous System

There are two main components to the human nervous system: the central nervous system (CNS) and the peripheral nervous system (PNS). The **central nervous system** is made up of the brain and spinal cord and is involved in making decisions about behavior. The **peripheral nervous system** includes every nerve outside the central nervous system. It carries information to and from the CNS. It has two functions: to sense stimuli, with the **somatic nervous system** and to regulate the "vegetative processes" in the body, like heart rate, with the **autonomic nervous system.**

The autonomic nervous system (ANS) integrates the central nervous system and bodily organs, linking the decision-making brainstem nuclei to target organs. It contains motor nerves, and regulates all manner of bodily function. It controls cardiac (heart) muscle and smooth muscles in the gastrointestinal tract. Humans cannot voluntarily control these nerves.

The ANS's **parasympathetic** division acts to increase the body's stored energy through **anabolic** processes. The parasympathetic division acts to increase salivation and digestion, slow heartbeat, and to decrease sweat activity, among other things. The **sympathetic** division acts in emergencies in **catabolic** processes, which expend energy to help the organism survive (you can remember the phrase "catabolic means catastrophe"). For example, if you were suddenly confronted by a rabid grizzly bear in the midst of your studying, your pulse rate would rise, your pupils would dilate, and you would breathe faster. Your sympathetic nervous system has prepared you to confront the bear—or run away very quickly.

Both sympathetic and parasympathetic branches have the common aim of maintaining **homeostasis,** or the equilibrium which allows the body's internal condition to stay constant. Keeping a steady body temperature, supply of nutrients, and heartbeat are all goals of autonomic homeostatic regulation. The two branches act antagonistically; if one branch opens a blood vessel, the other constricts it. Both systems send branches to the same organs.

The two branches involve different neurotransmitters. The parasympathetic system's terminal buttons secrete a neurotransmitter called acetylcholine (ACh); they are termed **cholinergic** neurons. ACh is also the transmitter chemical for synapses between neurons of the somatic nervous system. The sympathetic nervous system's terminal buttons which synapse directly onto "target" organs release noradrenaline, or norepinephrine, and are termed **noradrenergic;** in neuron-to-neuron communication, sympathetic neurons also use ACh. The exception to this rule is sweat glands; the sympathetic nervous system releases ACh onto sweat gland terminal buttons. The nerves for these divisions also leave the CNS at different locations. Sympathetic nerves emerge from the thoracic (rib) and lumbar (lower back) regions of the spinal cord, while parasympathetic neurons arise from the cranial (head) and sacral (buttocks) regions.

Psychologists measure sympathetic nervous system signals to detect agitation or deception. In lie-detection tests, heart rate, blood pressure, and sweat (measured through electrical skin-conductance measures) are used to determine if a subject might be lying. Unfortunately, subjects who are merely upset at being questioned often show the same symptoms as nervous liars. Thus, calm liars are at an advantage since their lying might not be detected.

THE ENDOCRINE SYSTEM

Exocrine glands release substances through ducts; they include sweat, tear, and digestive glands. The endocrine system consists of ductless glands which secrete hormones into the extracellular fluid around capillaries. Transported by the bloodstream throughout the body, these hormones affect behavior over minutes, hours, or weeks, instead of the nervous system's milliseconds. Though hormones circulate throughout the bloodstream, only certain types of cells respond to each hormone. These cells are known as target-organ cells.

Some endocrine glands, like the pituitary, need nervous system stimulation to begin releasing hormones. This stimulation is often provided by the **hypothalamus.** This forebrain structure regulates daily and monthly "biological clocks," controls feelings of thirst, hunger, and water excretion, and modulates aggression and sexual behavior.

The CNS controls much hormone production; in return, hormones influence neural function and behavior. **Hormones** control and coordinate functions like reproduction, metabolism and energy balance, and sexual behaviors.

Hormones generally fall into two categories: amino acid derivatives called polypeptides and steroids. **Polypeptides** vary in size from tiny molecules to very large proteins. They include pituitary hormones, insulin (which regulates sugar metabolism) and cortisone. Like neurotransmitters, pituitary hormones are accepted by receptor sites on target cells. **Steroids** are produced by the adrenal cortex, ovaries, and testes. They are small and enter target cells easily, changing protein production in the cell nucleus. Steroids include androstenedione, which affects sex drive, testosterone, and epinephrine, commonly known as adrenalin.

Many endocrine glands are governed by the **pituitary gland,** sometimes called the "master gland." Connected directly to the hypothalamus, the pituitary gland absorbs a concentrated dose of hypothalamic signals before they become diluted in the bloodstream.

The pituitary gland actually consists of three different glands: the anterior, intermediate, and posterior lobes. The anterior lobe produces at least six different polypeptides which cause target organs to secrete hormones like thyroid-stimulating hormone (TSH) to control the thyroid gland; adrenocorticotropic hormone (ACTH), to stimulate the adrenal cortex to secrete cortisol; and follicle stimulating hormone (FSH) and luteinizing hormone (LH), to control sex-hormone secretion by the gonads. The pituitary also produces prolactin, which stimulates milk production and growth hormone (GH), or somatotropin. The intermediate lobe is only rudimentary, and its purpose is not clear. The posterior lobe is in reality an outgrowth of the hypothalamus. It consists of neural tissue. The posterior lobe releases oxytocin, which stimulates uterine muscles prior to birth, and vasopressin, an antidiuretic, or drug which increases water retention by inhibiting excretion by the kidneys.

The **adrenal gland,** located just over the kidneys, is controlled by the sympathetic nervous system. The cells of the adrenal medulla, a set of cells near the center of the adrenal gland, produce epinephrine, or adrenalin, and norepinephrine. These hormones increase heart rate and constrict peripheral blood vessels, but also stimulate conversion of starch into glucose in muscle cells, increasing available energy. This conversion cannot be achieved by neurons alone.

Pheromones

Pheromones are hormones secreted by an organism which influence the behavior of other members of the same species. They are secreted by exocrine glands, which release substances through ducts, and are sensed by smell or taste. Pheromones evoke specific behavioral, developmental, or reproductive responses in other organisms.

Pheromones act on the recipient's CNS. Moths' sex attractants and ants' trail pheromones are **releaser pheromones** and cause an immediate behavioral change in affected individuals. **Primer pheromones** act more slowly and affect the recipient's growth and differentiation. For example, pregnant mice who smell the urine of unfamiliar male mice will spontaneously miscarry their litters.

GENETICS

From Mendel to Modernity

In the nineteenth century, an Austrian monk named Gregor Johann Mendel (1822–1884) observed the offspring of his garden peas. Mendel observed "true-breeding" pea plants which consistently produced, say, round or wrinkled peas. Mendel bred together one round-pea and one wrinkled-pea plant, producing a generation of plants, which he labelled F1, and counted how many of each type of pea the plants produced. Mendel then allowed the F1 plants to self-pollinate and produce a second generation, labelled F2. Again, Mendel counted the number of wrinkled and round peas from each plant.

This may sound dull, but with careful, well-organized quantitative data, Mendel was able to show the existence of dominant and recessive traits. **Dominant traits** are characteristics which are always expressed in organisms carrying that trait (given a healthy environment). **Recessive traits** only appear when the dominant gene is not carried.

In 1953, the science of genetics took its next great leap forward when James Watson and Francis Crick published their study of the structure of deoxyribonucleic acid (DNA), a chemical found in the cell nucleus. A segment of DNA is equal to a Mendelian gene. By discovering DNA's form, Watson and Crick opened the way for modern geneticists to locate individual genes. Scientists can now begin to manipulate the very basis for our genetic makeup.

Genes and Cells

Each human cell nucleus contains 23 pairs of **chromosomes,** microscopic bodies which carry genes. One set of chromosomes is donated by each parent. Each chromosome is believed to contain between 40,000 and 60,000 **genes,** or functional units which control protein synthesis.

Chromosomes which determine gender are termed X and Y chromosomes. One X-chromosome is donated by the mother's ova, and either an X or a Y chromosome is carried in the father's sperm. An XX individual is female; an XY person is male. An "x-linked" trait is a trait that is carried on the X chromosome and will always be expressed if the offspring is male. If the offspring is female, the trait will only be expressed if the gene occurs on both chromosomes. Examples of sex-linked genetic syndromes include hemophilia, color blindness, and perhaps autism.

Genes are made up of deoxyribonucleic acid **(DNA),** a chainlike molecule consisting of four chemical bases: adenine, guanine, thymine, and cytosine, in various combinations. In 1953, James Watson and Francis Crick discovered that two strands of this molecule form a twisted, spiralling ladder formation (helix). DNA strands can reproduce themselves, and proteins can cross from one strand of the spiral to another, forming new genetic combinations. These changes are called **mutations.** Ribonucleic acid **(RNA)** occurs in both the nucleus and cytoplasm of cells. It is concerned with actually manufacturing new proteins according to DNA instructions. **Messenger RNA** carries DNA instructions from the cell nucleus to **ribosomes,** which are sites where proteins are constructed. **Transfer RNA** ensures that the correct amino acid is attached to a protein being constructed at the ribosome.

Genes in fertilized ova come in pairs. Each variation of a single gene is called an **allele.** A dominant gene takes precedence over other, recessive alleles for a particular trait. The dominant trait will appear in offspring carrying that gene. For example, in humans, brown eyes are dominant. If either parent donates a gene for brown eyes, the child will have brown eyes. Blue eyes only occur when both parents donate blue genes.

In the case of Mendel's cross-bred peas, all the F1 peas were spherical, but ¼ of the F2 peas was wrinkled. The round-pea trait was dominant. When each parent has one dominant and one recessive gene for the same trait, and one gene from each parent is randomly selected for each offspring, on average ¼ will receive two dominant genes, ½ will receive one dominant and one recessive gene, and ¼ will receive two recessive genes, producing the wrinkled pea. You can see the distribution in this figure:

Parent 1

		B	b
Parent 2	B	BB	Bb
	b	Bb	bb

B = dominant allele

b = recessive allele

In some cases, **incomplete dominance** occurs. A snapdragon which receives one gene for red flowers and one for white will produce pink flowers. In this case, the **genotype,** or genetic constitution of the flower, is red and white; the **phenotype,** or observable characteristic of the flower, is pink. This sort of incomplete dominance determines human skin and hair color. Aside from genetic encoding, many environmental factors influence an organism's phenotype. These factors include the availability of food when the organism is growing, exposure to infectious diseases, stress, or the opportunity to develop and use skills.

Nature vs. Nurture

The environment does affect expressed traits, but how much? This is the **nature vs. nurture question.** Most psychologists now agree that both nature and nurture interact to determine behavior. Nature sets possibilities for behavior, while nurture determines how those possibilities will be realized. For example, when an intelligent individual fails to receive the books, education, or encouragement to learn that would lead her to achieve in school, or score well on tests, she has the nature but not the nurture. Stern (1956) likened the process to a rubber band; inherited traits are a rubber band. The environment determines how much the rubber band "stretches."

One way to test a trait's heritability, or how much it is determined by genetic influences, is through twin studies. In a country with accurate birth and adoption records, like Sweden, psychologists examine how traits correlate in identical twins (who share identical genetic codes), reared together or apart, fraternal twins reared together and apart, and siblings reared together and apart. If the identical twins in each situation show a higher correlation of traits than less genetically-similar fraternal twins and siblings, then that trait is more likely to be a product of nature than nurture. Schizophrenia, intelligence, and alcoholism have all been studied in this manner, with some support for heritability of each trait. However, there are no perfect +1.00 correlations; the results are mixed.

Genetics are often invoked in the study of sex or **gender differences.** There are definite differences between the genders in the United States. Boys are born larger and more muscular at birth than girls; they suffer more learning disorders and diseases than girls. Girls are more verbal earlier than men, who tend to develop better visual, spatial, and mathematical abilities. Though this is true, it is not relevant—a political variable is involved. It is very difficult to separate heritable traits from cultural experience and training, especially in the realm of complex social behavior like performance on standardized tests.

While lower animals, such as mice, may be ruled by their hormones, there is evidence that biology's influence declines as the individual climbs the evolutionary ladder. In terms of behavior, studies with hermaphrodites—people born with both ovaries and testes—are quite enlightening. Money et. al. studied 105 biological hermaphrodites, whose parents decided whether they would become female or male at birth. Only five of the 105 individuals deviated from the gender assigned to them at birth. The decision to raise these children as either boys or girls appears to be much more important than biological gender in determining behavior.

REVIEW QUESTIONS

1. Match the brain regions and structures.

    (a) hindbrain

    (b) midbrain

    (c) forebrain

    (1) tegmentum
    (2) pons
    (3) cerebral cortex
    (4) RAS
    (5) corpus callosum
    (6) medulla
    (7) tectum
    (8) cerebellum
    (9) limbic system
    (10) hypothalamus

2. A researcher who removes part of a brain to find out its behavioral function is practicing _____ .

3. Three ways to image the brain are:

4. True or False:

Neuron cell bodies have receptor sites.	T	F
All neurons have myelin sheaths.	T	F
Used neurotransmitter is absorbed by cells called cytophages	T	F

5. When the resting potential of a neuron changes by about +10 millivolts, it becomes rapidly _____ .

6. The central nervous system includes _____ .
   The peripheral nervous system includes _____ .

7. Do anabolic processes release energy or store it?

8. List two hormones produced by the pituitary gland.

9. A mother who carries one allele for hemophilia gives birth to a baby boy. What is the probability that the baby is a hemophiliac?

10. What is the "rubber band" in the rubber band theory of heritability?

ANSWER KEY

1. (a) 2, 4, 6, 8
   (b) 1, 4, 7
   (c) 3, 5, 9, 10

2. ablation

3. PET, CAT, and MRI scans

4. True, False, False

5. depolarized

6. brain and spinal cord, all other nerves

7. Anabolic processes store energy.

8. Luteinizing hormone, follicle stimulating hormone, prolactin, growth hormone, adrenocotricotropic hormone, thyroid stimulating hormone

9. 50%. Hemophilia is a sex-linked trait, carried on the X chromosome. If a fetus is male, the chance of it becoming hemophiliac depends on whether or not the mother has donated a hemophilia gene to the fetus. The father of the boy donated a Y chromosome, which ensures that all X-linked traits are dominant (there is only one of each gene on the X chromosome because there is only one chromosome). The chance of her donating either the hemophilia gene or its allele is ½, or 50%.

10. Genetics, or "nature"

Chapter 3

Sensation and Perception

DEFINITIONS

This chapter is concerned with two major concepts: sensation and perception. **Sensation** is an experience of sensory stimuli. **Perception** is the processing of sensation, the interpretation of basic experience. Perceptual processes receive, encode, store, and organize sensations. For example, Gestalt psychologists (see Chapter 1) researched how perception formed complete images out of sensations of broken lines.

Humans experience at least seven major senses: sight, hearing (audition), taste (gustation), smell (olfaction), touch (including temperature, pain, moisture, etc.), motion, and vestibular senses which maintain balance and adjust eye position to compensate for head movements. Each sense has its own receptor cells which transform physical stimuli into neural impulses. The senses detect a range of stimuli intensities. For example, a bright light has a greater intensity than a dim glow. Other species have different types of senses. Rats can taste the difference between the sugars glucose and fructose, though they cannot sense bitter tastes. Honeybees and other animals can see ultraviolet light. Migrating geese may be able to follow magnetic poles to lead them north and south.

Sensory transduction is the process by which stimuli—light entering the eye, heat on skin, a loud noise—are translated into neural impulses. Sensory stimulation is transduced (translated) into a change in the receptor cells' electrical charge, called a receptor potential. The receptor cells then release neurotransmitter into the synaptic cleft between neurons, beginning sensory coding, or the transformation of information into neural impulses.

Neurons translate receptors' messages through spatial or temporal coding. Simply put, in **spatial coding** receptor cells in different places carry different information, whereas in **temporal coding,** neurons communicate different information by firing at different rates. Spatial coding is used by all senses, except perhaps smell. For example, when different parts of your skin are touched, different neurons lead to separate parts of your spinal cord and on to specialized sections of the brain. But when, say, pressure-sensitive cells in your skin need to communicate the difference between the touch of a feather and an anvil resting on your thumb, they will use temporal coding. When the stimulus is more intense (anvil), in general the neuron will fire more rapidly.

THRESHOLDS, SIGNAL DETECTION AND SENSORY ADAPTATION

In the beginning, physiologists wondered "Just how little do you have to do to a person to produce a sensation?" They wished to find the absolute threshold, or the minimum intensity of stimulation needed to produce sensation, and differential thresholds, or how much a stimulus had to change in intensity before a person could detect the change. For example, an experimenter finding the absolute threshold might place a very tiny candle in a dark room and ask the subject if she could see it. An experimenter finding the differential threshold would first place one candle in the room, then two, and ask the subject if there was any difference between the two trials. A few absolute thresholds (also called the detection thresholds) have been approximated. The approximate detection thresholds, as reported by Galanter, 1962, are for vision, a candle flame seen at 30 miles on a dark night; for hearing, the tick of a watch 20 feet away; for touch, an insect wing falling on a cheek from a centimeter away.

Differential thresholds, on the other hand, change with the nature of the stimulus. The more intense the stimulus, the more of a change in the stimulus there has to be before you will notice the difference. The relationship between the change of intensity needed to reach a differential threshold and the intensity of stimulation already there is a constant ratio. This relationship, mathematically expressed as (delta I)/ I, is called Weber's law, after Ernst Heinrich Weber (1795–1878), who discovered the law through experiments in visual thresholds.

Weber's law of differential thresholds is beautifully, simply demonstrated in the eye. As light intensity increases, receptor potentials increase by a smaller amount, forming an exponential curve, i.e., the rate of firing for the intensity of 100 units of brightness is only twice the rate for 10 units, three times the rate for 1 unit. For every multiple of 10 units, the rate of firing increases by 100%. A very large range of intensities can be coded in a small range of firing rates this way.

The word "approximate" is important when discussing absolute thresholds. There are two problems with absolute thresholds. The first is the problem of signal detection theory. Some subjects will always say that they have sensed a stimulus, no matter how small. The second is the question of sensory adaptation and fluctuation. Sensory receptors are not constant, static turnstiles of sensation, but cells which actively respond to the changing environment. All absolute thresholds are statistical averages. One common estimate of an absolute threshold is a stimulus intensity which can be detected 50% percent of the time.

Signal detection theory raises the question of how subjects make decisions when sensory data is not clear-cut. Classical psychophysical theory assumed that subjects only reported their sensations. Yet in absolute threshold experiments, there are some cases where a subject is not quite sure if she has sensed the chosen stimulus or not. For example, in a visual threshold experiment, subjects may think they see a flash of light. Those subjects may want to show how good their senses are, or please the experimenter, or earn money for correct guesses. Each of these reasons makes subjects tend to say that they have seen the light, even in cases where they are not sure what they have seen, causing "false alarms." In ambiguous situations, subjects judge a stimulus according to both their sensations and their own motivations and expectations.

When receptor cells are constantly stimulated, they undergo sensory adaptation, or a loss of sensitivity to stimuli. Then, less intense stimuli cannot be sensed. In life, you may have noticed that the pressure of a wrist watch disappears moments after you put it on, or that sunlight looks bright when you first emerge from your dim, dusty study chamber, but seems less overpowering a few minutes later. Each sense has its own methods of adaptation. Conversely, time spent in less-intense-than-normal levels of stimuli (say, a dark room instead of a lit room) will make receptor cells more sensitive than normal. In the case of absolute threshold measurement, sensory thresholds vary according to how long a subject has had to adapt to a particular stimulus level. Sensory adaptation is not the only reason receptor response to stimuli varies, but it is the most common.

DEPTH PERCEPTION

Humans live in a three-dimensional world. To throw balls, dodge falling rocks, or drive cars, we need to be able to perceive depth, or the distance between ourselves and other objects. Both vision and hearing can detect depth. For sound, the main cues for depth are the intensity of tones and the time when they arrive at each ear. The body compares the differences to calculate which direction the sound came from, and how far away the object is. The intensity of the sound, and familiarity with the source of the sound (i.e., a stampeding herd of buffalo, your pet guppy's breathing), also help a person to determine how far away an object is. If you know that your pet guppy usually breathes quietly, but it sounds loud now, you will realize that it is much closer than usual.

How we see depth is slightly more complicated. Depth can be perceived using either one or both eyes. Certain cells in the brain's visual association cortex respond differently to information from each eye. In most cases, these cells respond most vigorously when slightly different parts of the retina are stimulated. The brain perceives depth through **stereopsis,** a process which occurs when identical images fall on slightly different parts of the retinas. Similarly, 3-D movies project two images in slightly different places to give an illusion of depth. Other depth cues traditionally used by artists include shadows and shading, linear perspective (picture a straight railroad track leading to the horizon), and interposition, where objects are placed in front of each other to give an illusion of depth. These cues are monocular, meaning that they require only one eye. However, there are no specialized cells in the brain for detecting monocular interposition or shading. Depth perception is not merely sensation, but a complex interpretation of visual cues.

VISION

The Stimulus: Light

For humans, visible light is electromagnetic radiation with wavelengths between 380 and 760 nanometers (a nanometer is one billionth of a meter). Different colors correspond to different wavelengths of light. An easy mnemonic for the colors' different wavelengths is ROYGBIV: red, orange, yellow, green, blue, indigo, violet. Red has the longest wavelength, violet the shortest. Other animals can see infrared light, which has a slightly longer wavelength than we can see, or ultraviolet light, which has a shorter wavelength than visible light. Light can have different wavelengths (hue), intensity (brightness), and saturation (purity). If all the radiation entering your eye has one wavelength, then the color will be saturated, and will seem "pure."

The Eye: Anatomy and Functions

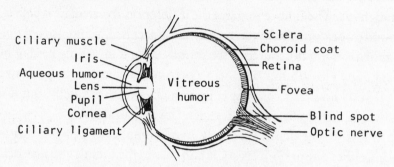

Diagrammatic section of the human eye.

The eyes are suspended in the front of the skull by six muscles. The outer layer of most of the eye, the **sclera,** is opaque. The front of the eye is covered by the **cornea,** the outer transparent coating which protects the eye's interior. Just beneath the cornea is the **lens,** transparent tissue that focuses images on the retina, the photosensitive layer of receptor cells at the back of the eye. The lens is controlled by the eye's ciliary muscles. The lens is normally stretched flat, and focuses images of distant objects on the retina. When the controlling muscles contract, they release tension on the lens, which springs back to a rounded shape suitable for focusing images of things nearby. This process is called **accommodation.** Light entering the eye passes through an opening called the pupil, the dark circle at the center of the eye. The colored portion of the eye, called the **iris,** is a ring of muscles which controls the size of the pupil.

The retina contains over 125 million **photoreceptors,** the cells which sense light. There are two varieties of photoreceptors, rods and cones, which are named for the shape of their receptive ends. Daytime vision relies on cones. There are about six million cones in the human eye, mostly located in the **fovea,** a small central region of the retina. When you stare at an object straight in front of you, you are focusing that image on your fovea. **Cones** respond differently to different wavelengths, or colors, of light. They are responsible for color vision. Each cone responds to only one of three different wavelengths of light: red, green, or blue. By combining reactions to long, medium, and short wavelengths, cone cells can indicate the color of any image. The cones are also very sensitive to small features in the environment; this detection is termed visual acuity.

Unfortunately, cones only function well when there is a lot of light available. At nighttime, or in dim light, humans rely on their **rod cells.** There are about 120 million rod cells in the eye, concentrated on the outer edge of the retina. Rod cells are very sensitive to dim light, though they do not provide much acuity. If you have ever seen a fleeting image of a ghost out of the corner of your eye at night, you were using your rod cells. If that dim image disappeared when you stared straight at it, you have witnessed the failure of cone cells as you inadvertently focused your ghost on your fovea.

Visual Transduction

Light entering the eye is **transduced** (translated) into neural impulses in three steps. First, light crosses the pupil's dark threshold to strike the retina. When light reaches the photoreceptors, light-sensitive substances in rods and/or cones undergo chemical changes. In rod cells, a rosy-colored substance called **rhodopsin** is separated into retinal (a lipid derived from vitamin A) and opsin (a protein). Researchers hypothesize that this splitting causes an intermediate substance to change the photoreceptor's electrical potential. The rod releases some neurotransmitter into the synaptic cleft, and a neural message is formed. Cones act similarly, though they contain one of three different chemicals which respond to red, green, or blue light.

Color Vision

Experimentation has supported two major theories of color vision: the "tricolor" theory, also known as the Young-Helmholtz theory, and the opponent-process theory, or Hering theory. The **Young-Helmholtz theory** states that the three types of color receptors in the eye—red, green, and blue—can form any color by mixing their responses. Remembering the ROYGBIV series of color wavelengths, receptors could encode yellow light by mixing some red responding with many green responses. The brain could "know" colors by interpreting receptors' responses.

The **Hering theory** states that there are only two kinds of color receptors in the eye: blue-yellow and red-green. These receptors would respond in opponent fashion, meaning receptors would become excited in the presence of one color, and inhibited in the presence of another. The brain would interpret the total activity of these receptors to see color.

The three types of color-receptor cone cells do respond to either red, green, or blue light, supporting the Young-Helmholtz theory. Yet when the cones send their information via bipolar (two-ended) cells to ganglion (neural) cells in the retina, there is evidence of opponent processes at work, in the X and Y cells. In the brain, there are cells excited by red and inhibited by green, excited by yellow and inhibited by blue, and vice versa. While the Young-Helmholtz tricolor theory holds for the retina, the Hering opponent process theory dominates in the brain.

Color Blindness

Defects in the three types of cones seem to cause color blindness. Most types of color blindness are sex-linked traits carried on the X-chromosome and, therefore, are much more prevalent in males (see Chapter 2). For Caucasians, about 8% of males and 0.4% of females suffer from color blindness. In **protanopia,** people confuse red and green, which both seem yellowish. These people see the world in hues of yellow and blue. All other aspects of vision are normal, suggesting that their red cones are filled with green-responding chemicals. In **deuteranopia,** green cones seem to be filled with red opsin, producing similar confusion. Green and yellow become red. **Tritanopia,** affecting fewer than one in 10,000 people, is not sex-linked. These people cannot detect short-wavelength colors, like blue and violet, and colors shift down the ROYGBIV scale accordingly. Blue becomes yellow, green becomes pink. Again, no type of color blindness affects visual acuity.

HEARING

Sound is defined as air in motion. When an object vibrates, it causes the air around it to move in waves which travel at about 700 miles per hour. Human ears can detect vibrations of a frequency between 30 and 20,000 hertz (cycles per second). Although our ears can detect vibrations through water and other media, no sound travels in a vacuum because no medium exists to carry vibrations to your ear. This is why in space, no one can hear you scream.

Like light, sound has three dimensions: pitch, loudness, and timbre. The **pitch** is determined by the frequency of the sound. **Loudness,** like light's brightness, is a result of the sound's intensity, or energy. **Timbre** refers to the nature of the sound, or the "shape." An example of this is the difference between an opera singer's trill and a hard-rock grunt. Most natural sounds are made of several different sound waves at many different frequencies, resulting in different timbres.

The Ear: Structure and Transduction

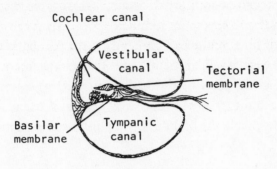

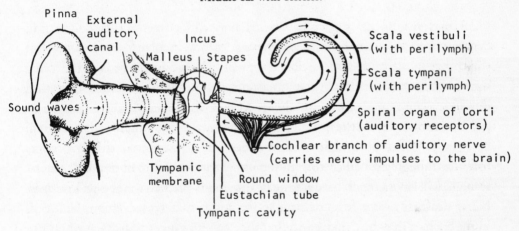

Middle ear with ossicles.

External ear   Middle ear   Inner ear

   The ear is divided into the outer, middle, and inner ear. Sound first enters the outer ear through an ear flap called the **pinna,** the sound travels through the air-filled auditory canal. The sound enters the middle ear as it hits the **tympanic** membrane, or eardrum, which vibrates with the sound. Just behind the eardrum are three small bones, the **ossicles** of the middle ear—the famed hammer, anvil, and stirrup, called malleus, incus, and stapes in Latin. The stapes vibrates onto the **oval window,** a membrane which covers an opening to the inner ear.

   The inner ear has two varieties of sense organs. One type is concerned with hearing, the other with balance. The **cochlea** transmits auditory information, and contains three separate fluid-filled canals. These canals spiral inside the cochlea, which wraps around like a snail's shell. The cochlea also comprises the organ of **Corti,** a part of the basilar membrane, which contains auditory receptor cells. These receptors have fine, hair-like extensions which bend as liquid strikes them. They bend in response to movement of the cochlear fluid. This bending creates a **receptor potential,** or change in the receptor cell's electrical charge, beginning the process of auditory transduction. High tones stimulate hair cells close to the middle ear; low tones stimulate more distant cells. There is a spatial representation of tone on the basilar membrane; a particular tone registers in a particular place on the basilar membrane. This arrangement continues in the brain, where specific parts of the basilar membrane correspond to specific locations on the auditory cortex. This arrangement is termed **tonotopic organization.** It may enable the brain to distinguish between tones.

Deafness

A person who has difficulty hearing may suffer from either conduction deafness or nerve deafness. Both varieties of deafness involve loss of hearing, but they differ in the cause and particular type of loss. When an ear is not carrying sounds from the outer ear to the inner portion, the victim suffers **conduction deafness.** The bones of the middle ear may be damaged, or there may be an accumulation of dirt in the ear. A person suffering from conduction deafness will be equally deaf to both high and low tones. The sounds have simply become softer, as though she had cotton stuffed in her ears. A victim of **nerve deafness,** though, will have a much harder time hearing high-pitched tones than low ones. Nerve deafness results from damage to the auditory nervous system. Hair cells in the cochlea may be damaged so that they can no longer transduce vibrations of the cochlear fluid into neural impulses. However, if only some of the hair cells are damaged, the person may still be able to hear certain tones quite well. Nerve deafness is most common among the elderly.

OTHER SENSES—TOUCH, TASTE, SMELL

Touch

Skin, that wonderful substance which covers your entire body, has four main senses of touch. These senses are called the **cutaneous senses:** cold, warmth, pressure, and pain. It is not clear which of the skin's receptor cells correspond to which sense. However, a few facts are clear. **Free nerve fibers,** not specialized receptor cells, seem to be responsible for temperature sensation. Generally, there is a difference of nine degrees Fahrenheit (five degrees Celsius) between your body temperature and blood temperature. An increase in this difference causes a response. Several different receptors probably respond to pressure. Like the auditory receptors in the organ of Corti, these cells create receptor potentials when the skin is bent or deformed. Like other receptors, **pressure-sensitive cells** undergo rapid sensory adaptation. The sensation of pressure of a watch on your wrist rapidly becomes unnoticeable. Possible pressure-sensitive cells include the Meissner corpuscle, a structure located near the surface of hairless skin, such as the palms. A structure called the **basket nerve ending** probably senses pressure at the roots of hairs. For deep pressure, felt far under the surface of the skin, like a skilled massage, small capsules called **Pacinian corpuscles** are likely to respond.

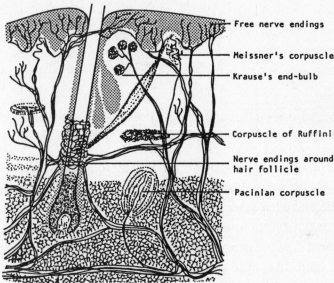

The skin senses include touch, pressure, pain, cold, and warmth (and perhaps itching and tickling). This drawing shows some of the important sensory receptors. There is some specialization among them: The Krause bulbs are most sensitive to cold; Meissner's corpuscles, to touch; and Pacinian corpuscles, to pressure. Free nerve endings are receptors for pain and any of the other sensations.

Pain has special significance. Pain can inspire learning, provoke unfocused aggression, and signal that something is terribly wrong with the body. Many different parts of the tongue are slightly more sensitive to some tastes than others, but you can taste any taste anywhere on your tongue. The tip of the tongue is slightly more sensitive to sweet tastes; the back of the tongue, bitter tastes; the sides of the tongue, sour tastes; and the front of the tongue, salty tastes. However, if you take a cotton swab and rub mixtures of water and sugar, salt, vinegar, or aspirin on different places on your tongue, you will see that you can taste any substance anywhere on your tongue. About one-third of taste buds are sensitive to all four tastes.

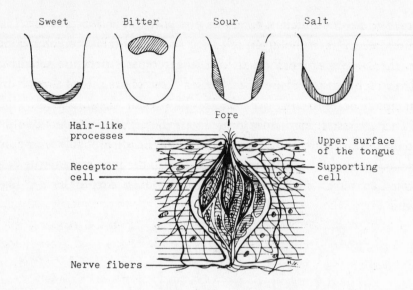

The distribution on the surface of the tongue of taste buds sensitive to sweet, bitter, sour, and salt. Below, cells of a taste bud in the epithelium of the tongue.

Some foods may seem too sweet. Different intensities of tastes are created by different concentrations of the stimulus, how much of the tongue's surface is stimulated, and what other tastes are present. A large mouthful of a strong flavor obviously will have an intense taste. But if that mouthful contains two strong flavors, those flavors will not taste as intense as if they were presented separately. Different kinds of stimuli produce pain, from pinpricks and bruises to inflammation and infection. Pain receptors in the skin seem to be unspecialized, free nerve endings which respond to body-tissue damage. However, capsaicin, the active ingredient in chili peppers that makes them "hot," does not cause tissue damage, yet causes burning pain. (Some researchers propose that mere damage does not cause pain, but damage cannot be repaired as quickly as it is created.) Yet acupuncture, hypnosis, and other treatments show that there is a large psychological component to felt pain. This sense that causes the most suffering of any human experience is still very much a mystery.

Taste (Gustation)

Four basic **taste receptors** determine how appetizing substances like spaghetti and cough medicine seem to you. They are sensitive to sweet, sour, bitter, or salty tastes. Both humans and other animals prefer sweet and salty tastes to sour flavors, though some animals, like rats, cannot sense bitter tastes. Psychologists believe that during evolution, creatures learned that sweet and salty tastes were generally nutritious, while sour and bitter flavors were associated with rotting, acidic food and poisonous alkaloids (certain chemicals contained in plants). There are receptors for each of these tastes on all parts of the tongue, the throat, and the soft palate of the roof of the mouth. (For example, lemonade tastes better than either lemons or sugar; and pickles more than vinegar and salt.)

This "cancelling-out" is a result of the properties of taste transduction. When food enters the mouth, it mixes with the liquid there, called **saliva.** The solution then flows into one of the many tiny "holes" in the tongue, called **taste pores.** Each pore contains slim, hairlike structures, which are part of the taste buds located under the taste pore. When these hairs are chemically stimulated, a receptor potential forms. The nerves which pass from the tongue to the brain almost all respond to more than one taste, and perhaps to changes in temperature. Neither taste buds nor nerves can respond to two tastes at once; therefore, strong tastes tend to be mutually exclusive. In general, tastes are distinguished by their different patterns of neural activity, which reflect the spatial distribution of the taste buds.

Smell (Olfaction)

Smell is a powerful, mysterious sense. The sense of smell is entwined with taste. With a congested nose, steak tastes like cardboard, onions seem to be apples, coffee becomes bitter, and peanut butter tastes rancid. Yet just how smell affects taste, and how a person can tell the difference between smell and taste, is unknown. The sense of smell can suddenly evoke distant memories and has direct connections to the temporal lobe (see Chapter 1). Yet this enigmatic sense defies understanding.

The stimulus for smell is air-born chemicals. The intensity of a smell is controlled by the quality or molecular shape of the substance, its concentration in the air, and its rate of flow in the air, which varies with wind currents, etc. Many psychologists have tried to create neat categories of basic smells, like the basic colors and tastes, but there is no solid evidence that a set of basic smells exists. One theory, by Amoore (1964), divided odors into seven categories: camphoraceous, musky, floral, pepperminty, ethereal, pungent, and putrid. The first five should have different receptors which are shaped to fit specific molecules, like a lock and key. Pungent and putrid-smelling molecules would be distinguished by different electrical charges on their molecules. Unfortunately, experimentation on this topic is not conclusive. Moreover, researchers who have tried to record responses of single receptor cells have found that no two receptors respond the same way.

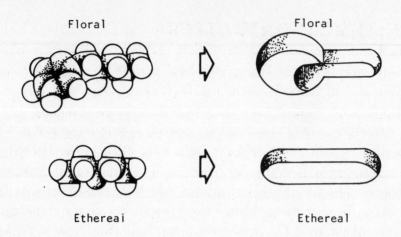

Floral   Floral

Ethereal   Ethereal

Examples of the molecular shape of two odorous substances, along with their hypothesized receptors.

Olfactory receptors lie behind the nose in two patches of mucous membrane, each with an area of about one square inch. Air entering the nostrils sweeps upward and onto these mucous membranes. Chemicals in the air then probably dissolve in the mucous and stimulate the olfactory hair cells, or **cilia.** The **olfactory mucosa** also contains free nerve endings, which probably sense pain when noxious substances like ammonia enter the nose. The axons of the olfactory receptors enter the skull and travel to the olfactory bulb in the base of the brain. Neurons project from the olfactory bulb to the temporal lobe, which is concerned with memory, and throughout the cerebral cortex, as well as to taste areas. These projections may explain flavor's dependence on both taste and smell.

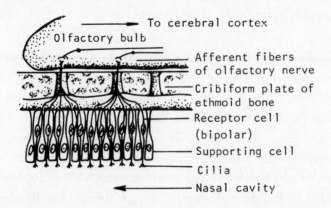

Receptors for the sense of smell (olfaction). Olfactory nerve fibers respond to gaseous molecules.

SENSORY DEPRIVATION

What would you do if you couldn't sense anything at all? In sensory deprivation studies, psychologists try to prevent subjects from having any sensory contact with the world. In the most perfect experiment, though, subjects can still hear the sound of blood flowing in their ears, changes in their body temperature, and moisture. Psychologists use three approaches to eliminate a subject's surroundings. In the first, the researcher tries to reduce external stimuli to a minimum. The subject may be placed in a soundproof room with no light. The subject may wear ear plugs, be bandaged to prevent touch, and be asked to lie on a bed and neither move nor talk. A second approach involves changing or distorting the subject's environment. The subject may hear a constant buzzing sound or wear translucent goggles that do not let the subject see any visual patterns. The third way to produce sensory deprivation is to create a monotonous environment, with no change in stimuli. Wexler, along with others, (1958) placed subjects' arms and legs in rigid cylinders to prevent movement and tactile stimulation.

Sensory deprivation causes certain standard symptoms in adults, and tragic developmental delays for infants. After deprivation, adults have problems thinking clearly and concentrating, and score low on intelligence tests. Many people find it difficult to count beyond 20 or 30. Visual deprivation by the translucent goggles leaves subjects reporting that objects seem wavy and moving after they take them off. They would see geometric patterns in the air, and could not tell if they were asleep or awake. By the end of sensory deprivation experiments, subjects began to hallucinate. Humans and other animals seem to need a basic level of stimulation; when it does not exist, the mind creates its own stimulation.

When infants or animals are deprived of sensation at critical stages of development, they may never develop normal abilities. For example, some people born with cataracts, or clouded corneas, never learn to use their vision once they receive corneal transplants. Spitz (1945) compared children in an orphanage, who had little sensory stimulation, to children in a nursing home. Children in both homes received good food and medical care. However, in the orphanage six nurses cared for 45 babies, while in the nursing home each mother took care of her own child. Children in the orphanage were only occasionally taken out of their cribs, which were draped with sheets that kept them from looking out of the cribs. In the first four months of life, both groups had the same scores on development scales. By the end of the first year, the orphanage children scored lower on development tests than nursing home children. Several of the orphanage babies became physically and mentally weakened, and the orphanage children began to have a high mortality rate. Most strikingly, most of the nursing home babies were walking and talking by ages two and three, while only two of the orphanage babies could walk and talk in the same period.

REVIEW QUESTIONS

1. What are the seven major senses?

2. An experimenter plays a tone softly. The experimenter then plays a slightly louder tone, and asks the subject if the second tone is as loud as the first. What is the experimenter trying to determine?

3. Are two eyes required for depth perception?

4. Images are focused on the retina by the _____ .

5. What are the two types of photoreceptors in the retina? What kinds of light do they respond to?

6. Match the structure with the sense.
   - (a) audition
   - (b) vision
   - (c) touch

   - (1) iris
   - (2) Pacinian corpuscle
   - (3) organ of Corti
   - (4) fovea
   - (5) cochlea

7. Will a person suffering from conduction deafness hear high tones better than low tones?

8. The four main cutaneous senses are _____ , _____ , _____ , and _____ .

9. What are the basic tastes? Are there basic smells?

10. Does sensory deprivation affect people after they return to normal circumstance? Explain how.

ANSWER KEY

1. Sight (vision), hearing (audition), taste (gustation), smell (olfaction), touch, motion, and vestibular senses

2. The differential threshold for loudness

3. No; monocular cues like interposition and shading are also used in depth perception.

4. lens

5. Cones respond to either red, green, or blue light. Rods respond to the presence of any light, especially dim light.

6. (a) 3, 5
   (b) 1, 4
   (c) 2

7. No

8. cold, warmth, pressure, pain

9. Salt, sour, bitter, and sweet; there is no good evidence that there are basic smells.

10. Yes. Children's development may be affected. In adults, the brain continues to produce its own stimulation after the experiment ends.

Chapter 4

Cognition

MEMORY

Sensory Registers, Short- and Long-Term Memory

Marcel Proust nibbled on a tea-cookie on a sunny afternoon. Upon tasting the melting sweet crumbs of the madeleine, as that particular sort of cookie is called, he suddenly found himself reliving his childhood in rural France. From these memories, Proust wrote the classic, lengthy novel *Remembrance of Things Past.*

To create the memories to write the book, Proust had to first store the information. Individuals use three different mental structures to build their memories: the sensory register, short-term memory, and long-term memory. Memory begins at the senses. Psychologists believe that memory starts at a **sensory register,** a very short-lived recording of sensory information. Sensations persist for a fraction of a second after they are experienced, then fade. Information is stored for about ¹⁄₁₅ of a second, so that a person can keep track of experience from moment to moment. If the individual was not distracted, and the information was either very different from normal events or very meaningful to him, that information was then passed to short-term memory, which can only store information for a limited time.

To keep information in short-term memory, people can practice rehearsal. **Rehearsal** simply means paying active attention to information by constantly repeating it, for example. A short interruption will destroy all the information in the short-term store. Most short-term memory fades in a matter of minutes.

Short-term memory is information storage a person would use to remember a phone number long enough to make a call. In general, people can remember seven items at a time, give or take a few. This is one reason why phone numbers are seven digits long. If, again, one paid attention to the phone number and kept rehearsing it in short-term memory, then the information would pass into long-term memory. **Attention processes** play a very large role in determining what information is transferred from short-term into long-term memory. If information is not very important or interesting to you, you are likely to forget it.

Encoding and Storage

When momentary sensory experiences are combined, information is recognized more easily. You can remember a visual image combined with a sound (like a car running its motor) more easily than the sound or the image alone. The process of mixing information is called **encoding,** or image representation. Essential features of an object or pattern are extracted so that the thing can be recognized later. For example, a single glance at a visual pattern can reveal color, texture, density, and shape. You may not be able to recognize a cherry just from the fact that it is red. However, by comparing its shape, size, and smooth surface to information about fruit stored in your memory, you can decide that it is not an apple, tomato, or cat.

Psychologists theorize that short-term memory is an ongoing process of neuron communication, while long-term memory is a permanent change in the locations of neurons' synapses, in the physical properties of the cells. Evidence suggests that the brain needs time for consolidation before information can be stored in long-term memory. Presumably, the neurons need time to change. Material in long-term memory can be brought into the short-term store and will not be lost if the thinker is distracted. However, the short-term store can still only hold a few items. This limited capacity may contribute to the difficulty people have with problem solving. Humans can only contain and examine a limited amount of information at a time.

Where short-term memory is immediate and easy to access, locating information in long-term memory can be slow and hard. Yet long-term memory's capacity is virtually endless. A person cannot "use up" her memory. There are no known limits to how much people can learn.

Other Types of Memory

Many people who suffer different types of amnesia can still perform certain memory tasks. To explain this phenomenon, psychologists have divided long-term memory into types of memory. Major categories include episodic and semantic memory and procedural and declarative memory. **Episodic memory** consists of personal experiences and events tied to particular times and places, while **semantic memory** contains facts like grammar, words, dates, and theories—the impersonal facts we use to go about our daily lives. In general, episodic memory is much more easily distorted and forgotten than semantic memory. **Declarative memory** is memory for conversations, facts and events, everything a person would normally think of as memory. By contrast, **procedural memory** is not memory for events, but ways of doing things, like solving a wooden puzzle, or how to knit, or casting a fishing reel. Certain amnesic patients who cannot remember conversations for more than a few minutes and will not recognize strangers no matter how many times they meet, can learn to solve wooden puzzles faster and faster. These patients will protest that they have never seen the puzzle before each time the psychologist brings it, yet they solve it more and more quickly nevertheless.

Retention and Recall: Rehearsal and Memory Hints

There are two basic variables which affect verbal learning: rehearsal and mediation. **Rehearsal** allows items in short-term memory to be retained, and facilitates the transferral of material from short- to long-term memory. The time allowed for rehearsal influences how well material is retained, though when material is very dramatic (i.e., embarrassing episodes) or well-organized (i.e., nursery rhymes), it is learned much more quickly.

Rehearsal can be helped by the process of chunking. Short-term memory can only store about seven items; however, some items are larger than others. **Chunking,** or grouping related items, can increase available short-term information. Chess masters can memorize entire boards of pieces in a few seconds through mentally grouping pieces by board location, function, and so on. For example, sentences are much easier to remember than 10 single words, because the meaning and grammar of the sentence provide instant ways to group and identify them.

Mediating factors are cues used to organize two items, and can be words or images. For example, "party" can be a mediator for "toga" and "politics," as can the word "republic." Many popular memory systems suggest that to remember a person's name and face, you should create a mediator. Visualize Ms. Smith at a forge hammering horseshoes, or Mr. Baker up to his elbows in flour and chocolate cream pies. When you later see Ms. Smith, your imagined picture will help you locate her name.

Retrieval

Once information is ready to enter long-term memory, it must be encoded and stored so that it can be retrieved. **Retrieval** can either occur rapidly with little or no active recall, or require attention and effort. The first type of recall is "effortless" and occurs when new information is similar to data previously stored. Word recognition is a good example of this type of retrieval. When new information is not like previously stored data, memory takes more effort. Seeing a familiar face does not guarantee remembering the name. The new information—the face—is visual and is not close enough a match to the verbal name stored in memory.

Information retrieval seems to come in stages. In response to the question, "What composer began writing his first requiem shortly before his own death?" some people can answer effortlessly, some require a few clues, and some can say immediately that they do not know. After an initial effortless search, a clue can help people who have found a particular area of memory (renaissance music, royalty) but have not located a specific association. The "tip-of-the-tongue" phenomenon shows what happens when the brain cannot locate a desired word. When a person has trouble remembering a word or a name, that person tends to guess words similar to the target. Words that either sound like the target word, start with the same letter, have the same number of syllables, or have a similar meaning come to mind. The more a person can narrow down the semantic (meaning) and phonetic (sound) characteristics of a word, the easier a time she will have guessing the word.

Forgetting

Are memories destroyed, or do they merely fade away? The **interference theory** would say that memories are prevented, while the decay theory supports the idea that memories disappear with time. In the **decay theory,** psychologists posit that like muscles, memories weaken over time if they are not exercised. This hypothesis is strengthened by studies showing that neural activity progressively weakens over time, also. And yet, experiments have demonstrated that forgetting is affected by the activities a subject engages in during the time between learning and the test for retention. The interference theory states that forgetting occurs because new, conflicting information interferes with an original memory. Memories, then, are lost not because they have disappeared, but because the brain cannot find them in the clutter of competing alternative responses. In **proactive interference,** previously learned information interferes with later learning. You may have observed this effect if you have tried to learn a foreign language and found yourself saying English words in the middle of a sentence. Your English knowledge interferes with your ability to learn new words for the same things. **Retroactive interference** refers to the effect the last items learned have on recall. In any list, the last few items learned tend to interfere with recall of earlier items. For a long list, items in the middle of the list are least likely to be recalled, since they are affected by both proactive and retroactive interference.

THINKING

Controlled and Automatic Processing

Imagine that you are an expert piano player. If you sit down with a new piece, you will play it easily, giving little thought to where each note lies on the keyboard, where your hands are, or how you are moving your fingers. If you are a novice, though, you may struggle to find each individual note, squinting and moving with a heavy hand. The piano virtuoso is using **automatic processing;** she barely notices that she is playing music. For her, interpreting music takes little effort, and almost no consciousness of her activities. The novice, on the other hand, is using **controlled processing** to determine just how and when she should play. She must consciously decide to play each note. Yet if the novice is interrupted in her controlled processing, she can easily find her place again. This is because controlled processing requires a great deal of attention. The automatic-processing expert, if distracted, will have a harder time finding her place because she is not paying as much attention to her task. Automatic processing, though faster than controlled processing, is best left to tasks which are less important to the survival of the organism, or are unlikely to go wrong.

Serial and Parallel Processing

Often, the development of models for thinking and new designs for computers emerge from the same basic idea. One important concept is that of serial vs. parallel processing. In **serial processing,** the brain solves one problem at a time and uses the solution of one problem as input for the next problem. In **parallel processing,** the brain solves many different independent problems at once. Saul Sternberg (1969) theorized that retrieving information from short-term memory involves **serial processing,** while searches through long-term memory take place in parallel. Serial searches are practical for short-term memory's seven items, but to search the entirety of long-term memory by serial means is impractical. It would simply take too long. Parallel processing takes up much more memory, as a computer scientists might say, than serial processing, but it is also much faster. At present, computer scientists are trying to program their machines for parallel processing.

Problem Solving

Creative solutions to problems do not necessarily flash effortlessly into an organism's brain. According to Karl Duncker (1945), there are three stages in problem solving. In the **preparation stage,** an organism assesses a problem. The **production stage** involves a search for possible solutions. The third stage, **judgment,** entails evaluating all possible solutions, and selecting the best one. Many psychologists add a fourth stage, called **incubation,** to this list. During incubation, a person withdraws from the problem. He may engage in some other activity, eat lunch, or take a vacation. When he returns to the problem, he may suddenly solve it with ease. One explanation for these unexpected solutions is that while the solver is distracted, her or his unconscious mind continues to work on the problem. Alternately, the incubation may allow the solver to "clear the mind," and escape any shortsighted or repetitious behavior that prevents him from finding the solution. Each stage may be repeated many times, depending on how complex the problem is.

People and other organisms may use algorithmic or heuristic approaches to solve problems. An **algorithmic** approach involves a set of rules which will guarantee a solution. For example, if you were deciding how to get to a party, you would use an algorithm, or standard procedure, if you took out a map and carefully traced out each possible route your could drive to get there. Algorithms are most useful in **deterministic problem models** where the outcome of each choice can be precisely predicted. However, in **stochastic models,** where the outcome of a decision cannot be discovered before the decision is made, an heuristic approach may be more useful. An **heuristic** is a problem-solving strategy which is likely to produce a solution, but does not guarantee an answer. A person may use heuristics to find out more information about each solution to maximize the possibility of finding the correct answer. An heuristic can be a shortcut, gimmick, or rule of thumb. For example, you might call friends more familiar with the area to find out if any roads are closed on the route to the party. Poker players only draw cards from the deck if they think they have a good chance of getting a better hand; their calculations of probability are an heuristic.

Another way to think of the difference between algorithms and heuristics is the distinction between **convergent** and **divergent** thinking. To converge is to come to one point; to diverge is to split, to follow different directions. There are two types of problems: those which have one correct answer and those which have more than one answer. Simple arithmetic is solved by convergent thinking, which determines one correct answer through applying consistent rules and categorizing events. Divergent thinking produces a variety of solutions. Writing, playing chess, creating pottery, or entertaining children all require divergent thinking to see the many possibilities of human endeavor.

Creativity

Creativity is the ability to produce novel solutions or objects. No matter how many other people may have thought of the same idea, a solution is novel if it is new to the person who thinks of it. There is, however, a distinction between creative and original behavior. Originality is a measure of the frequency of a response; an idea only one person thinks of is objectively original. Creativity involves a subjective judgment of how relevant, practical, feasible, or interesting an idea is. Most people can easily produce an original response to a question, but unless the response is directly or symbolically related to the question, it is not very creative.

There is no completely reliable test of creativity. One common test, the Minnesota Test of Creative Thinking, asks questions like "How many uses can you think of for an old tire? How can you improve a bicycle?" These tests are scored in terms of fluency, or number of responses, flexibility, or how often a person changes from one class of ideas to another (in the case of uses for a tire, a person could shift from ideas for playground equipment to concepts for clothing), and originality, or the number of unusual responses. Despite stereotypes of the "mad genius," studies show that as a group, exceptionally creative people are more emotionally stable than others. Yet people who score highly on creativity tests may not be viewed as the most "productive" people by teachers or peers. There may not be much construct validity to psychologists' measurement of creativity. Creativity does not correlate reliably with scores on intelligence tests.

Insight

Insight is the "Aha!," the experience people have when a solution to a problem unexpectedly becomes clear. Gestalt psychologists thought of insight as the sudden perception of relationships between parts of a problem. Because insight is so unexpected, it seems that problem solving relies on both conscious and unconscious processes. Conscious effort may serve as a retrieval mechanism spurring unconscious sources to produce the correct solution. While the unconscious processes work away, conscious processes rest. Wolfgang Kohler (1927) observed that chimps, given three sticks to be connected to reach a banana, first try to reach the banana with their hands, sit for a while, then suddenly fit the sticks together and reach their prize. The insight process may very well take place in other animals.

Habits, Preconceptions, and Functional Fixedness

Although past experiences can help in finding solutions, they can also interfere with successful problem solving. Habits can prevent problem solving. A method which worked before may not be appropriate to new situations. For example, it may be a good idea to give your friend extra blankets when she has a fever most of the time. But if the fever is extremely high, it is a better idea to put her in a tub of cold water with ice, to reduce body temperature and prevent brain damage. The term "set" describes a person's readiness to respond in a given way to a stimulus. You could ask a friend to pronounce the following words: pin, spin, win, bin, tin, sin, line. By the end of the sequence, your friend expects that the word will sound the same as the rest. Your friend's set makes him likely to say "lin."

Functional fixedness, a term invented by K. Duncker, refers to a set of ideas people have about the function and use of objects. It prevents people from using objects in new ways. If you have ever sat in a room with a can and no can opener, you know the difficulties involved in trying to find any other object to use the same way.

LANGUAGE

Elements of Language

Language is a form of communication. Language consists of symbols that can be arranged to derive meanings. In spoken language, sounds represent objects and ideas, while sign language uses hand motions for communication. Languages enable people to explore actual or potential relationships between parts of the environment. Though most animals communicate, psychologists vigorously debate whether or not they use language. Both chimps and dolphins have been studied, yet the best candidate for the study of language is the honeybee. When bees return to their hives, they perform complicated dances which may tell other bees where to find honey. Yet for reasons described below, most psychologists believe language is unique to humans.

Spoken language comprises four basic units of meaning: **phonemes, morphemes, syntax,** and **prosody. Phonemes** are the smallest units of sound, the single vowel and consonant sounds found in every language. These are the first sounds infants make. English has 45 phonemes, Japanese has fewer, other languages have more. Other languages involve very different sounds from English. The !Kung tribe of Africa uses a sort of clicking sound in their language, which is represented by an exclamation point.

Phonemes combine to form **morphemes,** the smallest units of meaning in a language. In English, morphemes can be whole words such as "death," or "tax," or prefixes and suffixes like "anti-," and "-less." There are more than 100,000 morphemes in English, and they do not begin to exhaust all the possible combinations of the 45 phonemes.

After constructing meaningful words out of morphemes, a person must be able to make understandable combinations of words. **Syntax** refers to the grammatical rules of a language which enable people to communicate. To see how important syntax is, take a sentence like "I walked the dog today," and change the word order. How easily can you understand the new sentence? Yet syntax does not mean strict "correct" grammar of the sort taught in elementary schools. Any sentence that can be understood by a native speaker of a language is syntactically correct. By using syntactical rules, a person can express and understand sentences that have never been said before. Syntactical rules allow humans to be creative with language. When honeybees dance, they do not seem to use syntactic rules; they never produce original, creative dances. Therefore, although they use symbols to communicate, they are not considered to be using language. So far, no animal has been definitely shown to use syntactical rules of language, even when trained by humans.

"Take care of the sense, and the sounds will take care of themselves," wrote Lewis Carroll in *Alice in Wonderland.* **Prosody,** the fourth element of spoken language, refers to the manner of expression. It includes features like intonation, accents, pauses, and variations in pronunciation that affect the meaning of spoken language. A sentence like, "You didn't do it, did you?" easily illustrates the different meanings prosody can serve. In sign language, the timing of and speed of gesticulations express emphasis.

Surface and Deep Structure

Language has two aspects or "structures." The **surface structure** is the actual spoken, signed, or written material of language. The **deep structure** refers to the patterns of meaning which underlie the surface structure. For example, "Mary's little lamb followed her to school" and "Mary was followed to school by her little lamb" have different surface structure, but since they have the same meaning, they have the same deep structure. On the other hand, two sentences with the same surface structure can have different deep structures, as in the sentence "It is drinking water." The deep structures for this sentence could be either "It is water for drinking," or "Water is being drunk by it."

Transformational Grammar

Noam Chomsky (1957) was the first linguist to distinguish between surface and deep structures. He constructed a theory of transformational grammar, or how rules could be used to communicate different meanings. Chomsky defined the "kernel" of a sentence as the basic declarative thought of the sentence. For example, "The girl kissed the boy" could be a kernel sentence. Chomsky showed how a basic structure could be transformed into different surface structures with the same kernel. The above kernel could be transformed into:

The boy was kissed by the girl.
The girl didn't kiss the boy.
Did the girl kiss the boy?
The boy wasn't kissed by the girl.
Didn't the girl kiss the boy?
Was the boy kissed by the girl?
Wasn't the boy kissed by the girl?

The kernel sentence and these eight transformations constitute the basic patterns of English surface structure. Although Chomsky's transformational grammar is a useful concept, linguists today believe that rules for language are much more flexible and related to context than Chomsky first thought.

Semantics

Semantics is the study of the meanings of words. More specifically, semantics is the study of how we infer deep structure from the surface structure of language. There are two kinds of meaning: denotation and connotation. **Denotation** is the concrete meaning of a word, or its external referent. **Connotation** refers to the verbal associations and emotional implications of a word. An old saying, "Horses sweat, men perspire, ladies glow," shows that words with similar denotations can have very different connotations.

The nature of meaning is still very much under debate. People from different backgrounds and cultures have different connotations for words. Even straight-forward-seeming denotation is a mystery. The word "car" denotes a gasoline-powered vehicle, to be sure, but in the absence of a specific car, how does a person think of the word? Is the representative "car" inside your head a tiny, foreign compact, a large shiny sedan, a Model-T Ford, or a Volkswagen Beetle? And how can you categorize all of these vehicles as being part of the same class; what do they share in common? Cognitive psychologists and linguists alike labor to learn about language.

REVIEW QUESTIONS

1. What are the three major memory structures?

2. How many items can be stored in short-term memory?

3. According to interference theory, _____ information interferes with _____ memories, while in decay theory, _____ memories _____ if they are not used.

4. Three stages of problem solving are _____ , _____ , and _____ . Some psychologists add a fourth stage called _____ .

5. You are solving an arithmetic problem by adding together a list of 50 numbers. Are you using an heuristic or an algorithm?

6. Is creativity correlated with intelligence?

7. The main elements of language are _____ , _____ , _____ , and _____ .

8. Do the following two sentences share the same surface structure?
    The cat ate the hat.
    The hat was eaten by the cat.

9. The opposite of connotation is _____ .

10. Match the pairs

declarative	serial
semantic	procedural
automatic	episodic
parallel	controlled

ANSWER KEY

1. Sensory register, short-term memory, long-term memory

2. Seven, plus or minus two

3. new, old, old, decay (or vanish)

4. assessment, production, judgment, incubation

5. An algorithm

6. No

7. phonemes, morphemes, syntax, prosody

8. No

9. denotation

10. declarative-procedural, semantic-episodic, automatic-controlled, parallel-serial

Chapter 5

States of Consciousness

DEFINITIONS

Conscious and consciousness are easily confused. To be **conscious** is to know. Yet consciousness is not knowledge; it is the total sum of mental experience. To be conscious is to be aware, yet consciousness is not awareness. William James spoke of **consciousness** as a "selecting agency," which chooses to notice certain phenomena in the environment and to suppress others. In **automatic behavior,** like riding a bicycle, a person is conscious of steering, pedaling, braking and so on, but she is not aware of them. She does not have to think about what motor responses to make.

Consciousness is not only wakefulness. There are many different states of consciousness, ranging from samadhi, the Hindu ideal of "total consciousness," to wakefulness, dreaming, sleep, and comas.

SLEEP AND DREAMING

Sleep is an active state of consciousness. The brain does not sit still and wait for awareness to return, but goes through four distinct stages. With the advent of electroencephalography, psychologists became able to measure changing patterns of electrical activity in the brain, including sleep. When a subject is fully awake, her EEG shows a pattern of **beta waves,** which have a low amplitude (height) but high frequency. A very relaxed subject's brain produces **alpha waves,** a pattern of waves which has high amplitude (height) and low frequency.

Basically, in alpha waves brain activity is synchronized. In stage 1 sleep, the alpha rhythm is replaced by slower, irregular waves. Stage 2 sleep begins when the waves speed up and develop **spindles**—sharply pointed waves recorded by the EEG. Larger and slower **delta waves** appear in stage 3, until they come to dominate in stage 4. The entire cycle of stages 1 through 4 is repeated four to six times during an average eight-hour period of sleep.

In stage 1, the sleeper also begins to have rapid-eye movement sleep, or **REM** sleep. A sleeper spends most of her time in non-REM, or **NREM** sleep. REM is jerky eye movement that is visible beneath the eyelid. During REM sleep, there is a massive inhibition of motor neurons. For the most part, people undergoing REM sleep cannot move. Dreams abound during REM sleep. About 80% of people woken during stage 1-REM remember their dreams, as opposed to less than 10% of NREM-woken subjects. Stage 1-REM sleep is also called "paradoxical sleep," because the EEG from a REM-sleeper looks very much like the pattern produced by an active, awake individual. As each cycle of sleep is repeated, the stage 1 REM becomes longer. The first REM stage occurs after about 90 minutes of sleep and lasts for five to 10 minutes. Every 90 minutes, REM gets longer. Many people awaken during their last stage 1-REM sleep, when they may be having a dream lasting half an hour or more.

Functions of Sleep and Sleep Deprivation

No one has ever managed to commit suicide by not sleeping. Although a few hardy souls have stayed awake for up to 10 days, most people find the need to sleep one of the most overpowering urges they have ever experienced. **Sleep deprivation** produces different effects in different people. Some people begin to develop psychotic symptoms, suffering hallucinations and paranoid hallucinations. Others are relatively unaffected, and motor abilities remain intact. Most begin to take **microsleeps,** naps which last only a few seconds, though they may believe they are continuously awake. Some psychologists suggest that it is the stress of staying awake, and not lack of sleep, which produces these symptoms. Overall, sleep deprivation studies have not shown that sleep serves any important, immediate psychological or physical function, aside from keeping people from feeling sleepy.

This does not mean that sleep does not have important physiological functions. Sleep may give the body a chance to construct tissue and repair itself. Athletes tend to have more NREM sleep after strenuous physical contests, yet people who reduce their physical activity (quadriplegics, subjects paid to spend six weeks resting in bed) do not sleep less than normal subjects. Oswald (1980) noted that sleep is a time for anabolic processes, including bone-growth in children. **Growth hormone,** a hormone produced by the anterior pituitary gland which increases the rate of cell division, is produced mainly during sleep stages 3 and 4.

One popular theory of sleep's function is that sleep simply keeps animals out of harm's way. By sleeping, animals conserve energy and keep from wandering around in the dark when predators are active. Small animals with safe hiding places, like squirrels, sleep a great deal of the time, as do large predators like tigers that can sleep safely whenever they choose. Large animals which are prey and cannot hide, like gazelles or cows, do not sleep much, and stay awake to watch for predators. Allison and Chichetti (1976) discovered that likelihood of being attacked and body size accounted for 58% of the variability of sleep times among different animals.

REM Deprivation

Psychologists have also deprived subjects of just REM sleep, the stage where most dreams occur. Using an EEG machine, psychologists awaken subjects as they enter REM sleep. When the REM-deprived subjects were allowed to sleep again, they dreamed for 60% more time than usual. This phenomenon is called **REM rebound.** Compared to control subjects, the REM-deprived subjects had problems concentrating and remembering. Despite early evidence, later studies found that there was no evidence that REM deprivation made subjects more irritable or tense than controls. Curiously, although REM deprivation did not impair performance in simple verbal tasks, REM deprivation did interfere with recall of emotionally toned words. When a violent film was shown prior to sleep, REM-deprived subjects also were more upset during the second viewing of that film than others. A good night's sleep really may make life seem less upsetting.

Sleep Disorders

The most common sleep disorder is **insomnia,** or the inability to sleep. Insomnia affects at least 20% of the U.S. population at some point in their lives. People need very different amounts of sleep. One 70 year old woman observed in a sleep laboratory only required one hour of sleep daily and felt that most people wasted time in bed. Therefore, there is no standard definition of insomnia; it depends on the individual's expectations. One odd syndrome, called **pseudoinsomnia,** occurs when people dream that they are staying awake. In the morning, they are not refreshed, despite having had a full night's sleep. They remember staying awake for hours.

Insomnia is not a disease; it is a symptom. It may be caused by pain, breathing difficulties, or, most commonly, by sleeping pills. Patients who take sleeping pills eventually develop a tolerance for the drug and suffer withdrawal symptoms or "rebound" if it is taken away. The drugs lose their effectiveness, and patients need larger doses to get to sleep. Any attempt to reduce the dosage leads to severe insomnia, and the patient begins to suffer from drug-dependency insomnia. Kales, Scharf, Kales, and Soldatos (1979) found that an insomniac can suffer rebound after taking sleeping pills for as little as three nights.

One dangerous cause of insomnia is **sleep apnea,** a breathing disorder commonly associated with snoring. Patients will fall asleep, and cease to breathe. The level of carbon dioxide in the blood rises until the person wakes up and begins to breathe. When the level of oxygen in the blood returns to normal, the person falls asleep again, and the cycle repeats itself. Victims may not realize they have slept at all, and will feel fatigued the next day. Sleep apnea may be the cause of sudden infant death syndrome (SIDS). In SIDS, infants may not wake up when there are high levels of carbon dioxide in the blood.

People suffering from **narcolepsy** may well wish they were insomniacs. Narcoleptics suffer from "sleep attacks"; they may suddenly fall asleep at any time, in any place, though they are more likely to fall asleep under dull, monotonous conditions. Very emotional or upsetting situations can also trigger attacks. A narcoleptic will commonly fall asleep in the midst of a fit of anger, or while laughing too hard. After a few minutes, the narcoleptic patient will wake up. Narcoleptics cannot drive and must carefully arrange their lives. The cause of this syndrome is not known.

Sleepwalking, or **somnambulism,** affects between one and five percent of the population. It occurs most often in males, children, and people who have suffered from enuresis (bedwetting) and have a family history of somnambulism, and usually disappears by the time the sleepwalker reaches adolescence. It is not a sign of a mental disorder. Sleepwalking is also not a way of "acting out" a dream; as in REM sleep, a person is paralyzed. Some psychologists believe somnambulism is a symptom of epilepsy, as there is a higher frequency of EEG abnormalities among sleepwalkers than non-sleepwalkers. There are continuing disputes as to what goes on during sleepwalking. Some psychologists believe the sleepwalker is awake, others believe he continues to sleep. In general, a single sleepwalking episode lasts between 15 and 30 minutes, and the sleepwalker has no memory of the incident.

Many investigators also consider **nightmares** to be sleep disorders. Although everyone dreams, nightmares are not terribly common. They are slightly more common in emotionally disturbed adults and young children. Nightmares tend to happen towards the end of an NREM period, not during REM sleep; thus, they seldom have very much of a "plot." People awakened during stage 4 NREM sleep do not report narrative dreams but some scenario in which they are being smothered or crushed. This sensation is accompanied by fear or dread.

DREAMS

Content and Interpretation: Freudian Theory

For thousands of years, dreams have been the stuff of legend. From the Biblical Pharaoh's visions of feast and famine, to Cary Grant in Alfred Hitchcock's *Spellbound,* people have credited dreams with special insights, even the ability to foretell the future if only properly interpreted. Nowadays, psychologists are more concerned with dreams' depictions of ideas a person cannot express in everyday life.

Sigmund Freud was the first major psychologist to consider dreams meaningful. Many other psychologists saw dreams as the "garbage" of mental life. Freud, on the other hand, believed that dreams provide the clearest example of unconscious processes at work, i.e., parts of mental activity of which the individual is usually not aware. Like past interpreters, Freud believed that he could tell the meaning of dreams. According to psychoanalytic theory, the psychological energy a person consciously uses is shifted to the unconscious portion of the brain while a person is asleep. The content of dreams is then dependent on emotions which have been aroused that day. These emotions are linked to primary sexual and aggressive drives, as well as repressed memories of these drives.

While studying children, Freud found that most dreams had to do with wish fulfillment. For example, a child who wanted a particular toy might dream that he would get it. However, adults' motives are not so clear. Though most adults reported that their dreams were nonsense, Freud believed he observed two types of interrelated content in those dreams. The **manifest** or **surface content** is the information about the dream that the dreamer can remember and report afterward. Beneath the manifest content lurks the **latent content,** the unconscious desires causing the dream. These desires are usually related to sexual or aggressive drives. Freud thought that these desires were too painful to recognize during waking hours. Thus, they enter dreams.

However, even in dreams unconscious wishes remain hidden and are indirectly expressed. They appear in a disguised form through what Freud called the dream process. A few common Freudian dream symbols are: Parents as emperors, empresses, kings, and queens; children (siblings) as small animals; birth as water; death as a journey. In this way, unconscious wishes are communicated in code. The problem is to determine what a particular person's code means.

Freud identified four ways that dreams disguise unconscious desires. The first of these dream processes is **condensation,** where one person or object represents characteristics of many different familiar things. A character in a dream may dress like one person, talk like another, and so on. A second process, **displacement,** carries psychic energy from sources of unconscious drives to other, less significant images. The most prominent elements of a dream do not carry much meaning with regard to unconscious drives, while small details are full of unconscious significance. **Symbolization** occurs when dream elements have common meanings for many people for example, a goblin or Santa Claus. Finally, in **secondary elaboration,** dream elements are arranged to form a "whole" dream. A story line or events from the day before are used to fill in transitions between events.

Freud's analysis of dreams was an art, not a science. No scientific method for proving or disproving Freudian dream theory exists, and it is difficult to believe that one ever will.

Daydreams

Daydreams are not like the fantasies of sleep. A daydream is a fantasy an individual creates while awake, to conjure up images that are gratifying. Daydreams are controlled by waking consciousness. Hence, they are usually closely related to reality and are logical and coherent. In daydreaming, unlike night-dreams, the dreamer willfully controls her thoughts. Also, in daydreams most people recognize they are fantasizing, while night dreams are, strangely, undifferentiable from real life. In some sleeping-dreams, called **lucid dreams,** people not only realize that they are dreaming, but act to change and control them. Many cultures teach people to increase their rate of lucid dreaming; however, among United States psychologists, the concept is controversial.

HYPNOSIS

Hypnosis is a sort of intermediate state of consciousness. Hypnotized subjects experience a relaxed mental state and lack the ongoing "stream of consciousness" which occurs in most waking states. It is not a form of sleep. Hypnotic subjects' EEG indicates that they are in a waking, active state. Subjects under hypnosis are in a state of **hypersuggestibility;** they readily accept almost any instruction and information from the hypnotist, no matter how bizarre.

Hypnosis was first popularized in the late 18th century by a Viennese physician named Anton Mesmer. Generally, hypnosis is induced while the subject is sitting or lying down. The hypnotists will ask the subject to relax, suggesting that the subject is becoming sleepy. The hypnotist builds on these suggestions, telling the subject that he is relaxed, until the subject enters a hypnotic state. This process, called the **induction procedure,** may involve an object—a swinging watch is a favorite—to focus the subject's attention while the hypnotist talks. Certain drugs, such as sodium pentothol, can bring on hypnotic trances if administered in small doses by depressing the central nervous system.

Hypnotists will then give the subject instructions to follow either during or after the session. For example, the hypnotist may tell an overweight subject to close her mouth any time in the future she sees chocolate. This sort of long-lasting instruction is called a **post-hypnotic effect.** A post-hypnotic effect is any phenomenon that occurs in ordinary, waking consciousness because of a suggestion made during hypnosis. Subjects often rationalize post-hypnotic behavior. At the end of the session, the hypnotist will tell the subject to wake up after a signal, like a finger snap, and the subject will return to a normal waking state.

Though hypnotic states can be faked for most observers, true hypnosis has distinctive characteristics. Subjects who are not "woken up" from their hypnotic states before their hypnotist leaves the room usually emerge from the state after 15 to 20 minutes; subjects merely simulating hypnosis wake up immediately. The hypnotic state itself can be diagnosed through eight major characteristics. Hypnotic subjects are **passive,** and quietly accept the hypnotist's suggestions. They have **selective attention,** and focus solely on one object or event to which the hypnotist tells them to pay attention. They suffer from **distorted perception;** if the hypnotist tells subjects that their vision is blurred, or that they will feel no pain, the subjects will follow the hypnotist's suggestions. This distortion can extend as far as sensing stimuli which do not exist, such as a cabinet-sized breathing tomato. The hypnotized subjects will undergo **altered awareness,** becoming keenly aware of their bodies or ignoring them at the hypnotist's whim. The subjects will display a **lack of emotion,** unless the hypnotist tells them to do otherwise. Hypnotists' subjects may have **altered memory,** and either remember formerly hidden information, or forget under the hypnotist's instruction. A hypnotist can instruct a subject to forget his own name or to forget the entire hypnotic episode when he awakens. A last feature of hypnosis is **altered identity** and **regression.** A hypnotist can suggest that a subject act like another person, or regress the subject to an earlier age of his or her own life. If a hypnotist asked a subject to act like a four-year-old, the subject would begin to act the way she believes a four-year-old acts, not necessarily the way four-year-olds actually act. In a few famous cases, like the Bridey Murphy affair, hypnotists have claimed to make their subjects regress to past lives. However, in the case of Bridey Murphy in particular and others in general, the subjects were found to be manufacturing interesting stories that could not be matched with actual past events or language for the hypnotists' benefit.

Applications of Hypnosis

Hypnosis has been applied to almost every branch of medicine, mostly for its effects on pain and stress. Hypnosis can be extremely useful to terminally ill cancer patients, since it can reduce pain so much that narcotics like morphine, which keep patients from thinking clearly, become unnecessary. Hypnosis is also used to relieve stress and overcome undesirable habits, like overeating. Aside from these humane uses, hypnosis is most often used for entertainment. People enjoy watching their friends and enemies behave in bizarre ways. Yet these public displays have encouraged people to think of hypnosis as a con game, or a form of magic. It is neither. Hypnosis is a real, distinct phenomenon of consciousness.

MEDITATION

Meditation is another altered state of consciousness. Through physical and mental exercises the subject achieves a relaxed and tranquil state, generally with the aim of having a religious experience. Yet meditation requires intense concentration to rid the mind of daily concerns and thoughts and achieve a state of complete relaxation. Meditation is typically associated with Eastern religions, but is widespread in Western religions, too.

Techniques

Meditative states are induced through a variety of special exercises. The meditator usually sits or kneels in a comfortable position. The setting is generally quiet and simple, to prevent distractions. The meditator then concentrates on something. In Zen meditation, the meditator thinks of her breathing. In Yoga, he may focus his attention on nonsense sound patterns called mantras, or objects, like a burning candle, called yantras. In transcendental meditation, a technique very popular in the U.S. in the 1970s, individuals sit quietly and try not to make an effort to concentrate on the mantra or anything else. The meditator shifts her consciousness to the mantra when unwanted thoughts intrude, though. In general, the idea is to concentrate one's attention to block out everyday thoughts.

Meditators undergo physiological changes when they meditate. Heart rate slows, and EEG alpha activity increases, as compared to control subjects who are told to simply sit quietly. The same type of physical changes can be found in people who practice transcendental meditation, a fairly simple technique, and in yoga experts and Zen monks who have been practicing meditation for 15 to 20 years. To take advantage of this fact, a psychologist has developed a system called clinically standardized meditation **(CSM),** so that people who wish to relax can take advantage of transcendental meditation techniques without having to subscribe to specific religious beliefs. Many people use meditation to help control anxiety and stress, and in treating certain illnesses worsened by stress, like asthma. Part of the interest in meditation was spurred by **biofeedback,** a system where people learn how to control their heart rate or brain waves by watching them on a screen. As the subject observes how the brain waves change in response to stress or relaxation, she learns how to tell when she is starting to become tense, and how to relax instead.

PSYCHOACTIVE DRUGS AND THEIR EFFECTS

Humans are fascinated with altering their mental state. Most of the **psychoactive drugs,** or drugs that produce subjective, psychological changes in consciousness, have been used for hundreds or thousands of years. Opium was probably used by ancient Sumerians, and the ancient Greek historian Herodotus describes how inner Asian tribes used marijuana. Spaniards invading Mexico found that the Native Americans there used a variety of drugs, including peyote.

There are four main categories of psychoactive drugs: central nervous system depressants, central nervous system stimulants, hallucinogens, and narcotics. If abused, some of these drugs will create an **addiction,** a state of physiological dependence on the drug. An addict who ceases to take the drug may suffer withdrawal symptoms, which include cold sweats, vomiting, convulsions, and hallucinations. Recovering heroin addicts are most prone to these symptoms. A drug abuser may also suffer from psychological addiction, where there are extreme psychological, but not physiological, reactions to withdrawal of the drug.

Depressants, or sedatives, are drugs which reduce anxiety. They do this by inducing muscle relaxation, sleep and inhibition of the action of cognitive centers of the brain. These drugs are also called "downers," as their primary effects are relaxation and drowsiness. Many sedatives have medical uses, such as anesthetics, and some are used to control epilepsy. Tranquilizers, barbiturate sedatives, anti-epilepsy drugs, and alcohol all come under this category. Though alcohol is a socially acceptable elixir in the United States, its effects on the nervous system are just as strong as any other drug. When depressants are abused, early symptoms include poor coordination, slurred speech, and drowsiness. Many sedatives are addictive, and people who stop taking them may suffer withdrawal symptoms and convulsions.

Narcotics are a special variety of depressants. Narcotics may produce euphoria but always relieve pain and make users insensitive to their surroundings, in a sort of stupor. They are also physiologically addictive and have been withdrawn from most medication. Morphine, heroin, and codeine all fall in this category. The human brain produces its own narcotic-like chemicals, called **endorphins,** that can relieve pain.

Stimulants, or "uppers," counteract fatigue and produce mood upswings. By increasing the activity of the sympathetic nervous system, they promote physiological activity and alertness. However, abusers show symptoms of nervousness, argumentativeness, pupil dilation, loss of appetite, and dry mouth and lips. Over the long term, chronic abusers may have hallucinations and psychotic reactions. Common stimulants include caffeine, nicotine, amphetamines, and cocaine (which is addictive).

Hallucinogenic or psychedelic drugs, needless to say, cause hallucinations. These illusions include voices, visual images, and sometimes **synesthesia,** a state where information from one sense causes an image in another. For example, many LSD (lysergic acid diethylamide) users report that music seems "colored," that the sounds they hear are actually accompanied by colored lights floating before their eyes. These drugs also affect cognition (thought processes) and emotion, as well as perception. They may produce pleasurable or depressive emotions, or a sense of detachment from the body. Common psychedelics include marijuana, LSD, psilocybin or "shrooms," and mescaline. Abusing hallucinogens can result in panic attacks and disorientation. Long-term abuse may contribute to psychoses. LSD has the interesting effect of sometimes promoting flashbacks, LSD experiences that occur suddenly and randomly years after the user took the original dose. Recent research implies that these are not memories, but new "trips" resulting from LSD residue in the brain.

REVIEW QUESTIONS

1. True or False: During sleep, the brain is in a constant resting state.

2. REM occurs during _____ sleep.

3. Most muscles are/are not paralyzed during REM sleep.

4. What is the most common cause of insomnia?

5. Match the terms and descriptions. Some terms may be matched with more than one description.

   (a) Daydreams   (1) Lacks the "stream of consciousness"

   (b) Meditation   (2) Characterized by selective attention

                                        (3) A relaxed state

   (c) Hypnosis   (4) Involves concentration

                                        (5) Controlled by waking consciousness

6. List four symptoms of drug withdrawal.

7. What is the name of the phenomenon in which LSD abusers suddenly re-experience a "trip" long after they have stopped taking the drug?

8. Complete the following sentence with a phrase: People who utilize biofeedback learn to control their heart rate or brain waves by _____.

9. Does hypnosis have any practical applications? What are they?

10. A child who dreams that she has a toy she desperately wants is acting on
_____.

ANSWER KEY

1. False

2. stage 1

3. are

4. Sleeping pills

5. (a) 5
   (b) 3, 4
   (c) 1, 2, 3

6. Cold sweats, vomiting, convulsions, hallucinations

7. Flashbacks

8. watching them on a screen and observing the changes

9. Yes: pain reduction, stress relief, overcoming habits, and entertainment.

10. wish fulfillment

Chapter 6

Learning

BASIC CONCEPTS

Learning is a change in behavior caused by experience. Consequently, much of our knowledge of learning has been discovered by **behaviorists,** psychologists who believe that only observable external behavior is a valid topic for study. Behaviorists who practice behavior modification change behavior by working with the environment; they are known as **behavior analysts.** Many behavior analysts work with developmentally disabled children or patients in psychiatric institutions. Others help people to end bad habits like smoking or overeating.

Historically, the psychological study of learning began in Ivan Pavlov's (1849–1936) laboratory in Russia in the late 19th century. Pavlov invented a teaching technique called **classical conditioning.** Using this technique, he taught dogs to salivate at the sound of a bell. In classical conditioning, organisms first display a response to a stimulus that they have not been taught, something they do "naturally"; in this case, dogs salivated when they were fed. The object or signal which provokes the response is called the **unconditioned stimulus,** or UCS. The pre-existing response is called the **unconditioned response,** or UCR. Pavlov's UCS was food, and his dogs' UCR was salivating. Pavlov then started ringing a bell each time the dogs were fed. This bell-ringing was a **conditioned stimulus** (CS) to which an organism would not normally respond. However, since Pavlov paired the bell-ringing (CS) with feeding the dogs (UCS), the dogs learned to associate the two stimuli. The dogs began to salivate whenever the bell was rung, with or without being fed. This new salivation is a **conditioned response** (CR). The new, double-drooling dogs are said to have **acquired** the conditioned response.

This, then, is the principle of all classical conditioning: a conditioned stimulus is paired with an unconditioned stimulus for a particular number of trials. When the subject produces a conditioned response to the conditioned stimulus, it is said to have acquired the CR. Operant, or **instrumental conditioning,** designed by B.F. Skinner, works on different principles. Here, a response is increased by a **reinforcer,** a reward which both follows a behavior and increases the rate of that behavior. For people, a reinforcer could be food, a chance to perform some favorite activity (reading, mountain climbing, etc.), an object, or money, which could be used to obtain any number of rewards. A food pellet is a reinforcer for a rat in a cage. If a child is given a peanut as a reinforcer for setting the table, the child will set the table more and more often. When the organism produces the response often enough, the trainer will withdraw the rewards. The organism will continue to produce the response for a time (see "Extinction" on page 83).

PUNISHMENT

The opposite of reinforcement is **punishment,** which decreases the rate of the response it follows. Both reinforcers and punishments can be divided into two categories: positive and negative. A positive reinforcement or punishment involves adding something to an organism's environment, like a piece of candy, or a stream of freezing cold water very early in the morning. A negative reinforcement involves taking something away from an organism, such as a very loud buzzing noise (reinforcement). Negative reinforcement is NOT punishment; it is a removal of something unpleasant, an "escape" from an unwanted condition.

In general, behavior analysts try to avoid using punishment. There are several good reasons to do this, even though delivering punishment can be a very quick and effective way of changing behavior. In terms of conditioning, obviously, punishment creates unfortunate emotional effects in the punished subject, which can interfere with any behavior the analyst is attempting to teach. In addition, punishment does not teach any new behavior to replace whatever response is being punished; it only teaches what not to do. Any stimulus that accompanies punishment, even random decorations in the room, can become punishing itself, a fact which partly explains some people's fear of schools and dentist offices.

Many psychologists believe that phobias develop this way, and treat them through a conditioning process titled **systematic desensitization.** In this conditioning, the person with the phobia is taught relaxation techniques. When the person can control his or her state of relaxation, the psychologist gradually introduces stimuli that are more and more similar to the object of the phobia. A person who is afraid of dogs might be shown pictures of a dog at first, then perhaps a stuffed toy dog, then stand in the same room with the dog. Gradually, the person associates relaxation with the phobic stimulus instead of fear.

Punishment also affects organisms in ways which have nothing to do with conditioned responses. Strong punishment leads to aggressive behavior; humans and animals who are punished tend to "lash out" and attack the first available victim after they are punished, even if that victim had nothing to do with the punishment. Children who are punished will model the adults who punish them and may learn to be aggressive (see "Observational Modeling" on page 86). Finally, punishment is addictive. A punishment may produce a quick end to a response and tempt the punisher to ignore positive reinforcement. When the behavior returns, the punisher has no choice but to continue to punish, starting a vicious cycle. Punishment should be a last resort.

Four major factors affect a reinforcer's (or punishment's) effectiveness. The **Principle of Contingency** states that a reinforcer is most effective if that reinforcer is delivered only when the desired response occurs. If the behavior analyst gave a child a peanut for doing nothing, no new response would arise. To make sure that the organism learns that the response and the reinforcer are associated, the **Principle of Immediacy** states that reinforcers must be delivered immediately after the response is made. If you feed your little brother a peanut a day after he has set the table, he may be grateful for the peanut, but he will not set the table any more often. The **Principle of Size** states that the more of a reinforcer is delivered after a response, the more effect it will have on behavior. Wouldn't your little brother be delighted if you gave him a whole bag of peanuts after he set the table, instead of just one? Unfortunately, you would then confront the **Principle of Satiation,** that the more an organism is deprived of a reinforcer, the more effective it will be. Conversely, an organism that has received a reinforcer too often or too recently will not respond as often as it might. If you feed your little brother a bag of peanuts for setting the table for lunch, he will not be very much inspired by your offering a peanut for setting the dinner table. Depending on his size, he might not wish to come to dinner at all.

In this example, your brother's peanut is a **primary reinforcer,** a reward he enjoys without having to learn to enjoy it. Other reward items are not inherently desirable. Money is merely a collection of pieces of paper and hard metal disks, and a designer suit may be worse looking and more cheaply made than its more economical peers. Yet these objects can be traded in for food, shelter, changes in social status, a better job, and so on. Money and designer clothing are **secondary reinforcers,** which become reinforcing through their association with primary reinforcers, in a process similar to classical conditioning. Money belongs to a special class of reinforcers called **tokens,** which can be accumulated and exchanged for other reinforcers. Other examples of secondary reinforcers include gold stars on a grade-school teacher's spelling chart and praise, which are associated with better treatment from teachers and parents. In a laboratory, a rat may push a lever to turn on a green light, which is associated with a time when lever-pushing will bring food.

One interesting demonstration of the power of secondary reinforcers is **higher-order conditioning,** also known as second-order conditioning, a variant of classical conditioning. When a neutral stimulus is paired with a conditioned stimulus, the subject will learn to produce the conditioned response to the neutral stimulus. The new neutral stimulus will provoke the CR, even though it was never paired with the original CS. In his original experiment, Pavlov used the sound of a metronome as a conditioned stimulus, with meat powder as the UCS to produce the UCR of salivation. In the higher order conditioning experiment, Pavlov used a card with a black square on it as his new neutral stimulus, pairing it with the sound of the metronome. No meat powder followed the sound of the metronome, though. Yet the response to the metronome had been so strongly reinforced previously that the card with the black square produced salivation after only a few pairings with the metronome. Usually it is not possible to teach a third stage of higher-order conditioning, since the original conditioned stimulus and the second conditioned stimulus are no longer followed by the UCS.

BEHAVIOR MODIFICATION

In any case of behavior modification, it is important to have a clear **behavioral definition,** a clear description of exactly what behaviors are to be observed, and changed. For example, if you complained to a behavior analyst that your little brother was "too whiny," the behavior analyst could not easily observe the behavior. She might believe that your little brother was just whiny enough. Together, you and your behavior analyst might decide that your brother cries very loudly far too often and for far too long. Then, with that definition in hand, you could directly observe the behavior, and record how often it occurs. In other words, you record the behavior's **baseline,** the usual rate or level of a behavior. Behavior analysts record the baseline for a behavior so they can objectively judge if the rate behavior changes when they introduce the **treatment,** a method that changes the rate of behavior, either reinforcing or punishing it.

The rate of learning can be shown on a graph called a **learning curve.** It was originally developed by Bryan and Harker (1897) to show the improvement in telegraphers' performance over time. The graph shows their results:

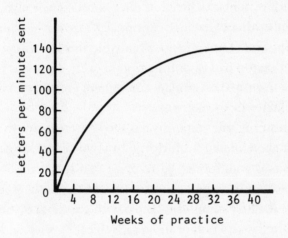

In early weeks, the telegraphers made dramatic improvements. Then, the gains became smaller and smaller, and gradually leveled off. This particular pattern, where improvement slows down after a certain point, is termed a negatively accelerated learning curve. Many types of learning show this pattern, though not all of them are negatively accelerated. The fact that this sort of curve is found in so many types of learning has led to speculation that all forms of learning follow the same laws.

After an organism has learned a CR to a stimulus, it will make the same response to stimuli which resemble the original stimulus. This process is called **generalization**. The more similar the new stimulus is to the original, the more likely it is that the CR will occur. For example, J.B. Watson, the father of American behaviorism, once demonstrated generalization in an experiment which might be considered unethical today. Watson took an 11-month-old boy, named Albert, and made a loud clanging sound while he touched a white rat. Poor little Albert was very frightened by the noise and would cry and avoid the rat after only seven pairings of the noise and rat. This was a classical conditioning procedure, where the UCS is the noise, the CS the rat, and the CR fear and crying. A few days later, Albert not only feared the rat, but a white rabbit, a dog, and a white sealskin coat, as well as a Santa Claus mask and Watson's white hair. Albert generalized his fear of the white, furry rat to include all manner of white, furry things in his environment. Some phobias also generalize. For example, a person who is afraid of spiders may become frightened of dark places or the woods (spiders may live there), or other arachnids (they look similar). Again, systematic desensitization is a useful treatment for phobic disorders.

In some cases, an organism will learn **discrimination,** or to respond differently to similar stimuli. Unlike generalization, discrimination must be learned. Conditioning discrimination can backfire, though. If an experimenter rewards a rat for pushing a black circle but does not reinforce pushing a white circle, the result could be that a rat which continually chooses the white circle will cease to push anything at all. Experimenters can avoid this behavioral trap, as will be shown below. An example of discrimination in every day life is responses to traffic lights. People learn to discriminate among red, green, and yellow lights, and they respond differently to each one.

In some cases, learning one response can keep an organism from learning another in a phenomenon known as **blocking.** In a typical blocking experiment, one group of subjects is conditioned to respond to a specific CS—say, a red light—while another group is not conditioned. Then, both groups are put through trials where the first stimulus is paired with a second, distinct CS. The red light could be paired with a puff of air on the subject's eyelid, and both could be paired with a UCS electric shock. In later trials, only the second stimulus (the puff of air) is presented to the subjects from both groups. The subjects who were initially conditioned (the red-light subjects) do not respond to the second stimulus. The training for the first stimulus (red light) blocks these rats from learning that the puff of air is also associated with shock. A rat in the first group will cringe, anticipating the shock, when presented with a red light, but only wink at the puff of air; a rat from the second group will cringe at both CSs.

Blocking is an important concept because it shows that learning the relationship between a stimulus and response is not a matter of simple association; then, the animal would learn to respond to the second stimulus easily. According to Rescorla and Wagner (1972), classical conditioning is a process of learning the relationship between events. There is not only a time relationship between events (the shock comes after the red light), but what Rescorla and Wagner call informational relationships. When a rat learns that a red light means that a shock is coming, a puff of air gives the rat no new information about the relationship between the red light and the shock. Thus, the rat does not learn.

EXTINCTION

The process of eliminating a response is called **extinction.** In classical, Pavlovian conditioning, a response is extinguished when the CS is presented without the UCS many times. Then, the rate of responding falls to the level present before classical conditioning began. In Pavlov's case, this would involve ringing the bell and not giving the dogs food afterwards. Gradually, the dogs would learn that the bell no longer signalled food and would cease to salivate at its sound.

Another way to stop the dogs from drooling is to ring the bells constantly for a little while. Like humans, animals stop noticing a stimulus if it is constantly present. You may have noticed a loud clock ticking when you first entered a room, or dull music when you entered a supermarket, and found that you simply did not hear it after a few minutes. This adaptation to a constant stimulus is called **habituation.** It can happen with smells, sounds, or any other sensation and can occur when there is a fairly intense stimulus, like the smell of a skunk. With stronger stimuli, it merely takes longer for an organism to habituate. In operant conditioning, responses are extinguished by ceasing to give rewards. In the case of the rat and the lever, the experimenter extinguishes the behavior by not giving the rat any more food pellets.

Pavlov believed that CRs were only inhibited during extinction and not forever lost. Conditioned behavior can reappear later, even though extinction had seemed successful. This is known as **spontaneous recovery.** If a rest interval follows the extinction of a CR, that response will reappear spontaneously, though it will be weaker. Then, if conditioning is redone using the same stimuli, the original CR will be strengthened quickly. Reconditioning is a faster process than original conditioning. This fact supports the theory that extinction is an inhibition of a learned response. However, in most cases, there is no reason to choose an inhibition theory over the idea that a new, competing response replaces the original CR, a process called counter conditioning.

SCHEDULES OF REINFORCEMENT: CONTROLLING BEHAVIOR

Psychologists not only control whether or not a behavior exists, but how often it occurs. A child who shouts out the answers in class, a student who dawdles on the way to school, a pupil who writes all her papers at the very last minute, a child who cleans her room once a year—these are all examples of behaviors which exist but need to be brought under control.

Time plays an important role in operant conditioning. The schedule or rate of reinforcement has a profound effect on the rate of response and must be carefully considered in any discussion or explanation of operant behavior.

Experimenters sometimes use the continuous reinforcement schedule, where each correct response is reinforced, but more commonly resort to partial reinforcement schedules. Though continuous reinforcement is the fastest way to learn, it is least effective for long-term learning because a rigid expectation of reward is created. The learned response is rapidly extinguished when reinforcements are stopped. Partial reinforcement schedules called **interval schedules** vary the frequency of the reward according to time intervals, while the number of responses is irrelevant. In **ratio schedules,** on the other hand, reinforcement is given according to rate of response, while the time it takes to make responses is irrelevant. In both these schedules, a reinforcer can be delivered on either a regular basis, called a **fixed schedule,** or intermittently, on a **variable schedule.** Combining these schedules yields four basic kinds of partial reinforcement schedules.

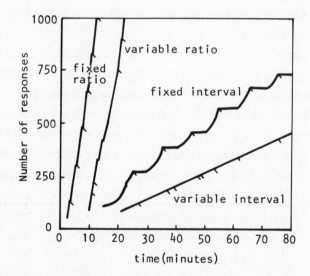

In a **fixed ratio schedule,** reinforcement is given after a set number of responses is emitted. This schedule produces a strong, durable response pattern, though responses tend to drop off immediately after reinforcement. Paying workers after a certain number of baskets of fruit are picked is an example of a fixed ratio schedule.

The number of responses needed before reinforcement is given is intermittent and irregular in a **variable ratio schedule.** This type of schedule produces the highest rates of performance. Response continues at a high, nearly constant rate, sometimes approaching the maximum physical capabilities of the organism. Slot machines provide an example of this type of schedule; the gambler never knows when she will receive the reward. Dishonest gamblers and three-card monte sharks also hook their victims with this type of schedule. At first, the opponent is allowed to win fairly often; eventually, the mark continues to play even when she is not winning at all.

In a **fixed interval schedule,** an organism is rewarded for the first instance of a response after a certain fixed period of time. No matter how much or how little work is done, reinforcement is given after a set period of time. This schedule has the lowest yield in terms of performance. However, just before reinforcement time, activity increases. Most people with salaried positions are reinforced with a weekly or monthly check and are operating on a fixed interval schedule. This sort of schedule is useful for dealing with a child who constantly shouts out answers in class. If the teacher gives the child a reinforcer for answering only once every 15 minutes, then the child will learn to respond near the end of the 15-minute cycle, and not interrupt the class so much in between.

In **variable interval schedules,** the time that must elapse before a response is awarded varies. This schedule tends to have consistent performance but a slightly lower frequency than a variable ratio schedule. Trying to call a busy number is an example of this type of schedule. No matter how often you try, the time (interval) that the line is busy determines when you will be rewarded with an opportunity to speak.

Shaping, Chaining, and Fading

When a response does not exist in an animal's behavioral repertoire, a psychologist must create it. This can be done through either shaping or chaining, two methods of operant conditioning. In **shaping,** a series of responses is taught by reinforcing closer and closer approximations of a behavior. For example, a dog does not learn how to fetch a stick by watching training videos. At first, the trainer may reward the dog for just approaching the stick. Then, the reinforcement may depend on picking up the stick; later, a reward may be given only for carrying the stick toward the trainer. Thus, behavior is shaped gradually until the desired response is produced.

Chaining is a way of teaching a series of responses where each response cues the next. There are three major methods of teaching chaining: forward and backward chaining, and total task presentation. In **forward chaining,** a person learns one response at a time in the usual order that they are produced. Learning the words to a song is one example of forward chaining. The end of one line, together with the melody, serves as a stimulus for the next line. The sequence of responses becomes very important, as you can see by trying to start singing in the middle of a song. However, subjects may not be very motivated to learn each successive response if they are not inherently reinforcing. In **backward chaining,** training begins with the last step of a sequence, which is reinforced. Each step becomes a secondary reinforcer, because producing the right response leads one step closer to gaining a reward. For example, if a toddler is learning how to put on her pants, the behavior analyst might start by putting the pants on the toddler but leaving the zipper and button undone. When the toddler zips and buttons her pants, she gets a reward. Then, the toddler starts with her pants at her ankles. She then must pull up her pants to get to the zipper-and-button step, to get to her reinforcer. The behavior analyst can extend this chain back as far as she likes, as long as completing each step in the chain is sufficiently reinforcing, and prompts the subject to keep going. In **total task presentation,** the subject tries to accomplish the entire series of responses in each learning trial.

Sometimes, once a response is established, a psychologist wants to remove the prompts or stimulus that helped the subject learn the response. For example, in the backward chaining example, a parent may tire of saying "That's great!" to reinforce the response every time the toddler pulls up her pants. The parent could start **fading,** or removing the interrupting stimulus in this operant conditioning procedure, by saying "That's great!" more and more softly over time, until the toddler gets dressed without any prompting.

OBSERVATIONAL LEARNING

Miller and Dollard first developed social learning theory, an attempt to combine principles of social analysis of behavior with principles from behavior analysts' laboratories. Albert Bandura and R.H. Walters refined the theory, emphasizing learning through "modeling." Modeling consists of imitating the behavior of another person. When accompanied by positive reinforcement, modeling is an efficient technique for learning the social roles that are expected of a person in different situations.

Bandura and Walters observed four processes which are involved in modeling. The first is the **attention process.** Exposure alone does not ensure that learning will occur. It is also necessary for the learner to pay attention to the model. Several variables affect attention, including distinctiveness and the likability of the model, the learner's history of reinforcement for paying attention to similar models, the psychological state of the observer, and the complexity of the behavior to be modeled. Next, the **retention process** refers to the observer's capacity to recall what the model did. In the **reproduction process,** the observer must use memory to guide an actual performance. The student driver may recall the steps he observed when learning to parallel park: "Align the front wheels of your vehicle with the back wheels of the car in the space in front of the one where you are going to park." Even with correct recall, the performance will be influenced by the learner's physical abilities. If the teacher is with the learner and is able to give feedback on parts of the parking process that have been incorrectly retained or for which a particular skill needs to be refined, the learning becomes more rapid. Thus, abilities and feedback are important guiding processes during a learning experience.

In the **motivational process,** although an individual may have acquired and retained the observed behavior, she will not translate it into behavior if that behavior is punishing. The student driver will find herself avoiding the need to parallel park if the first few times she tries it other drivers honk impatiently or yell at her for holding up traffic. If, on the other hand, the attempts at parking yield successful results or are reinforced by encouragement, the learner may be positively motivated to exhibit the behavior she has learned.

REVIEW QUESTIONS

1. What do these abbreviations stand for? What is the relationship between them?

    UCS CS CR UCR

2. A reinforcer makes a response more/less likely.

3. Four major factors affecting a reinforcer's effectiveness are _____ , _____ , _____ , and _____ .

4. Is a diploma a primary or secondary reinforcer?

5. True or False: a learning curve starts off steeply, then flattens out.

6. A young boy is painfully bitten by a spider as he steps into the basement one day. Soon, he begins to avoid all dark, enclosed spaces. This is an example of _____ .

7. Rank these four partial reinforcement schedules in terms of frequency of responding: fixed ratio, variable ratio, fixed interval, variable interval.

8. True or False: in shaping, a trainer teaches an organism a sequence of responses one at a time, so that each becomes a stimulus for performing the next.

9. In modeling, a learner _____ the behavior of another person.

10. True or False: negative reinforcement is a form of punishment.

ANSWER KEY

1. Unconditioned stimulus, conditioned stimulus, conditioned response, unconditioned response. If an US which produces a UR is paired with a CS, then the CS will in turn produce a new instance of the UR termed the CR.

2. More likely

3. contingency, immediacy, size, satiation

4. Secondary reinforcer

5. True

6. generalization

7. Highest to lowest: fixed ratio, variable ratio, fixed interval, variable interval

8. False

9. imitates

10. False

Chapter 7

Intelligence

THE NATURE OF INTELLIGENCE

Cultural Definition

Our society believes that intelligence is very important. Intelligence tests are used to decide what schools people should attend, what jobs they can get, and whether or not they are just plain "smart." However, psychologists generally cannot agree on what exactly intelligence is. E.G. Boring once declared, "Intelligence is what intelligence tests measure." If that were the only meaning of intelligence, no one but psychologists would care about it.

Broadly defined, intelligence seems to be the ability to adapt. This ability can be described as a set of abilities, or just one factor in an organism's mental make-up. This may seem a far cry from scribbling in little egg-shaped spaces to show a computer that you know the answers on your Scholastic Assessment Test, but Western Society has equated intelligence with education, and there is nothing you can do about it. With the growth of public schooling, it became important to judge both individual students and their performance as a group, to rate school performance. American intelligence tests like the Stanford-Binet scales were developed to fill this need.

Still, though intelligence test scores may correlate with performance on many intellectual tasks, such as school grades, they do not measure other abilities that people in many other cultures would consider as requiring intelligence, such as finding your way home on a dark country road under a new moon, or negotiating with a salesperson to get the best price. If your job requires more negotiating than studying, your score on an intelligence test may not be the best indication of your ability—or intelligence.

Intelligence and Creativity

Creativity and intelligence are simply not the same thing. Thurstone observed that creativity is influenced by many nonintellectual aspects of temperament and encouraged by a receptive (as opposed to critical) attitude towards new ideas. Barron (1958, 1969) was curious to know how highly creative people differed from their equally intelligent colleagues. Barron assembled two groups from four professions: science, architecture, literature and mathematics. One group consisted of individuals who were considered "highly creative" by their colleagues, while the other group contained individuals who were not thought to be "highly creative." There was no significant difference in IQ between the two groups. Barron found that creative people were more likely to be able to integrate diverse stimuli, to be high in energy, to be able to think of many different words quickly, to be dominant and assertive, to be impulsive, to be interested in music, art, literature, and social service activities, to prefer complex to simple stimuli, to perform in different kinds of situations effectively, and to be less susceptible to social influence in making decisions.

There are many aspects of creativity which cannot be measured on intelligence tests. Tests of **divergent thinking,** i.e., the ability to generate a variety of solutions to one problem, are the best psychological method of measuring creativity. **Convergent thinking,** or thought designed to produce just one end result, is not generally used during creative thinking. The question of whether or not a creative person must also be intelligent remains. Are creative people necessarily intelligent, or is it possible to be a genius in one field and have normal or subnormal general intellectual ability? Correlations of creativity with current intelligence test scores are fairly low. An intelligent person would naturally have more information at her disposal to use creatively. Yet the secret of creativity seems to be the *way* a person thinks, not what she thinks of.

TWO THEORIES OF INTELLIGENCE

Can intelligence be reduced to just a few "smart" factors, or are there many different aspects of intelligence? Charles Spearman favored the more reductionistic approach in his two-factor theory of intelligence. Spearman believed that all intellectual activities share a single common factor which he called the general factor, or "g." In addition to "g", he posited several specific, or "s," factors which belong strictly to a single activity. Positive relationships between any two intellectual functions, like mathematical and reading ability, are a result of "g." Spearman claimed that a two-factor theory meant that psychological testing should aim to measure each individual's amount of "g." Similarly, L.L. Thurstone believed in just seven primary abilities, including spatial ability, computational speed, perceptual speed, grasp of word meanings, speed of manipulating single words, rote memory ability, and logical reasoning.

In contrast, Guilford believed that intelligence was the result of multiple factors, or a set of traits. To explain his theory, Guilford developed the **"structure of intellect"** model of intelligence. This model describes the factors of intelligence by classifying them according to three dimensions, termed operations, contents, and products. The **operations dimension** specifically describes what a person does when she is using that particular intellectual factor. These factors are categorized as cognition, memory, divergent production, convergent production, and evaluation. Contents are the materials on which operations are performed. These contents can be figural, symbolic (letters, numbers), semantic (words), or behavioral (information about the way other people act). Products are the end result of operations, or the form in which information is processed. Products are classified as units, classes, relations, systems, transformations, and implications.

There are 120 (5 operations x 4 contents x 6 products) categories of cells in Guilford's three-dimensional theoretical "structure of intellect" model. There is at least one, and possibly many, intelligence factors for each cell. Thus, at least 120 factors make up intelligence in Guilford's theory. Each factor of intelligence is described in terms of all three dimensions. For example, verbal comprehension corresponds to the cognition (operation) of semantic (content) units (product). Another intelligence factor would be memory (operation) for symbolic (content) units (products), or the ability to memorize and recall a string of numbers.

Of the 120 factors of intelligence Guilford stated must exist, 98 have been identified. Guilford's method of assessing intelligence includes specifically measuring each separate factor of intelligence, to account for unique and individual differences in intelligence. For example, people who are lacking verbal skills because of a particular cultural background can be assessed on other non-verbal factors.

HEREDITY VS. ENVIRONMENT

Misconceptions about the relationship between heredity and intelligence have caused pain for millions of people. In the U.S. alone, Irish, Italians, eastern European Jews, Chinese, African-Americans, and women have all been accused of being less intelligent than white men, and have been denied jobs, education, and legal rights in part because of these claims.

It is true that in the U.S. the IQ scores of African-Americans are on average 15 points lower than those of whites. However, the range of IQ for European Americans and African-Americans is the same: every race contains genius. The mean IQ difference has no meaning for specific individuals, only the distribution of scores for the entire population. Approximately 16% of the African-American population scored above the mean for the European-descendents.

The problem with comparing different racial groups is that IQ tests have traditionally been tested only on one population: relatively affluent Americans of white European ancestry. IQ tests may be as effective tests for cultural similarity to this population as intelligence. In one famous study, a group of black infants, whose natural parents' IQ was average for blacks in general, was adopted into white middle class professional homes. Their group IQ increased to 105. Whether it was the case that the babies' biological parents grew up in a deprived learning environment, or that their adopted parents taught them to adapt to the cultural norms expected on IQ tests, it is clear that the environment has a strong effect on intelligence.

The highest average correlation of intelligence test scores, the correlation between identical twins raised together, is .87. Clearly, they have similar scores on intelligence, though they are not exactly the same. Yet for parents and children, or siblings raised together or apart, the average correlation is about .50, but measured correlations range from .20 to .80. Though there clearly is a genetic component to intelligence, at this point it is impossible to tell how important it is, and if it is more important than environment.

MEASURING INTELLIGENCE

IQ, Tests, and Intelligence

Intelligence is not IQ. Intelligence is a complex concept which is still under debate. An IQ, or intelligence quotient, is a score on an intelligence test, which may or may not be an accurate measure of intelligence. Psychologists still disagree as to whether intelligence is a single function or several different abilities. If intelligence is the same as academic achievement, then an IQ is an excellent way to measure intelligence, since IQ tests are usually validated by comparing them to subjects' school grades.

The test that introduced the term "intelligence quotient" is the Stanford-Binet Intelligence Scale. First developed by Alfred Binet in 1905, Binet's original tests were meant to separate intellectually normal and subnormal children. Repeatedly revised, the scale is still used today. The Stanford-Binet test is known for its high reliability and predictive value. It is very accurate in predicting future academic achievement and may be best thought of as a measure of scholastic aptitude or achievement, not of intelligence per se.

The Stanford-Binet test is individually administered. There are 20 sets of subtests for 20 levels of ability. There is a separate set of tests for every half year from ages 2-5, for every year from 6-14, and for four adult levels. The items on the subtests are selected so that children of that age or older can pass them, but younger children generally cannot.

To score the test, an examiner determines the child's **basal age,** or the highest level at which the subject passes all the subtests. Testing continues until all the subtests are failed; this is called the **ceiling age.** Items on the Stanford-Binet test are scored on an all-or-nothing basis. For example, an 8-year-old must define eight words on a vocabulary subtest to pass. Many of the subtests are the same for almost all ages, except for the passing requirement. The mental age of the subject is determined by adding to her basal age several months of credit for each subtest passed beyond the basal age.

IQ was once calculated as the ratio of mental age over chronological age (MA/CA). Now, IQs are calculated in terms of deviation from the mean mental age for people of a certain chronological age. It is standardized, so that the average IQ is always 100. Ninety-eight percent of the people who take this test fall in the range between 70 and 130.

The most commonly used intelligence test for adults is the Wechsler Adult Intelligence Scale (WAIS). It was constructed for adults, and thus its test items are often more appropriate for adults than the items from the Stanford-Binet, which was designed for children.

The WAIS consists of 11 subtests which comprise two subscales: General Information, General Comprehension, Arithmetic Reasoning, Similarities, Digit Span, and Vocabulary comprise the Verbal subscale, and Digit-Symbol Substitution, Picture Completion, Block Design, Picture Arrangement, and Object Assembly comprise the Performance subscale. In similarities, the subject is asked to explain how two given objects are similar. The subject's memory is tested on the Digit Span test, where she is asked to repeat a string of three to nine digits read to her. In the Digit-Symbol substitution subtest, nine symbols are paired with nine digits; the subject uses this as a key to fill in as many symbols as he can under the numbers on the answer sheet in 1 and ½ minutes, in a sort of primitive version of newspaper "cryptograms."

Each subtest on the WAIS is scored separately so that areas of weakness are quickly identified. People who are at a cultural disadvantage are also easily identified by poor performance on the General Information, General Comprehension, and Vocabulary subtests. Final test results are broken into three scores: verbal, performance, and total.

The three WAIS scores are converted into deviation IQ scores, with the mean set at 100 and a standard deviation of 15. The correlations between Stanford-Binet IQs and WAIS IQs are not as high as one might hope. Younger and "brighter" people score higher on the Stanford-Binet, whereas older and "less intelligent" people score higher on the WAIS. One reason for this difference is that the WAIS does not have a "floor" or "ceiling" for scores, and discriminates poorly among people at the high and low ends of the distribution. It is not clear why there are age differences. The WAIS has high reliability and validity findings are good, yet it is not as good a predictor of future academic performance as the Stanford-Binet.

One series of tests of intelligence, but not IQ, is the Bayley Scales of Infant Development. While adult intelligence is gleaned from academic achievement, infant intelligence obviously has nothing to do with school. No academic achievement or IQ can be predicted from these tests. The Bayley Scales are used to assess an infant's developmental status and discriminate between mentally retarded children and normals. Basically, these scales measure if the child is acting normally for her age. There are three different tests: the mental scale, the motor scale, and the infant behavior record. The Bayley Scales are a list of behaviors; the examiner checks whether they are present.

The mental scale tests functions like perception, memory, learning, and problem solving. Bayley and her associates observed many infants over years to determine when, on average, certain abilities developed. For example, at what age does an infant begin to recognize familiar faces? At what age does a child begin to speak in two-word sentences. The test is a schedule of mental development and how the tested infant compares.

The motor scale provides measures of gross motor abilities such as sitting, walking, stair climbing, and hand and finger coordination. Specific motor skills do develop at specific times, and it is important to notice interruptions in motor development. Often a delay in motor development is the first sign of mental retardation. The intellectual signs of mental retardation are not easily observed until early childhood (2 ½ – 4 years).

The infant behavior record is designed to assess various aspects of personality development, such as emotional and social behavior, attention span, and persistence. It is a good measure of how well the child is being socialized, and how much the infant's environment is socially and emotionally enriched.

Aptitude vs. Achievement

Achievement tests do not only measure the effects of learning, and aptitude tests do not solely measure "innate capacity" independent of learning. The distinction between aptitude and achievement tests is fuzzy at best. Examiners use the term "aptitude" to refer to tests that measure the effects of learning under uncontrolled or unknown conditions. People who take aptitude tests usually have not undergone a uniform past experience, unlike people who take achievement tests. One example of a uniform past experience is a geometry class; the New York State Regents Examination in geometry is an achievement test given to all students who have undergone the uniform prior experience of taking a geometry test in a New York state public high school. An aptitude test, by contrast, is administered to students with a variety of unknown experiences.

The uses of achievement and aptitude tests are also different. Aptitude tests are used to predict later performance, e.g., to determine if an individual will profit from the education at a particular college, if someone will perform well in a training program, etc. Achievement tests, on the other hand, are generally given after training to evaluate what the examinee has learned.

Since achievement tests and aptitude tests have different uses, they are validated in different ways. An achievement test is judged on its content, while aptitude tests are compared to other tests of the same behavior. For example, an aptitude test might be designed to predict college performance. Therefore, its scores would be checked against college grades to make sure that those scores correlate with the examinee's future academic achievement. However, the line between achievement and aptitude tests is thin. Achievement tests also can be used to predict performance, even though they may have been designed only to measure past achievement.

Cultural Bias

There has been concern that intelligence tests are unfair to culturally disadvantaged groups which are not assimilated into or knowledgeable about the dominant culture in the U.S. It is unfair to judge groups which comprise a different culture on tests which are inherently "culturally biased." There seems to be no question that IQ tests, achievement tests, and aptitude tests are culturally biased. The mere fact that a person needs to have good English skills to do well on them is evidence of cultural bias.

The advantage of developing cross-cultural tests is that it is possible to compensate for the differences between cultures, or the disadvantages many people have been subjected to and to measure innate abilities, such as Spearman's proposed general intellectual ability. Then, people from many different cultures can be compared fairly on their innate ability.

To deal with this problem, psychologists have developed cross-cultural tests. First of all, they attempt to eliminate the problem of different languages by either translating the test, or eliminating language altogether. Language may be eliminated in cases where people may have very different educational backgrounds but perhaps similar intelligence.

Different cultures place different values on speedy performance. In some cultures, or rural environments, the tempo of life is slower, and there is less emphasis on finishing tests quickly. Thus, cross-cultural tests often allow long time limits and give no credit for fast performance, while standardized tests typically have rigid restrictions on time and may be scored according to the total number of items completed.

The most important way that cross-cultural tests differ is in test content. Many tests require that the subject be familiar with objects which are absent in her culture, or which have different uses or values. For example, a person raised with the British game of cricket would assume that a baseball bat is used for hitting balls on the ground, and perhaps fail a portion of a test.

The Leiter International Performance Scale is one cross-cultural scale given to one person at a time. There are no instructions: the subject's understanding of her task is part of the test. The Leiter Scale consists of a frame with an adjustable card holder. The examiner slides a particular card with printed pictures into the frame. The subject is given a set of blocks with printed pictures on them, and is supposed to choose the blocks with the proper response pictures on them. Among the tasks on the Leiter Scale are matching identical colors, shades of grey, forms, or pictures; copying a block design, completing pictures, estimating numbers, completing analogies and series, recognizing age differences, spatial relations, and footprints, remembering for a series, and classifying animals according to habitat.

The Leiter Scale has no time limit, and is scored in terms of the ratio of mental age (MA) over chronological age (CA)—MA/CA. The Leiter Scale IQ does not always correlate highly with the Stanford-Binet and Wechsler IQs and may be measuring different intellectual functions. This fact does support Guilford-type theories of multiple intelligence factors.

Stability of Measurements

If you take an IQ test twice, you may not get the same score both times. Your score may not show stability or consistency over two or more samples. In general, two variables affect IQ stability: the interval between the initial test and retest, and the subject's age. The shorter the interval between test and retest, the more stable the IQ. The older a person is at the time of the initial IQ test, the more accurate that IQ score will be. Intelligence changes during childhood, and the greatest changes occur early. The difference in intelligence between a three-year-old and a four-year-old is greater than the difference between a 15-year-old and a 16-year-old.

In general, IQ scores are fairly stable measures. In a Swedish study, Husen (1951) found a correlation of .72 between the best scores of 613 third grade boys and their test scores 10 years later. The Fels Research Institute (Sontag, Baker & Nelson, 1958) found a correlation of .83 between the Stanford-Binet score of the same individuals at age three and four. At age 12, though, the scores had a correlation of .46 with the scores from age three. The stability of the IQ is effectively the same as its reliability.

One explanation for the increasing stability of IQ with age is that intellectual development is cumulative. A person's skills at any one age include all the skills and knowledge she had at a younger age plus all her newly learned skills and knowledge. Having learning skills like knowing how to read also contributes to IQ stability. The more learning skills a person has, the more she will profit from later learning experiences, and the more stable her IQ will be. One reason behind childhood intervention programs like Head Start is that they help provide children with learning skills.

Environmental stability, or intellectual advantages a person has which persist, such as a house full of books, also account for IQ stability. A large upward or downward change in IQ may be the product of an environmental change (Jimmy broke his leg and had to spend the whole summer reading books), or that the child is developing more quickly or slowly than normal. Drastic changes in the family (divorce, loss of parents, adoption into a foster home) and illness have negative effects on children's intellectual development. Parental concern with a child's educational achievement and general welfare can also shift IQ.

Certain personality traits are also linked to IQ. During preschool years, emotional dependency on parents seems to have a negative effect on intellectual development. During school years, high achievement drive, competitiveness, and curiosity, or the traits associated with an independent child, are associated with IQ gains. Also, emotional stability seems to have a beneficial effect on IQ.

The purpose of determining the stability of an individual's IQ is to anticipate problems she might encounter in her intellectual development. Then, it is often possible to develop intervention programs and change that person's intellectual future.

EXTREMES OF INTELLIGENCE

Retardation

Mental retardation is the lower extreme of intelligence as determined by IQ tests. There are five levels of classification of mental retardation: borderline, mild, moderate, severe, and profound mental retardation. Altogether, they make up about eight percent of the population.

Borderline mental retardation implies an IQ of 68 to 83. During school years they are often "slow learners." Although a large percentage of this group fails to complete high school and can often achieve only a low socioeconomic status, most adults in this group blend in with the rest of the population. This group is not sufficiently retarded to be eligible for specialized services.

People suffering **mild mental retardation** have IQs of 52 to 67. As children they are eligible for special classes for the educable mentally retarded. Adults in this group can hold unskilled jobs or work in sheltered workshops, although they may need help with social and financial problems. Only about one percent are ever institutionalized.

In **moderate mental retardation,** people have an IQ of 36 to 51. Brain damage and other disease is frequent. During childhood, they are eligible for special classes for trainable retardates in which self-care is emphasized instead of academic achievement. Few hold jobs except in sheltered workshops, and most are dependent on their families.

A person who has **severe mental retardation** has an IQ of 20 to 35. Most are institutionalized and need constant care. They need prolonged training to learn to speak and take care of their basic needs. As adults they are friendly but can only communicate on a very concrete level. They engage in very little independent activity and are often lethargic. Genetic disorders or severe environmental insult account for this degree of retardation.

Profound mental retardation describes an IQ below 20. People at this level require total supervision and nursing care all their lives. They can learn little except to walk, say a few phrases, feed themselves and use the toilet. Many have severe physical deformities as well as neurological damage. There is a very high mortality rate during childhood in this group.

The most common cause of mental retardation is **Down's syndrome,** which accounts for 10 to 20 percent of moderately to severely retarded children. Another major cause is **fetal alcohol syndrome,** which results when the mother drinks alcohol during her pregnancy.

Down's syndrome children seldom have an IQ above 50. They have many physical abnormalities: slanting of the eyes, flat face and nose, overly large and deeply fissured tongue, stubby fingers, fingerprints with L-shaped loops instead of whorls, underdeveloped genitalia, and arms and legs that are smaller than normal.

Down's syndrome is caused by a chromosomal abnormality. The vast majority of Down's syndrome children have 47 chromosomes instead of 46. During the earliest stage of an egg's development the two chromosomes of pair 21 fail to separate. When the sperm and egg unite, chromosome pair 21 has three chromosomes instead of the usual two. This is referred to as a **trisomy** of chromosome 21.

Giftedness

On a happier note, gifted children make up about three to five percent of the population. Although traditionally defined as children who score in the top one percent of the population on IQ tests, the term "gifted" is also commonly used to refer to people who have special talents, creativity or leadership ability. Gifted does not mean "genius," though; in psychology, the term refers to children who score over 140 on the Stanford-Binet Intelligence Test.

As gifted people are presumed not to require special aid or education, psychologists have not classified them or studied them as extensively as people suffering from mental retardation. For example, when gifted children grow up, they are no longer termed "gifted." In 1926, however, Lewis Terman published his book *Genetic Studies of Genius,* a longitudinal study of one thousand gifted children. Contrary to expectations of "mad geniuses," Terman found that children with high IQs grew up to be better-adjusted adults than the average-IQ population.

Yet, gifted children do have special needs. Intelligent children may be bored with repetitive, unchallenging classes and become disruptive, or ignore their schooling altogether, becoming "underachievers" who do not fulfill their intellectual potential. Many drop out of school; according to a study by D.S. Bridgman (1961), 55 percent of females and 70 percent of males identified as gifted at the time either dropped out of high school, finished high school but did not enter college, or did not complete their college work once started. If their society or peer-group does not value intellectual ability, gifted children will commonly try to hide their intelligence. Many children don't want to play with a peer who is a "dictionary brain" or "too smart." Conversely, gifted children who are put in classes up to their intellectual ability with older children may not be as socially, physically, or emotionally mature as their older classmates. Rejected by their intellectual and same-age peers, a gifted child can become alienated and very much alone. Ideally, a program for gifted children will take account of these children's wildly different rates of development.

REVIEW QUESTIONS

1. What one phenomenon spurred American psychologists to develop intelligence tests?

2. True or False: Creativity and intelligence are the same ability.

3. Spearman developed a _____ _____ theory of intelligence.
    Guilford believed that intelligence was the result of _____ _____ .

4. When you know that the American white population scores 15 points higher on average than the American black population, what can you predict about a single black individual?

5. True or False: IQ equals intelligence.

6. True or False: The Stanford-Binet intelligence test is a fairly good predictor of future academic achievement.

7. Which IQ test tends to give better results for adults? Which test is used to measure early childhood development?

8. Aptitude tests are given to subjects whose past educational experience is _____ .

9. Is speed of task completion a valid cross-cultural measure of intelligence?

10. The most common cause of mental retardation is _____ _____ , also known as _____ _____ .

ANSWER KEY

1. The growth of public schooling

2. False

3. two factor, multiple factor

4. Absolutely nothing. Population means cannot predict an individual's performance.

5. False

6. True

7. The Wechsler Adult Intelligence Scale (WAIS), the Bayley Scales of Infant Development

8. unknown

9. No

10. Down's syndrome, trisomy 21

Chapter 8

Motivation and Emotion

MOTIVATION

Why do people act the way they do? The study of factors which influence the arousal, direction, and persistence of behavior is the psychology of motivation. It is generally agreed that motives energize behavior, but how they operate and where they come from are still debated. There are basic biological drives such as hunger, thirst, and sex, and there are learned motives such as need for achievement and affiliation. There are also emotional motives such as pleasure, pain, anger, fear, and frustration.

Generally, motivation for behavior is directed towards maintaining **homeostasis,** or a constant internal environment, and establishing both internal and external equilibrium. The idea is that drives or motives indicate a need that must be satisfied to maintain homeostasis. The process of personal adjustment and the criteria for leading a happy and productive life are dependent on finding and using acceptable solutions to various drives (motives).

Needs or tensions rise from primary (basic) drives and secondary (learned or acquired) drives. **Primary drives** are the same for everyone. They consist of visceral or survival functions, kinesthetic (activity) functions, and sensory functions, which deal with reactions to external stimuli. **Secondary drives** vary with the individual because they are acquired through experience. The tendency to alleviate a need or tension will give rise to a motive for behavior. The way a person handles a motive to seek relief determines the degree to which personal adjustment has occurred and whether immature or mature behavior results. Gaining relief or satisfaction from a need involves the following sequential pattern: a motive provokes goal-seeking behavior, which is directed towards relief. For example, young children tend to eat with their fingers. The motive is to seek relief from hunger through goal-seeking behavior (picking up food with fingers and stuffing it into a tiny mouth). Older children are expected to use forks, knives, and spoons. The motive remains the same, but the behavior that brings relief is different. The means and manner of goal-seeking behavior become increasingly complex as a person grows and is influenced by society.

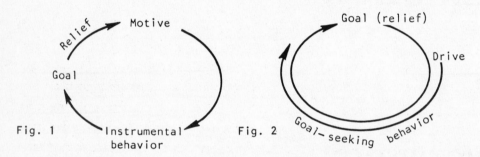

Prior to Darwin, many thinkers throughout the ages and the world differentiated between animal and human motives by claiming that animal behavior was controlled by physical forces, while human behavior was subject to both physical and spiritual forces. In the early nineteenth century, Jeremy Bentham and James and John Stuart Mill founded an English school of thought and said that the basic motive behind all behavior is to avoid pain and seek pleasure. Yet another approach before Darwin is typified by the work of Machiavelli and Hobbes. These thinkers formulated a list of motives which they believed were responsible for most human behavior. Machiavelli maintained that egotism, fear, love, hunger, and sex were the basis for political leadership. Hobbes felt that the contradictions in human desires made it necessary for people to have a strong leader to protect them from themselves.

Darwin's theories of evolution dispensed with the distinction between human and animal motivation. Many thinkers abandoned the concept of will, and their main concern became the internal and external environmental stimuli that cause behavior. These stimuli could be manipulated and changed to change behavior. This new approach facilitated the development of systematic experimental approaches to the study of motivation.

Drives and Instincts

A **drive** is a goal-directed tendency based on a change in an organism's organic processes. A drop in the water content of your blood will make you thirsty, invoking the thirst drive. Primary drives are associated with innate bodily mechanisms. Examples of stimuli having a primary motivational effect are food, water, air, temperature, and almost any intense stimulus such as loud noises or electric shocks. All secondary drives are learned. For humans, these sources of drive include learned desires such as success, power, affection, money, appearance, and security. Some theorists believe that fear, anxiety, and certain verbal cues are also learned drives.

Drives are probably first acquired when a person learns to be discontented or anxious when an object is not present. Eventually, the drive is directed towards this object. Cues such as lack of money, affection, and prestige, could arouse an anxiety reaction with drive properties. When the object is nearby, the anxiety is reduced, and relief is had. For example, a child whose parents are anxious about having no money could become anxious herself. To this child, money could become a higher order conditioned stimulus, which could reduce the anxiety response. In first-world culture, it is no longer common to experience hunger, thirst, or great amounts of pain. Acquired drives appear to be central to any explanation of modern life.

An **instinct** is an unchanging sequence of behaviors that is observed in all members of a species and released by specific stimuli without learning. Behaviors produced by instinct are not affected by practice. The idea was important to Darwin's work, but William McDougall developed the concept. McDougall proposed that each instinct is a response to certain stimuli and contains a tendency to behave in a certain way. This receptivity to certain stimuli and the tendency to respond could change as a function of learning. McDougall also maintained that each instinct has an emotional core that does not change and generated a list which paired instincts with emotions. For example, flight was paired with fear, and the fighting response was paired with anger. During the early part of the century, hundreds of "instinct" theorists published long lists of new "instincts" that were supposed to determine the arousal and direction of behavior. There was no attempt to measure the predictability of these instincts or go about systematic empirical research into their existence. Indeed, the entire concept led to circular reasoning: we love, they would say, because we have a love instinct, and we know we have a love instinct because we love. Today, psychologists generally accept that innate tendencies interact with experience to produce behavior.

Freud and Instinct

Freudian motivation theory assumes that all behavior results from basic innate biological drives. In Freudian terms, an instinct is characterized by four qualities: its source, impetus, aim, and object. The source of tension may be internal or external. The internal sources originate in the body itself and consistently recur, while external sources of tension are irregular. The impetus of an instinct is the force that energizes the instinct. Its force depends on the intensity of the motivating need, since the aim of every Freudian instinct is to reduce or eliminate tension. Sometimes the aim is approached in a number of steps, where each step brings a person closer to reducing tension. For example, a drive for sex can be somewhat reduced simply by making a date with the object of one's desire. The object is anything that will reduce or eliminate the tension. The choice of object is influenced by many variables, including the individual's past learning and expectations.

Hunger and Sex

At the surface, seeking food and sex are basic instinctual behaviors common to all warm-blooded animals. Yet there is evidence that both are drives and possibly learned.

At first, it was thought that hunger was simply a result of having an empty stomach. Yet people who have no stomach get hungry, as do people whose neural links between the stomach and brain have been severed. Both humans and rats seem to prefer good-tasting food over less interesting food, even when the tasty food has less nutritional value. In the early 1980s, Bland (1982) even identified "overconsumption-undernutrition" syndrome, where a person who eats a sugary and unnutritious diet of junk food begins to have a variety of ailments. Certain brain tumors are associated with hyperphagia (causing a voracious appetite) or aphagia (causing inadequate food intake). And yet, Schacter (1971) found that some people overeat because of external cues. According to Schacter, international pilots who ate at their current countries' mealtimes were obese, while pilots who ate according to their internal clock stayed thin. Obese people in highly lit surroundings eat more than their normal-weight counterparts, who eat more when lighting is dim. More obvious cues, like family prompting ("Eat, you look so thin!") or smells associated with delicious food, contribute to heightening the appetite as well as the hunger drive.

If sexual behavior were completely innate, and purely instinctual, it would not be easily manipulated by altering the environment. Yet though the mating season for animals is thought to be innate, altering the amount of artificial light that cats, for example, are exposed to can cause them to demonstrate mating behavior in November and December, when their usual season is from February to June. The role of experience in sexual activity also supports the idea that sexuality is partly learned. While sexually mature rats that have been reared in isolation can copulate normally, monkeys and apes with the same background fare poorly. It appears that the more evolved a creature's brain is, the more important learning is to sexuality. Sexual behavior is more easily influenced by learning than hunger or thirst. In higher animals at least, the survival of the species is dependent on the particular experiences of its individual members.

Incentives: Achievement and Fear of Success

Some psychologists believe that secondary drives are the result of incentives, or reinforcing outcomes of that behavior. Henry Murray used this theory when developing his theories of motivation in the 1930s. Murray observed individual differences in needs, and the question of how these needs develop. Why does a person develop the need to harm others, or be a high achiever? What are motives such as affiliation and achievement supposed to achieve?

David McClelland extended Murray's work to address these questions, specifically the achievement motive. Essentially, he stated that anything that leads to positive affect (emotion) produces approach, and anything that leads to negative affect produces avoidance. McClelland went on to state that experiences which are moderately different from past experience in any way will lead to positive affect and approach, while situations which are very different from past experience lead to negative affect and avoidance.

McClelland easily applied these ideas to the Achievement Motive, or need for achievement (nAch). Individuals who have a high need for achievement would approach, stay in, and perform well in situations with opportunities for achievement, because these achievement environments are similar to environments where their previous learning had taken place. Individuals with a low need for achievement would tend to find these situations negative and tend to both avoid them and perform less well in them, again because their past experience did not include similar environments. Therefore, some environments can be measured as providing more or fewer achievement opportunities. Achievement-oriented individuals prefer environments with moderate risk, need feedback to know what they have accomplished, and need to have individual responsibility for any results. Thus, achievement-oriented people should cluster in entrepreneurial pursuits.

When McClelland first published his results, though, psychologists explained that the findings were not really applicable to women. Some researchers suggested that motives for task-oriented achievement are different for males or females. Much later, in 1968 Matina Horner published a series of experiments on this question. She concluded that women with high abilities and high nAchs have "the motive to avoid success," which is not commonly found in men with the same attributes.

The "motive to avoid success" is supported by certain socialization practices in this society. Supposedly, high achievement is incompatible with "femininity." Women in the U.S. commonly hide or play down their abilities to remain attractive to men, who may feel threatened by smart women. Women with high nAchs have conflicting drives; they need to be involved in achievement-related endeavors, but they also don't want to challenge society's mores. Thus, for high nAch women, optimal achievement situations paradoxically produce both approach and avoidance behavior. Therefore, the achievement behavior of females is more difficult to predict than for males. This area of research is becoming increasingly important today as opportunities for women change dramatically.

Maslow's Hierarchy of Needs

Abraham Maslow, a chief proponent of psychology's humanistic school, is most widely known for his hierarchy of motivations. In this five-stage model, primary needs control an organism's actions until those needs are fulfilled. Then, the next higher needs become dominant until they, too, are satisfied, and so on.

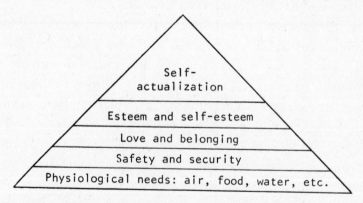

Most of these needs are self-explanatory, except self-actualization. This need refers to the process of developing one's potentiality, achieving awareness of one's identity, and fulfilling one's self. Most of peoples' time is directed towards lower-level needs; the percentage of self-actualizing individuals is thought to be quite small. The higher level needs are expressed more subtly than the lower needs and are thus more difficult to measure systematically. Theoretically, it is possible to assess a person's dominant needs at any point in her life and use this information to predict a pattern in her behavior. Yet Maslow's theory lacks empirical support. An individual's behavior will not reflect her needs unless incentives exist which promise fulfillment of that need. The role of the environment in the fulfillment of Maslovian needs must still be demonstrated.

EMOTION

Emotion is a complex state, generally characterized by a heightened level of arousal. The term **emotion** can be defined in three basic ways: in terms of feelings, responses, and motivation. As a feeling, emotion is a highly subjective state which cannot be objectively or consistently measured. An emotional response, though, not only refers to overt behavior, but to an internal process that occurs as a result of a particular stimulus. Some psychologists consider emotion as a response to one's perception and judgment of a particular stimulus. For example, if a person perceives and judges a particular situation to be very threatening, fear will be the emotional response. Some investigators, such as William James, believed that emotion is a response to the body's internal state. A person who perceives that his heart beats fast will respond by becoming upset. If emotion is considered as a motive, though, the organism is induced to do something to reduce or eliminate that emotion, i.e., rats will pull a lever to dispel a shock, eliminating the emotion of fear. Conversely, emotion can be viewed as a way of energizing a motive. According to Sylvan and Tomkins, when a goal is associated with a particular physiological state, it must be amplified by emotional excitement. In sexual motivation, for example, the motive is ineffective unless it is accompanied by emotional excitement, the energy required for the act.

Emotion can be objectively measured through changes in physiological arousal. During arousal, one or more of the following changes may occur: heart rate (pulse rate) increases, breathing becomes faster, blood pressure rises, pupils dilate, the electroencephalograph (EEG) pattern changes, and galvanic skin response **(GSR)** changes. GSR is a measure of conductance, or how well skin transmits an extremely weak electrical current. When people sweat, their skin conducts electricity better, and the GSR increases.

Different emotional states lead to different bodily changes. For example, fear produces higher blood pressure and heart rate changes than anger. In a phenomenon called directional fractionation, heart rate decreases while other measures (GSR, EEG, etc.) show greater arousal. In a normal arousal state, both heart rate and GSR would increase. Directional fractionation usually takes place in experiments where subjects cannot actively react to stimuli, such as a tape recording of an actor portraying a dying woman.

General Adaptation Syndrome and Stress

When a person undergoes great emotional stress, that person's body will go through three stages of physical response that are collectively called the general adaptation syndrome. The first stage of this syndrome is the **alarm reaction.** This stage consists of the body's usual reactions to heightened emotion, such as increased heart rate. Usually, if the individual continues to be stressed, she enters a second stage called **resistance.** She recovers from the stress of the first stage and attempts to endure it to the best of her ability. There is an excess of epinephrine, one of the hormones secreted by the adrenal gland, which increases heart rate and blood pressure. In this stage, diseases such as hypertension (high blood pressure) and heart disease become likely. If the stress continues even longer, and the individual continues to endure, her body's resources are strained so that the third stage begins; the stage of **exhaustion.** The body's internal resources for dealing with stress are exhausted, and the body cannot tolerate any further stress. Death may result.

When the body reacts to a change in environment, that body is under stress. The emotion associated with stress is anxiety. The severity of stress is related to its quantity (how much stress, how long it goes on, and how strong it is), its predictability, and how soon an anticipated stressful event will occur. Individuals typically react to stress in one of two ways, as **Type A** or **Type B** responders. Type A individuals are usually in a rush. They respond to stress by working harder, or competing more, or with aggression. Type A's tend to be impatient and intolerant of slowness. These are the people who will blow their horns and swear during a traffic jam. Type B's, on the other hand, tend to be more relaxed and patient. They allow stress to "roll off their backs," and are generally less hard-driven. Consequently, Type A people are more severely affected by stress than Type B's. Type A's have a higher incidence of heart attacks, ulcers, and other stress-related diseases.

Types of Emotion and Expression

It is hard to tell just how many different emotions there are. Davitz (1969) counted over 400 different words for emotions in a Roget's Thesaurus. Not all emotions can even be classified as being pleasurable or unpleasurable. Surprise is neither; it depends on the context in which it arises. Classifying emotions by intensity is also problematic. Joy, happiness, fascination, elation, and gratitude are all pleasant emotions, but they cannot be easily ranked.

However, certain types of emotional expression are relatively constant and may be constant throughout the human race. In Ekman's 1973 study, it was noted that over 90 percent of subjects in the U.S., Brazil, Argentina, Chile, and Japan agreed that specific facial expressions showed happiness, disgust, or surprise. Ekman also found wide agreement on the signs of sadness, anger, and fear. These facial expressions do not seem to be culture-specific. Their accompanying facial expressions may be biologically determined.

There are three types of emotional expression: the startle response, facial and vocal expression, and posture and gesture. The **startle response** is usually experimentally elicited by a loud and sudden noise. The response begins with a rapid closing of the eyes and a widening of the mouth. The head and the neck thrust forward while the muscles of the neck stand out with the chin tilting up. The entire response occurs very quickly, and has the most consistent pattern of any emotional response. **Facial and vocal expressions** are much less consistent. Three different dimensions of emotional expression can be observed. In pleasant emotions, the eyes and mouth slant upward; in unpleasantness, both slant downward. In the second dimension, attention is characterized by wide-open eyes, flared nostrils and an open mouth, while in rejection or disgust, eyes, nostrils and mouth are all tightly shut. The voice also indicates emotion through laughter, sobbing, screaming, and groans. A low voice or a tremor may indicate deep sorrow. Anger is usually expressed in a sharp, loud, high-pitched voice. As for **posture** and **gestures,** in happiness or pleasantness, the head is held high, and the chest out. In sorrow, posture is often slumped with the face tilting downward, while in anger aggressive gestures such as fist clenching occur. In fear, the individual either flees or remains frozen in one spot.

Theories of Emotion

Over the years, psychologists have developed several theories of emotion. The James-Lange theory, named in part for William James, asserted that the individual's perception of his physical reactions creates his emotions. The emotional experience occurs after the bodily change and as a result of it. According to William James, if we see ourselves trembling, we are afraid, and if we find ourselves crying, we are sad. The sequence of events is this: the perception of a situation that will produce a bodily reaction; the actual bodily reaction to the situation; the perception of the reaction; and the onset of the emotional reaction as a result.

According to the Cannon-Bard or emergency theory, bodily reactions do not cause emotional reactions; rather, the two occur simultaneously. The emotion-producing situation stimulates nerve cells in certain lower portions of the brain, which in turn activate the cerebral cortex and the body structures. Activity received by the cerebral cortex is felt as emotion, and the activity received by the body structures causes bodily changes typical of the emotion. Physiological states which result from lower brain activity prepare the organism for emergency reactions to threatening or emotion-arousing situations.

The Schacter-Singer theory, or **cognitive theory,** is similar to the James-Lange theory. In this theory, emotion is the result of the individual's interpretation of her aroused bodily state. The main idea is that bodily states which accompany many emotions are similar, and even when these states do differ, the differences cannot be sensed. They seem different because we interpret them or have thoughts about them, and we feel the emotion we believe to be the most appropriate to the situation. The sequence of events according to cognitive theory is: perception of the situation that will produce emotion; arousal of an ambiguous bodily state; interpretation and naming of the bodily state in terms of perception of the external, arousing situation. In Schacter and Singer's experiments, subjects were injected with adrenalin, which makes a person feel nervous and excited. Half the subjects were told what adrenalin would do; the other subjects were merely told that the injection would make them feel numb. Then, the subjects were left in the room with a confederate who was enthusiastically flying paper airplanes around the room. Subjects who knew they had been injected with adrenalin merely sat in chairs and stewed. But subjects who did not know the true effects of adrenalin assumed that they felt aroused because they, too, enjoyed the paper airplanes. These subjects would get up and toss the planes with abandon and seemed to truly enjoy themselves.

To preserve homeostasis, there are optimal levels of various behaviors. According to the **opponent process theory,** this is true of emotions, too. The opponent-process theory says that all emotions are accompanied by an opposite reaction. Fear is followed by relief, sadness by happiness. According to Solomon and Corbit, with each experience of the same emotion, the dominant emotion becomes weaker, while the opponent emotion becomes stronger. Solomon and

Corbit studied sky divers, who were frightened on their first jump. Over repeated jumps, though, the parachutists became more and more relieved, then overjoyed at each jump. In terms of drug addiction, the first dose of heroin might be very pleasurable, yet over time the opponent negative reaction takes over. To achieve the pleasurable state and avoid unpleasant emotion, the addict must take higher and higher doses of the drug.

Yet another explanation for the genesis of emotion is **cognitive dissonance theory.** This theory, originated by Leon Festinger, states that humans have many cognitions (attitudes, perceptions) about the world that can have one of three relations to one another. Cognitions can be **consonant,** in that they follow one another and support behaviors related to one another. For example, a woman who enjoys repairing automobiles will repair her mother's car. The cognitions can be irrelevant to one another, as when a woman who enjoys fixing automobiles calls the hairdresser. Finally, cognitions can be **dissonant,** when two cognitions are contradictory. For example, if the woman who enjoys fixing cars hires a mechanic, she will not be repairing automobiles as much any more. This woman will experience a dissonant state. Dissonance is a negative experience; it produces a motivational state that aims at reducing the dissonance. The greater the dissonance, the more likely it is that the person will try to reduce the dissonance in one of several ways. The woman who hires a mechanic may begin to focus on the positive reasons for hiring a mechanic and deemphasize the fact that she herself likes to fix cars. Dissonance theory predicts that an individual's dissonance-reducing satisfaction with a decision escalates as any of the following factors is increased: the importance of the decision, the negative side-effects of the decision, and the differences between the alternatives the person had to choose from in making her decision.

Another equilibrium theory is Neal Miller's **"approach-avoidance"** situation. According to Miller, when an organism is confronted with a situation that is both attractive and aversive, that organism is likely to experience conflict. This state is called an "approach-avoidance" situation. He postulated that an organism's behavior when choosing among conflicting motives would vary depending on the physical distance from the goal and the relative strengths of the approach and avoidance drives. With motives of equal strengths, the further away the organism is from the goal, the more likely it is to approach it. The closer it gets to the goal, the more likely it is to avoid it. There is a stable equilibrium point where the two forces exactly cancel each other. For example, a person who wants to swim in a cold ocean may spend 10 or 15 minutes trying to decide whether or not to go in. Some other variable usually enters, such as a friend's coaxing or a hot dog vendor, to make one of the motives stronger. This same model can be applied to

approach-approach situations, where an individual must make a choice between two equally desirable alternatives, and to **avoidance-avoidance** situations, where a person must choose between two equally undesirable decisions.

Yerkes and Dodson also had an interesting outlook on equilibrium and arousal. Several animal studies have shown that increased arousal, produced by food or water deprivation, greatly improves performance in learning tasks. An extremely high level of arousal, however, can impair performance in situations that require discrimination among cues or responding appropriately at different times—in other words, complex tasks. Up to a certain point, as arousal level increases, so does performance. This performance increase is reflected in increased alertness, interest, and positive emotion. After the optimum level is reached, as the arousal level becomes greater, there is an increase in anxiety and emotional disturbances, and performance declines. In a graph, the relationship between arousal and level of performance is an inverted U-shape. In real life, students who have high levels of anxiety about tests often do not perform as well as students who are less anxious. The anxious students have a level of arousal which is higher than the optimum.

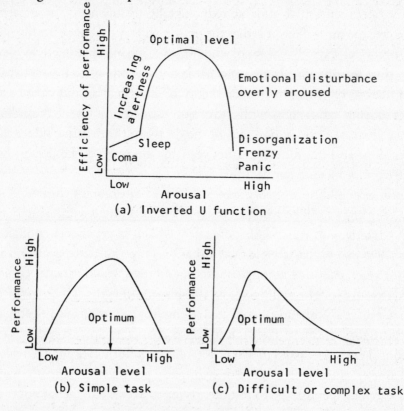

(a) The general relationship between arousal and efficiency can be described by an "inverted U" curve. The optimal level of arousal or motivation is higher for a simple task (b) than for a complex task (c).

Romantic Love

Love may be the least understood, most troublesome emotion on earth. Social psychologists understand it as a special case of interpersonal attraction. Rubin (1973) tried, like thousands of fifth-graders around the world, to differentiate love from liking. Liking, according to Rubin, involves a sense that someone is similar to one's self, and judging that person positively. Love is a matter of not only affiliation, or associating with a person, but dependence, exclusivity and absorption, as well as a desire to help that person. Love can create jealousy; liking seldom does. When Rubin developed his loving and liking scales, he found that couples who score high on the love scale are more likely to plan marriage than couples who just score high on the liking scale.

Walster and Berscheid (1971) conducted a Schacter-Singer like study of labelling and love. They believed that arousal would be labelled love if conditions were appropriate. They had male subjects interviewed by an attractive female interviewer either on an unstable suspension bridge 230 feet above a canyon, or on a low, stable bridge just 10 feet above the ground. The subjects were given the interviewer's phone number in case they had any questions. Half of the unstable-bridge subjects called the interviewer, while less than 12 percent of the stable-bridge subjects called. It seems that an arousing environment may bring people together.

REVIEW QUESTIONS

1. The motivation behind behavior is to maintain _____ .

2. True or False: Many primary drives are learned.

3. Do animals have to practice instincts?

4. According to Freud, all behavior is the result of _____ drives.

5. Which can be more easily influenced by the environment: human sexual or eating behavior?

6. True or False: While both men and women work to achieve success, many women also avoid it.

7. In general adaptation syndrome, the body goes through three stages: _____ , _____ , and _____ .

8. Are emotional facial expressions always specific to particular cultures?

9. Match the answers.

    (a) James-Lange   (1) Emotions and physical reactions are simultaneous

    (b) Cannon-Bard   (2) A moderate level of arousal produces the best performance

    (c) Schacter-Singer   (3) Emotions follow physical reactions

    (d) Festinger   (4) Many emotions involve similar physical states

    (e) Miller   (5) Emotion results from cognitive dissonance

    (f) Yerkes-Dodson   (6) Emotion is produced in approach-avoidance situations

ANSWER KEY

1. homeostasis or equilibrium

2. False

3. No

4. biological (These drives are also unconscious, but they are biological in origin.)

5. Sexual behavior

6. True

7. alarm, resistance, and exhaustion

8. No

9. (a) 3   (b) 1   (c) 4   (d) 5   (e) 6   (f) 2

Chapter 9

Developmental Psychology

THEORIES OF DEVELOPMENT

The study of **development** is the study of how children grow and mature. Growth refers to changes in the size of the body and its various parts, changes which can be quantified. **Maturation** refers to qualitative changes through subtle rearrangement of structures that are already present. For example, maturation of the brain is not typified by adding new cells but by rearranging and reorganizing connections between existing brain cells.

Theorists have questioned development for ages. Historically, in the Middle Ages in Christian Europe, infants were considered miniature adults. Development was only a matter of physical growth, and children were expected to behave as adults. Given that the average life expectancy was about 30 years, this is not as unreasonable an idea as we modern folk might think. Children who misbehaved were often thought to be inherently evil and were beaten. At the end of the eighteenth century, Jean-Jacques Rousseau promoted a theory that children were innately good, and naturally endowed with a sort of blueprint for development. Rousseau saw the duty of parents and teachers as protecting children, and creating an environment where their natural development could occur. One hundred years later, G. Stanley Hall declared that individual development parallels the evolution of the species, in a doctrine called **recapitulation.** Each child would pass through all earlier stages of human existence before reaching the present evolutionary stage as an adult.

The first major figure to stress the importance of environment in human development was John Locke, in the seventeenth century. He believed children were born as a blank slate, or **"tabula rasa,"** and that environmental experiences would determine the course of their development. J.B. Watson, in 1928, founded behaviorism with this concept in mind.

Today, both endogenous (biological) and environmental factors are recognized as necessary to human development. A developing embryo is affected by the environment in its mother's womb. The stresses, such as drugs present in the mother's blood stream, are different for each fetus. This sort of organism-environment interaction is the basis of human development. One widely accepted theory was introduced by Stern (1956). He stated that genetic factors are flexible, like a rubber band, and the amount it stretches (develops) depends on its interaction with the environment.

Another controversy in developmental theory is whether development is **continuous** or **discontinuous.** In broad terms, development is continuous, that is, it occurs gradually in small steps. Children rarely change overnight. And yet, there are clear differences between 10-year-olds and 12-year-olds. Thus, many models of human development rely on the concept of stages, qualitative descriptions of certain states. Then, a researcher can tell whether or not a child is in a certain stage, if not exactly when that child entered the stage, or when the child will leave it.

Piaget's Theories

Jean Piaget described development in terms of four stages. The first stage, of **sensorimotor development,** occurs during infancy; the second stage, **preoperational,** is a childhood stage; **concrete operations** takes place in middle childhood; and **formal operations** occurs during adolescence.

The Conceptual Period of Intelligence

Stage		
1. Preoperational (2-7 yrs.)	a. Preconceptual (18 mos. -4 yrs.)	First such use of representational thought and symbols, such as words, for objects; classification of objects.
	b. Intuitive thought (4-7 yrs.)	Beginning of reasoning, but thinking is fragmented, centered on parts of things, rigid, and based wholly on appearances.
2. Concrete operations (7-11 yrs.)		Can perform mental operations and reverse them. Can add up "all the marbles." Operations are however confined to concrete and tangible objects that are immediately present.
3. Formal operations (12-15 yrs.)		Can perform hypotheses, can go beyond appearances to deal with the truth or falsity of propositions.

The sensorimotor stage refers to the development of the child's perception and physical movements and takes place until the second year of life. The child then progresses to the preoperational stage, which lasts until about age 7. Then, the child enters the age of concrete operations, where the child is capable of invoking a mental representation of an object or event that she previously experienced. She begins to understand numbers and logic and can think about real objects and things which can be easily imagined. This stage lasts until about age 11. Around adolescence, the stage of formal operations sets in. The teenager can now think about things he has not perceptually experienced, hypothetical states, and advanced logic. Adolescents are better at thinking of possible solutions to a problem. When Piaget asked 10-year-olds and 14-year-olds to figure out what combination of four different liquids would produce a yellow color when a catalyst was added, the 10- year-olds only came up with pairs of chemicals. The 14-year-olds thought of combinations of two, three, or four chemicals, until they had found the complete solution. According to Piaget's theory, adolescents can solve problems in a logical, organized way that younger children cannot.

Freudian Theory

Freud's theories stress sexual and aggressive drives, and both internal development and environmental influences. Freud believed that each individual passes through three **psychosexual stages** of development, so named because Freud felt that the bodily focus of a person's sexual energy changed over the course of development.

Freudian Stages of Development

Stage	Age	Body Focus
1. Oral stage	0-8 mos.	mouth, sucking
2. Anal stage	8-18 mos.	anus, urination, defecation
3. Phallic	18 mos.-6 years	genitals, opposite-sex parent
4. Latency	6-11 years	same-sex parent, loss of sexual interest
5. Genital	11-	adult sexual pleasure

In the first stage, the **oral stage,** the mouth is the most sensitive part of a baby's body. The baby is most concerned with mouthing and sucking things through about the age of eight months. Then, the child enters the **anal stage.** In this stage, the child's energy is focused on the parts of her body which are concerned with urination and defecation. This is the stage when toilet training takes place. Then, in the **phallic stage,** children discover that their genitals can be a source of pleasure. Boys enter the **Oedipal stage,** where they sexually desire their mothers, while girls enter the **Electra stage,** where they desire their fathers. This love for the opposite-sex parent causes anxiety in children, because to win their desired object, they would have to fight and supplant their powerful same-sex parent, their mommy or daddy. Eventually, most young boys decide to identify themselves with their fathers, so as not to feel threatened by their stronger, jealous fathers, and perhaps win their mothers' affection. The outcome of this stage is not so clear for girls. By the beginning of elementary school, though, children have begun to repress these desires, and enter the **latency stage,** when they are sexually dormant. Children concentrate on their intellectual and social skills. At puberty, sexual forces can no longer be controlled, and in the **genital stage** people once again focus their sexual energy on their genitals and on finding opposite-gender sexual partners their own age. This stage continues for the rest of their lives. If the child does not progress smoothly from one stage to the next, that child may fixate on that stage. The conflicts at that stage will become the core of the child's personality. For example, a child who had a difficult toilet-training can develop an **"anal-compulsive"** personality, and become overly concerned with rules and control.

Freudian developmental theory is not widely accepted as the complete truth. Freud's theory of female development is incomplete, and his ideas on homosexual development seem primitive and insulting in current analyses.

Kohlberg's Stages

Kohlberg's developmental theory focuses on the formation of moral beliefs and principles. Kohlberg believed that morality is a decision-making process and not a fixed set of behaviors. In Freudian terms, morality reflects the strength of the ego, which makes compromising decisions between the id and the superego. Kohlberg devised a sequential design to explain the development of morality based on this idea. According to Kohlberg, morality emerges through three levels, which each consist of two stages of moral orientation. The three levels are termed pre-moral, conventional role conformity, and self-accepted principles, also termed preconventional, conventional, and postconventional.

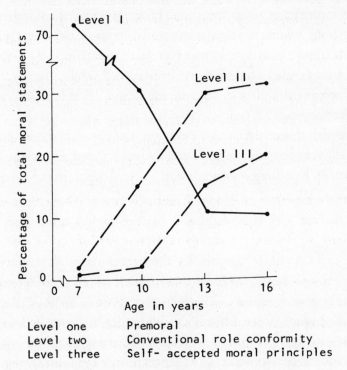

Level one   Premoral
Level two   Conventional role conformity
Level three   Self-accepted moral principles

Mean percent of moral statements on Kohlberg's three levels made by boys aged 7 to 16.

The first level is **premoral.** At this stage, a child believes that evil behavior is behavior which is punished, while good behavior is behavior which is not punished. Moral behavior is based on its subjective consequences. The second stage of level I is **hedonism.** To children at this level, good is something pleasant and desirable, while evil is something unpleasant and undesirable. This level of morality characterizes infants and preschoolers.

The second level of morality is the morality of **conventional role conformity.** In the first stage, the child practices the sort of morality which wins approval from parents, teachers, and peers. Whatever the child is praised for doing is considered moral, be it turning in homework on time, eating worms, or throwing eggs at a neighbor's windows. In the second stage, a child believes that being moral is conforming to rules and norms of society and obeying authority figures. Obeying the teacher, traffic signals, and "playing by the rules" are now moral acts.

The third and highest level of morality in Kohlberg's scheme is the morality of **self-accepted principles.** At this level, the individual judges her own moral standards. She can see beyond the literal interpretation of rules and laws, and distinguish between good and bad laws. The second stage reflects individual principles of conscience. This stage is typical of adolescents.

The development of morality is part of the process of **socialization,** or learning behavior which is appropriate and inappropriate for a particular culture. In addition, moral development is related to intellectual development. The child cannot develop a moral system until certain intellectual abilities have developed, such as the ability to imagine the results of their actions and their effect on others.

Kohlberg feels that many people never get past the early stages of development, and that very few individuals actually reach the highest stage of moral development. In Kohlberg's own studies, about 10 percent of 24-year-olds operated at level III.

Erikson's Stages

Erikson studied Freudian theory; hence, his ideas about psychosexual development resemble Freud's constructions. Erikson believes that human behavior and personality result from a combination of heredity and cultural influences. He divides development from birth to maturity into eight basic stages. Each stage consists of a crisis which indicates a major turning point in the individual's life. This conflict is usually one between individual instinct and external restraints. Successful development depends on choosing the right alternative. If an individual does not resolve a crisis successfully, that individual will become "stuck" at that crisis, and develop psychopathology related to that stage of her childhood. Erikson's stages are: (1) oral-sensory (birth to one and a half years), (2) muscular-anal (one and a half to four years), (3) locomotor-genital (four to six years), (4) latency (six to eleven years), (5) adolescence, (6) young adulthood, (7) adulthood, and (8) maturity.

Erikson's Stages of Development

Age	Stage	Conflict
0-18 mos.	oral-sensory	trust vs. mistrust
18 mos.-4 yrs.	muscular-anal	shame, self-doubt vs. independence
4 yrs.-6 yrs.	locomotor-genital	initiative vs. guilt
6 yrs.-11 yrs.	latency	industry vs. inferiority
adolescence		identity vs. identity confusion
young adulthood		intimacy vs. isolation
adulthood		generativity vs. stagnation
maturity		ego integrity vs. despair

During the **oral-sensory stage,** the basic crisis centers on either trust or mistrust. The infant is dependent on others to fulfill his needs. If these needs are consistently satisfied, the child will develop trust. If these needs are not satisfied regularly, or he does not receive love, attention, and stimulation, he will develop mistrust, become timid and withdrawn and give up hope of achieving his goals. In the second stage of psychosocial development, the **muscular-anal stage,** the central crisis is between establishing autonomy and dealing with doubt and shame. The child who has successfully resolved the trust-mistrust crisis now has gained some control of her bodily functions. She begins to assert herself, and learns to say "No!" If parents are overprotective of the child, and overdemanding about her controlling her urination and defecation, the child will develop feelings of shame and self-doubt. If the child passes through this stage successfully, she will become an independent adult who can make her own decisions.

Erikson's third stage, the **locomotor-genital stage,** is characterized by the formation of guilt, the development of motor skills and locomotion, language development, and curiosity. Children at this stage are particularly curious about bodies and the difference between male and female bodies. The crisis at this age is the question of initiative vs. guilt. The parents' response to this age of exploration determine whether the child will feel competent taking initiative, using his imagination, and dealing with new situations, or feel guilty and restrained.

In Erikson's latency stage, like Freud's, the child is concerned with social and intellectual accomplishment. The crisis here is between industry and inferiority. A child develops a sense of industry if she receives attention and praise for accomplishments. In contrast, a child who fails consistently at various tasks and receives little or no attention or praise develops a sense of inferiority.

Erikson's fifth stage of development is **adolescence,** where the major crisis is the identity crisis. Adolescents change clothing styles, joining groups or gangs, or experiment with different roles in an attempt to answer the question, "Who am I?" Otherwise, the adolescent slips into confusion over his or her role in the world.

For Erikson, development continues into adulthood. In **young adulthood,** Erikson's sixth stage, the basic crisis is intimacy vs. isolation. At this time, the individual is concerned with establishing intimate, long-term relationships with others. If she has successfully resolved the identity crisis, she will be open and warm toward others. If she has not resolved the identity crisis, she will not be willing to open herself up to others. Successful resolution of the crisis in young adulthood leads to a healthy intimacy with another, such as a long-term relationship.

The seventh stage of Erikson's psychosocial development is **adulthood,** where the question of generativity vs. stagnation comes to the fore. Success in resolving this crisis is evident in someone who takes an active role in parental guidance of the next generation and in community affairs. Unsuccessful adults may suffer depression and loneliness. The eighth, final stage of Erikson's scheme is **maturity.** The basic crisis during this stage is ego integrity vs. disgust and despair. A sense of integrity develops if the individual, looking back on his life, believes it has been meaningful and relatively successful. If the individual sees his life as meaningless, wasted, and unsuccessful, a feeling of disgust will arise. He will feel despair if he feels that it is too late to change.

INFANCY AND CHILDHOOD

Physical Development

Physically, the neonate (newborn) child is already quite developed. The child has many reflexes, such as sucking anything placed in her mouth or fanning her toes when the soles of her feet are tickled. After birth, the most important development in infancy is the ability to walk. A sequence of motor acquisitions precedes this: crawling, sitting, grasping, and climbing. Though the sequence is relatively constant, the age at which each step is acquired varies considerably from one child to the next.

Most children follow a standard motor sequence of development, including (Shirley, 1933):

Month	Ability Acquired
1	Can hold chin up
3	Can reach for an object
4	Can sit up, with support
7	Can sit alone
8	Can stand with help
11	Can walk when led
14	Can stand alone
15	Can walk alone

By the time a normally developing child reaches preschool age, her feet have moved closer together while walking, and her arms and hands have moved closer to the body. Her balance during locomotion thus improves. By age two, the child's grasping ability also improves. She can easily pick up objects, carry them, and carefully set them down again. Drawing ability improves as well. A three-year-old can now draw a circle and a straight line where a two-year-old generally cannot. A four-year-old can draw a cross and a diamond, and button her clothes, while a five-year-old can draw triangles and lace her shoes.

During middle childhood, the child's body grows rapidly. Boys are slightly taller and heavier until about age 10, whereupon girls match their growth, then exceed it as they enter adolescence. Motor skills continue to improve. On average, boys possess superior motor skills, a fact which is probably an artifact of cultural training. For example, though boys have been found to be able to run farther and faster than girls during middle childhood, girls are better at "cable jumping"—an exercise which involves jumping over an object which is held in front of a person. Essentially, the boys are better at playing kickball, and the girls are better at jump rope. Reaction times improve considerably. A five-year-old's reaction time is about half an adult's. Most five-year-olds have difficulty catching balls but improve as they get older.

Social Development

When speaking of cognitive development in childhood, most psychologists are overwhelmingly influenced by Piaget's theories of infant and childhood cognition. Social development is another matter. Social development refers to the development of behaviors the child engages in when he interacts with others. This area of study includes topics such as games, morality, learning society's rules, and language acquisition.

In the beginning, children are quite egocentric. Preschoolers and infants are primarily interested in themselves. They cannot see the world as someone else might see it; they simply have not reached the stage where they can consider the thoughts and feelings of others. Any morality at this stage comes from Kohlbergian acceptance of rules and authority.

In the beginning, parents and their new baby form a bond, or attachment, especially if they are kept together in the first few hours after birth. Yet young infants are not necessarily afraid of strangers. It is only at age five or six months that children stop smiling at all strangers and show fear in the presence of unknown people. There is evidence that though children are perfectly happy with several caretakers in the first months of life, they need to make and maintain a few stable relationships during the second six months of existence. According to Mary Ainsworth et. al. (1978), infants who have a secure attachment explore the environment and interact with strangers as long as their mothers are present. If their mothers leave, the children calm down shortly after she returns. Some babies have an anxious-avoidant attachment and avoid and ignore their mothers after a separation. Others, with an anxious-resistant attachment, seem angry at their mothers after separation and resist being comforted. Children who have secure attachments tend to show greater resilience, self-control, and curiosity when they become preschoolers.

Infants show their attachment to the mother by clinging to her and objecting when she is out of sight. The good feeling a baby feels near a warm, soft object is called **contact comfort** and a very important fact of her young life. In a sad study by Harlow (1958), baby rhesus monkeys were raised in a cage with no live mother, only surrogates. One surrogate was made of wire and held a bottle filled with milk. The other was made of fuzzy cloth but did not have any milk. The baby monkeys preferred the cloth mother, spending over 15 hours a day on it, and would stand on that surrogate while feeding from the wire monkey. Clearly, the monkeys were not responding only to a biological need for milk; the monkeys felt a need for softness and warmth. Some psychologists would say this behavior shows a need for attachment, or cuddling.

Over time, the child (or baby monkey) becomes socialized. First, the child develops a **self-concept,** often through identification with parents, or adopting their parents' qualities. If the parents have high status, or power and competence; warmth, or affection and regard for the child; and similarity to the children, then the children will tend to incorporate the parents' attitudes and beliefs.

The family is the first and most powerful socializing agent the child has. The family not only fulfills the child's physiological needs, but teaches culture and the rules which govern acceptable and unacceptable behavior in his society. After about age five or six, though the family still provides for the child's physical needs, the child's peers provide much of his psychological support. These peer relations are very important. Harlow's sad monkeys were seriously disturbed and could not successfully interact with other normal monkeys in later life. Children will conform to their peers' expectations and false judgments in middle childhood. As the child spends more of her time in school and with friends, the parents' influence gradually diminishes, and the child's main concern becomes acceptance by her friends. Yet through middle childhood, most children are still willing, even eager, to internalize the norms of her culture.

ADOLESCENCE

Physical Maturation

Adolescence begins at the onset of puberty (sexual maturity), and spans the teen years. **Puberty** is defined as the ability to reproduce. Various physical changes, called **pubescence,** occur during the passage from middle childhood to adolescence. The beginning of puberty, or the age when a person becomes fertile, is hard to determine. Many researchers have defined the start of puberty for girls at the time of their first menstrual period, called **menarche.** However, this definition is not entirely accurate, since a girl remains infertile for about a year after menarche. Pinpointing the start of puberty for boys is even more difficult, though some researchers claim that it begins with a boy's first ejaculation. Today, however, most psychologists agree that adolescence follows a period of rapid growth, or the "growth spurt" which heralds sexual maturity. Generally, adolescence begins at age 14 for boys and age 12 for girls.

During **pubescence,** both primary and secondary sexual characteristics develop. Primary sexual characteristics are traits directly related to reproduction. They include the enlargement of the genitals or sex organs. Secondary sex characteristics, which have no effect on physical reproduction, include the appearance of pubic hair and axillary (armpit) hair, the enlargement of the female's breasts, the lowering of voices (especially for boys), and the appearance of facial and chest hair in males.

Cognitive and Social Development

According to Piaget, during adolescence, thinking becomes more scientific. The adolescent follows the steps of scientific method, including formulating and testing an hypothesis. This stage is also characterized by **idealism.** The adolescent can contemplate hypothetical, possible worlds. They may become concerned with ideas or ideals over reality, which may not meet their high standards. Adolescents also reach higher Kohlbergian levels of moral development, and begin to question morality based on rules and authority.

In social development, an adolescent's social skills become increasingly important as she makes more frequent contact with members of the opposite sex. The adolescent progresses from middle childhood, where she mostly had friends of her own sex, to a more mature stage where she learns the social etiquette necessary to behave appropriately in the adult world. Adolescents also become less dependent and concerned with their parents and more involved with their peers.

Adolescents who are undergoing an Eriksonian identity crisis may become especially involved with an individual or group which can provide simple answers to their questions. They may join a gang, religious group, or political organization. However, they may come to resent these others' codes and to feel that they want to do only what they personally want to do. If these adolescents cannot decide what it is they want to do, they often return to the identity crisis.

ADULTHOOD

Adulthood is inevitably a process of decline. Childhood skills are not practiced, and the body begins to show its wear. Some of the symptoms of aging include: brain size reduction, deterioration of visual acuity and hearing, a lengthened reaction time, reduced motor control, poorer concentration, and reduced short-term memory. However, certain other abilities improve. Spatial skills decline after age 40, but verbal skills improve between ages 25 and 64. Intellectual tasks that require the application of learned material are maintained through the 60s.

As older people enter retirement and watch their children leave home, they go through considerable change. Aside from Erikson's theory of generativity vs.

despair, some theorists feel that older adults go through a process of disengage-ment (Cumming & Henry, 1961). Older people may become more focused on internal processes and less invested in the world around them. But in general, life functioning and satisfaction is directly, positively related to their state in younger years. People who were happy in their youth tend to be happy in their old age.

SEX ROLES AND SEX DIFFERENCES

Psychologists have always argued over whether gender roles, or different ways of acting according to one's biological sex, are inherited or learned. In human society, it is very difficult to tell whether gender roles reflect some inherited tendency or are a result of simple socialization. Socialization to sex roles begins at birth. The first question about any new baby is not "Is it healthy?" but "Is it a boy or a girl?" The introduction of pink or blue blankets begins socialization. Children under the age of three tend to judge what gender a person is according to environmental cues, not that person's genitalia, according to research done by Daryl and Sandra Bem. In the eyes of a young child, a boy who wears a dress becomes a girl, even if his external genitalia are clearly visible.

There are some observable differences in male and female development. One clear biological fact is that girls tend to mature earlier than boys, at age 12 as compared to 14. Other differences are less clearly caused. For example, girls who mature early suffer much more anxiety than boys who do so. Girls who mature early are often rejected by their peers, whereas boys respect and admire the greater strength and height of early blooming males. Girls tend to speak more fluently earlier than boys and suffer from fewer speech defects. Boys tend to behave more aggressively than girls. Adolescent boys also tend to have a more difficult time (more stress, family disharmony) gaining autonomy from their parents, mostly because girls demand less independence. Since both of these trends reflect complex social interactions, there is considerable room for environmental and cultural influence.

REVIEW QUESTIONS

1. John Locke believed that children were born as a blank slate, or _____
   _____ .

2. True or False: In the Piagetian stage of concrete operations, children begin to solve problems by imagining hypothetical states.

3. According to Freud, at age three, boys enter the _____ stage, where they desire their mothers.

4. What are Kohlberg's three levels of morality?

5. How old are children in Erikson's latency stage?

6. The Eriksonian _____ crisis takes place during adolescence.

7. The most important physical development in infancy is _____ .

8. True or False: Three-month-old babies will cry when confronted with a stranger.

9. What were the two alternatives given to baby rhesus monkeys in the Harlow experiment?

10. True or False: Girls often take a negative view of early physical maturation.

ANSWER KEY

1. tabula rasa

2. False

3. Oedipal

4. Premoral, conventional role conformity, and self-accepted principles OR preconventional, conventional, and postconventional

5. Six to eleven years

6. identity

7. learning to walk

8. False

9. Wire and cloth surrogate mothers

10. True

Chapter 10

Personality

THEORIES AND APPROACHES

Generally, psychological theories of personality could just as well be called theories of human nature. The personality psychologist is trying to make sense out of human conduct, discover the uniformities of character among people, and devise general principles to explain particular motives. Each theorist approaches this area with somewhat different assumptions, strategies, and objectives. To date, there is no way to empirically test competing theories for their validity and reliability; some theories are constructed in such a way that they defy testing. Yet these theories form a strong basis for beginning questioning and formulating hypotheses. A student should approach the study of personality theories with the knowledge that they are useful, though expendable, guidelines to research and thinking.

Historically, personality has been most commonly described in terms of traits. **"Traits"** are enduring and stable characteristics that provoke a person to act in some consistent way. Trait psychology looks for consistencies in behavior. Examples of traits that have been studied include extroversion-introversion (first popularized by Carl Jung), submission-dominance, honesty-dishonesty, and intelligence. One problem with these characterizations is that they omit individual variation and mixtures; a person reading a description of introverted and extroverted behavior is likely to find both within herself.

Another historical approach to personality is **type psychology,** which attempts to isolate individuals according to particular characteristics. The ancient Greeks Hippocrates and Galen classified people according to the dominance of one of four body fluids, called **humors.** The **sanguine,** or happy personality, had a preponderance of blood; **choleric,** angry personalities, had too much ordinary bile; **melancholics,** who produced overmuch black bile, were unhappy and depressed; while **phlegmatics** were apathetic due to their overproduction of phlegm. However, this theory was certainly not empirically tested and is not currently used. Yet some theorists continue to work with type concepts today.

The danger with both trait and type theories is that labels can be misleading when environmental variables are not taken into account. Their predictive power is limited except in the case of extremes. Traits tend not to be consistent from situation to situation. Another criticism of both theories is that any trait that is observed is more easily explained by the observer's personal opinions about the subject rather than some inherent quality in the subject. The average person is believed to judge others by assigning them traits. The actual presence of these traits is irrelevant; what is important is the traits the observer chooses to assign. Careful analysis of this attribution process helps psychologists in studying the person's values and attitudes. Another problem with these theories is that people tend to overestimate the influence of a person's inherent traits, and underestimate the influence of the environment. This tendency to "blame the person for everything" was termed the Fundamental Attribution Error **(FAE)** by Ross (1977).

Psychoanalytic Approaches

According to Freud, humans have two basic tendencies. One is survival; the other is procreation. Freud coined the term **"libido"** as the source of energy for the sexual urge. Freud was most interested in the reproductive urge, since this one is constantly being thwarted by the environment. He considered many different activities, including cigar smoking and thumb-sucking to be sexual behaviors, which give physical satisfaction to the actor. Later in his life, Freud identified two human instincts, **Thanatos** and **Eros,** the Greek terms for death and love. Eros is the life instinct, or the will to live. Thanatos is the death instinct, which competes with Eros. The death instinct operates invisibly and is rarely observable in pure form. It can only be inferred from its effects—aggressive and violent tendencies. The organism, according to Freud, is designed to return naturally to its original, inanimate state; thus, Thanatos.

These instincts wage war within the basic elements of any human personality: the **id, ego,** and **superego.** According to Freud, an infant's personality is governed by the id, the sum of all instinctual urges. The id has no ethical and moral rules and demands immediate satisfaction. Yet no child is always imme-diately satisfied, and the id comes into conflict with reality. The ego is the intermediary between id and reality and develops between the age of eight and 18 months, as the child begins to understand what is and is not possible. The ego also distinguishes between long- and short-range goals and decides what actions will be most beneficial. The id and the ego work together to determine the individual's goals. After a time, though, the child also acquires a moral sense. This sense is embodied in the superego. The superego represents the taboos and mores of the child's society and develops from the ages of 18 months to six years. Since these rules are learned through social contact, the development of the superego represents the socialization of the child. The id and superego are often in conflict, since fulfilling many of the id's urges would be socially unacceptable. The superego is often described as having two divisions. One is the **conscience,** which consists of internalized rules. The other is the **ego ideal,** which represents strivings and goals the parents admire.

There is always some frustration and anxiety in passing from one stage of development to the next. According to Freud, if the child's anxiety about moving on to the next stage becomes too great, development can halt, and the child will become **fixated** at that stage, as we saw in Chapter 9. An overly dependent child is one example of someone who is fixated at the oral stage. Anxiety over feeding and being fed (the infant state) led to the person's unwillingness and inability to move on to the next stage. Development ceased at an early stage, preventing that person from becoming independent.

To compensate for some need which cannot be immediately fulfilled, the ego creates **defense mechanisms.** These structures mediate between the id and the superego to resolve conflict in an acceptable way. Examples of defense mecha-nisms include repression, displacement, reaction-formation, intellectualization, projection, and denial. **Repression** occurs when an individual unconsciously tries to forget a painful incident or event. For example, you may simply "forget" that your prom dress tore in half on a nail on the door. **Displacement** results when a person wishes to gratify a socially unacceptable desire but chooses a more acceptable alternative instead. A person who feels aggression toward his boss may exercise his aggressive energy away through jogging. In **reaction-formation,** a person consciously tells herself that she feels the opposite of her socially unacceptable feelings—a particularly common reaction to homosexuality. **In-tellectualization,** or rationalization, occurs when a person fears his behavior is abnormal. He then searches for ways or excuses that will "rationalize" his behavior and make it appear perfectly normal. In **projection,** a person attributes her anxieties onto other people. A person who is afraid of her own homosexuality may start accusing others of being homosexual. Finally, in **denial,** a person tries to make a behavior seem more normal by believing that everyone engages in that behavior, or by denying that he is committing these behaviors. For example, a person may excuse his cheating on taxes by claiming that everyone does so. Any of these defense mechanisms may become very strong, depending on the individual and the situation.

Post-Freudians

After Freud's death, several theorists continued to work with his theories, and make important modifications. Karen Horney is perhaps the most famous of the post-Freudian "cultural school" psychologists, who argued against Freud's claim that developmental stages are biologically determined (see Chapter 9). Instead, Horney and her fellows argue that culture has an important role in development. Horney is especially well known for her criticisms of Freud's views on female development. Freud believed that girls develop into heterosexual women on the basis of their desire to possess their father's penis. Horney argues that this desire for male organs is merely an outgrowth of western culture's devaluation and oppression of women.

Alfred Adler also had differences with Freud. For Adler, the central core of personality is not the question of repressed sexual drives but a sense of inferiority, for which the individual strives to compensate. Under Adler's schemata, healthy people are motivated by goals related to others, while neurotic personalities are self centered. In his view, the ego is not the id's servant, but a creative intelligence attempting to make a healthy adaptation. The Oedipus complex in Adler's work is not only a sexual phenomenon but a need to be better than the father. Personality, for Adler, is fragmented. Instead of being motivated by biological tension, Adler thought of individuals as having a drive to grow, to become whole, and to realize themselves fully. Adler preferred to think of the person as a whole rather than considering the separate parts of a personality.

Carl Gustav Jung also found it more and more difficult to accept that sexual motives were the chief force in human behavior. Jung felt that the concept of sexuality should be reserved for extreme forms of libido, and that the more generalized expressions of libido should be considered in a different framework entirely. Jung discovered forces and content within the unconscious unlike anything Freud had ever mentioned. Jung began to explore universal symbols of the human race's experiences that transcend the individual's immediate concerns. Where Freud was concerned with biology, Jung was obsessed with the spirit.

In his theory of personality structure, Jung wrote of the **collective unconscious,** the inherited images common to all humans. These images are called "**archetypes.**" The archetypes Jung mentions most frequently are the shadow, the anima and animus, and the persona. The **shadow** represents the repressed, unconscious drives and desires of the personal unconscious, the "dark side" of all humans. However, only men are supposed to have an **anima,** an internalized feminine image. The anima is based on a man's real experiences with women, particularly his mother, sisters, and other family members, as well as the collective male experience throughout history. This anima determines a man's relationship to women, and helps compensate for his otherwise one-sided view. Similarly, a woman has an **animus,** her internalized personification of all masculinity.

The **persona** is the front a person presents to other people. It is a mask that makes the person and others believe that she is an individual, when she is actually acting a role through which the collective unconscious speaks. An individual's persona is only one of the many themes available from the collective psyche.

Trait Theory

Allport was the first psychologist to stress the difference between **nomothetic personality studies** involving large numbers of subjects and generating basic principles of behavior, and **idiographic studies** which select methods which will not conceal each individual's uniqueness. Nomothetic studies are more concerned with quantitative laws and theories, while idiographic studies involve more descriptive analyses of individuals. Allport preferred to use the ideographic method to examine individual traits that determine personality.

Allport's theories stress conscious motivations. In his theory, the individual's intentions are the most important key to his current behavior. Allport's personality structure is represented by traits, which develop as a result of a person's interaction with the environment. These traits are structures which produce consistent behavior by making different stimuli functionally equivalent for the individual. For example, a person who carries the trait of friendliness will tend to react in a friendly way to a variety of situations, because he sees each of these situations as places to make friends; they are functionally equivalent. There are both **common traits,** which are universal to all people within a culture, and **special traits** which are unique to individuals. These individual traits are referred to as **disposition.**

Raymond Cattell divides traits into **surface traits** and **source traits.** Surface traits are clusters of highly related behaviors, while source traits are the underlying causes of these behaviors. For example, a person who carries the surface trait of introversion may be shy at the doctor's office, take many solitary walks, and avoid crowds. These are not the same behavior, yet they seem to be related to each other. Source traits, on the other hand, can only be extracted through statistical analysis. The source trait for surface introversion may also cause a tendency towards quiet activities, a high degree of attention to detail, and intolerance of others' views; source traits often are not easily categorizable and may not have common names.

Hans J. Eysenck's theory of personality emphasizes the introversion/extroversion split in personality types. His theory has three separate **levels of influence.** At the first level, **personality types** are classified by introversion and extroversion, neuroticism or emotional stability, and psychoticism, or impersonal hostility. This level is the type level where a person's general tendencies emerge. On the next level, the **trait level,** specific responses such as sociability and impulsiveness are detailed. Eysenck believed that individual differences in the introversion/extroversion realm were due to differences in a brain structure called the ascending reticular activating system **(ARAS),** which produces arousal in the cerebral cortex. According to Eysenck, introverts are more highly aroused in normal conditions than extroverts. Thus, introverts tend to act in a restrained, quiet manner to avoid excess arousal.

Some psychologists, though, believe that entirely too much attention has been given to biological factors. Walter Mischel explores the cognitive aspects of personality theory, emphasizing the importance of understanding the environment that gives rise to behavior. According to Mischel, people tend to behave certain ways in certain situations, such as when they are stopped by a police officer for speeding, or dressing in a locker room. Mischel argues that traits are inferred from preconceptions of how people ought to behave, not how they actually act. Mischel has also listed several **cognitive dimensions** he feels are necessary for understanding a person's behavior, such as cognitive competencies, or a person's knowledge, and self-encoding, or the way that person sees herself. Interestingly, Mischel found that depressed subjects judge themselves more realistically than control subjects. Their preconceptions of themselves are not tainted by optimism.

And yet, tests of self-perception may not be the best measure of personality. Just after World War II, E. Kelly and D. Fiske tried out several psychometric testing methods on clinical psychologists being trained by the Veterans' Administration. Kelly and Fiske found that two tests were better indicators of personalities than any other test, observation, or interview. They found that the Miller Analogies Test did a very good job of predicting intelligence, while the Strong Vocational Interest Blank was the best personality test. This test asked for persistent interests, such as past jobs, books read, tools bought, hobbies, and so on. Since the scale focused on environmental stimuli that interested the men, the scores were more accurate in relating past, present and future tendencies, than scores on self-observation inventories. Mischel could have predicted this result, if he had been an adult at the time of the testing.

Humanistic Theories

Humanistic psychology emphasizes humans' capacity for goodness, creativity, and freedom. Humanistic theories see humans as spiritual, rational, autonomous beings, and emphasizes the "whole" human, instead of component parts. The most famous proponent of humanistic theories is Carl Rogers. Carl Rogers believed that the structure of personality is based on two constructs, the organism and the self, which is a portion of the phenomenal field. The organism is where all experience, every sensation in awareness, occurs. The total sum of experience is the **phenomenal field,** a concept that includes both conscious and unconscious experiences. The phenomenal field is the person's subjective reality. For a person to act realistically, he must find out if his phenomenal field represents objective reality. If there is a difference between the phenomenal field and the real world, the person will behave unrealistically, and harm himself in some way. The **self** refers to the consistent set of perceptions which refer to the self, i.e. "I" or "me," as well as the relationships between "I" or "me" and other people. This self does not control behavior. Rather, it is the person's attitudes and feelings about herself. There is also an ideal self to which the individual aspires.

Roger's distinction between organism and self becomes important in the issue of **congruence** and **incongruence.** Incongruence between the perceived self and the organism's actual experience (e.g., failing a test you thought you would do well on) results in the individual feeling threatened, anxious, and defensive. Incongruence between the perceived self and the ideal self also results in dissatisfaction and frustration. Rogers considers an individual to be mature when there is congruence between the organism's experience and the self.

Erik Erikson is also considered a humanistic theorist, though much of his work derives from Freudian psychoanalytic thought. His work is covered in depth in Chapter 9.

Another theorist, Abraham Maslow, is famous for his hierarchy of needs (see Chapter 8: motivation). His theory of self-actualization holds some interest for personality theorists, because it emphasizes healthy behavior, not just psychological symptoms. According to Maslow, there is a marked difference between behavior patterns of people motivated by lower needs (aimed towards correcting deficiencies) and the behavior of people driven by self-actualization, or growth-oriented needs. The person who is still motivated to satisfy lower needs is characterized by a tendency to be self-centered and concerned with her own needs, to behave mainly on the basis of external cues, to look for gratifications that are short term and temporary, and view others in terms of how they can satisfy their needs. Growth-oriented people, on the other hand, are likely to be more concerned with the world at large than themselves, to accept their own impulses, to attain unique, individual goals, and to view people for what they are, and not just as useful objects.

Behavioral Theories and Socio-Cognitive Learning

Behavioral theories of personality are not theories of personality per se: they are theories of patterns of observable behavior (see Chapter 6 for a more thorough explanation of behaviorism). What is more, as behaviorists assume that behavior is learned, and not innate, they credit personalities with almost infinite flexibility. A child can be conditioned to fear objects or people, as happened to J.B. Watson's poor little Albert, or to admire and enjoy almost anything. J.B. Watson, the popularizer of behaviorism in America, is famous for having stated that he could make a child into any sort of person, if he had complete control of the environment. Another behavioral personality theorist, B.F. Skinner, did not create a systematic theory of child development. Yet Skinner believed that each new experience helps to determine a person's future responses that, in turn, form the popularly-termed personality. Implicit in Skinner and other behaviorists' theories is the idea that the environment is responsible for individual development. Healthy personalities can be programmed through a healthy environment. Thus, behavioral scientists focus on controlling environmental variables that act on the individual.

Social learning theory, originated by Miller and Dollard, grew out of behaviorist theory. In this theory, children learn responses through imitating others. This imitation is reinforced by others around them. This process is influenced by the fact that children are completely dependent on others. This dependency is extremely important to socialization. Like Freudian theory, social learning theory involves the channeling of aggression and other energy into socially acceptable outlets.

These theories inspired Bandura and Walters's theory of modeling. In modeling, people acquire new responses through imitating another person's behavior, though the imitator must have the motivation and skills necessary to reproduce the response. Bandura and Walters emphasize that a whole range of behaviors, both acceptable and antisocial, can be learned this way.

Biological Influences

Traditionally, it has been difficult to devise measures to assess the effect of heredity without the influence of the environment. Some believe that the environment is the major factor in individual development because members of a society share expectations about people. People in a given community will act towards a fat, short, or bald person in a particular way, which lead that person to behave the way they expect him to. What is labelled as hereditary personality traits may only be the result of self-fulfilling prophecies, the sort of results one would expect from a social learning process.

Twin studies have helped in understanding this problem. Psychological research has demonstrated an interaction between hereditary capacities and environmental opportunities for IQ (see Chapter 7). Nineteen pairs of twins were studied by Newman, Freeman, and Holzinger. The results showed that the greater the educational advantage, the greater the IQ of the twin with that advantage. A study by Shields and Slater demonstrated that when both members of a twin pair were neurotic, there was much greater similarity in symptoms if the twins were identical than if they were fraternal. Heredity provides a capacity for a wide range of behavior that may be encouraged or thwarted by the environment.

ASSESSMENT

Objective Tests

Two major objective personality tests exist in psychology: the Minnesota Multiphasic Personality Inventory (MMPI) and the California Psychological Inventory (CPI). They are objective in that each person is given the same, standardized test and can only respond to the test in a few controlled ways.

The **MMPI** is a self-report personality test. It was originally designed to discriminate between "normals" and people in psychiatric categories. It is now also used to assess personality. The MMPI consists of 550 statements to which the subject is asked to answer "true," "false," or "cannot say" in respect to herself. Examples of typical MMPI statements include "I do not tire quickly," "I am worried about sex matters," and "I am sure I am being talked about." The statements on the MMPI are divided into 10 scales based on psychiatric categories. The scales are hypochondriasis, depression, hysteria, psychopathic deviate, masculinity-femininity, paranoia, psychasthenia (troubled with excessive fears and compulsive tendencies to dwell on certain ideas), schizophrenia, hypomania (tending to be physically and mentally overactive), and social introversion. In addition to these scales there are three validity scales which represent checks on lying, carelessness, misunderstanding, among others. The lie scale consists of statements where a particular answer is socially desirable but also extremely unlikely, such as answering true to "I never lie." The test is considered invalid for individuals who score too highly on any of these validity scales.

The MMPI's items were originally selected on the basis of whether they differentiated between normals and people specifically diagnosed as depressives, schizophrenics, and so on. Statements which did not differentiate among the groups were eliminated. Thus, the MMPI has a high degree of criterion validity (it measures what it is supposed to measure). Yet most of the standardization of normal samples was done on rural Minnesotans in the 1950s, and may not be characteristic of today's population.

The **CPI** is another personality inventory. It was developed for use with less clinical and less deviant groups of subjects than the MMPI. There are several forms of the CPI for different age groups. Most of the CPI was developed using the method of contrasted groups, like the MMPI, though four of the subscales were calculated from the consistency of responses within the questionnaire. Some of the representative scales include self-control, responsibility, well-being, flexibility, tolerance, and intellectual efficiency. The items were not designed to measure gross psychopathy, but to measure minor forms of maladjustment, especially those common among adolescents and young adults.

Projective Tests

A projective test may provide as valid and reliable personality data on an individual as a paper-and-pencil personality inventory. In a **projective test,** the subject is given some vague or unexplained stimulus and is asked to respond, often with a story. Projective testing allows symbolic expression of conflicts and impulses. Unlike an objective questionnaire, the projective test is unstructured. The subject cannot give conventional answers. Projective tests, though, are very open to bias on the part of the examiner, who may have her own ideas about how the subject ought to respond.

One famous projective test is the **Rorschach Inkblot.** The subject is presented cards with blots of ink on them one at a time in a specified order and is given the ambiguous instructions, "Tell me what you see. What might this be?" The subject is given as much time as he wishes and is allowed to look at the cards from any perspective. The observer records the time taken. After the subject has responded, the examiner questions him to find out where the item was seen in the blot, or location; what aspects of the blot determined the response (form, color, shading, and movement), or the determinant; and the content of response (what was seen). The interpretation of these results is supposed to reveal how a subject solves problems, the subject's intellectual level, and emotional stability. However, the validity of these associations has never been satisfactorily proven, and the test is currently of questionable diagnostic value.

The **TAT** is another questionably-valid test, designed by Murray and Morgan in 1935. The TAT consists of 31 cards, with one left blank. The remaining 30 cards show some interpersonal involvement between two or three people and represent a variety of gender and age groups. The subject's task is to provide a setting for the action in the picture, what the future outcome will be, and the characters' feelings. Traditionally, the TATs are interpreted according to the needs of the "hero." The subject assumes the action in the picture revolves around the "hero" figure. Scorers usually take into account characteristics of the story, recurrent themes, choice of "hero," the description of specific interrelationships, and the handling of authority and gender relationships. Whatever the subject chooses to discuss is considered to be important to him. This differs from the Rorschach test, where the subject's characteristics are inferred from different aspects of her response, not merely from content.

Where objective tests emphasize Allport's nomothetic method of study, where large numbers of subjects generate basic principles of behavior, subjective tests tend to emphasize ideographic study, where methods do not conceal or blur the uniqueness of a particular individual.

Self-Concept and Self-Esteem

Self-concept is a person's picture of herself, a la Carl Rogers (as described above). **Self-esteem** is the amount that one values oneself, for good or for bad. Coopersmith (1967) studied the self-esteem of 85 boys. He found that individuals with high self-esteem were more likely to lead group discussions, make friends, be nonconformist, and be less self-conscious than other boys. Clearly, self-esteem plays an important role in personality. However, it is not clear whether having many good traits gives a person high self-esteem, or having high self-esteem promotes the development of beneficial traits.

REVIEW QUESTIONS

1. "Traits" are _____ characteristics that make a person act in a _____ way in certain contexts.

2. Hippocrates's four humors are an example of _____ psychology.

3. What is the major flaw in both trait and type psychology?

4. Match the following:
   - (a) superego
   - (b) libido
   - (c) Thanatos

   - (d) id
   - (e) Eros
   - (f) ego

   - (1) the death instinct
   - (2) the sum of all instinctual urges
   - (3) the intermediary between instinct and morality
   - (4) the life instinct
   - (5) the moral sense
   - (6) sexual energy

5. True or False: According to Jung, the female archetype every man holds in his mind is called the persona.

6. If Gordon Allport decided to study the Rorschach ink blot responses of 10 subjects for a year, to see how each person's unique inkblot showed their personality, he would be using _____ methods.

7. Hans J. Eysenck examined the brain's physical correlates of the personality traits _____ and _____ .

8. Which personality test was designed to distinguish "normal" people from the mentally ill: the MMPI or the CPI?

9. The Thematic Apperception Test and the Rorschach Test are both
    _____ tests.

10. A very fat person who is told that fat people are jolly all her life finally
    becomes jolly. This is an example of _____ .

ANSWER KEY

1. stable, consistent

2. type

3. Failure to consider environmental variables

4. (a) 5   (b) 6   (c) 1
    (d) 2   (e) 4   (f) 3

5. False

6. ideographic

7. introversion and extroversion

8. CPI

9. projective

10. self-fulfilling prophecy

Chapter 11

Social Psychology

INTRODUCTION

Social psychology focuses on the psychology of the individual in society. Social psychologists may draw from sociology and cultural anthropology, though their primary interest is still the psychological level of thought and action. Using the scientific method and objective study, social psychologists have produced a body of knowledge about the underlying psychological processes in social interactions.

Within social psychology, there are two major schools of thought. **Cognitive theorists** concentrate on an individual's internal processes and thoughts. They believe that a human being organizes and processes experience, and that her "world view" greatly influences her social behavior. **Behaviorists,** on the other hand, put more emphasis on external events, and tend to believe that people react to events that occur around them.

ATTITUDES AND ATTRIBUTIONS

An **attitude** is a person's beliefs about an object or a situation. An attitude both precedes behavior and causes behavior toward an object. The average adult probably has thousands of attitudes of which he is not aware. Attitudes usually occur in clusters or sets around a particular issue or situation—for example, taxes or abortion—supporting and reinforcing each other. A **value,** on the other hand, is a person's enduring belief about how she should act, and what goals are appropriate or desirable. Values direct behavior on a long-term basis. Examples of values (from Rokeach's Value Survey) are pleasure, wisdom, and a sense of accomplishment. A person generally holds many more attitudes than values.

Attitudes are generally formed through imitation, classical conditioning (see Chapter 6), or operant conditioning (op. cit.). Learning often occurs by imitation without obvious reinforcement. Hence, children often take on their parents' behavior and attitudes. In a study of Bennington College students, Theodore Newcomb found that incoming freshmen held conservative political attitudes, like those of their reference group—their parents. By graduation, though, they had acquired significantly more liberal attitudes, like those of their new reference group: classmates. One example of attitudes acquired by classical conditioning is the connotation of words. If you give a person a neutral word and immediately follow it with a word that evokes a strong negative or positive reaction, this will eventually cause the same type of reaction to the previously neutral word. In operant conditioning, a subject emits a behavior. If the behavior is reinforced, it will likely reoccur; if it is punished, it will not recur as often. If your child says, "I want to be a fireman!" and you respond with a smile and an assurance that she'll be just like Mommy then, the child will continue to have a positive attitude about firemen. If, on the other hand, you scowl and admonish her for even considering such a thing, you have punished her response, and the chances are that she will develop negative attitudes about the firefighting profession and all emergency-rescue careers.

Though it may seem that the principles of attitude acquisition are simple, the actual process is quite complex. An adult's attitudes are quite difficult to trace to their source. This is complicated by the fact that attitudes can change, even quite significantly, in the course of a person's lifetime. There is much yet to be learned about attitudes and their acquisition.

Persuasion

Persuasion refers to a type of social influence that involves attitude change. Persuasion is not necessarily the result of conscious communication: a person can be persuaded that a street is dangerous if he sees a person being mugged there. In general, though, three factors affect how persuasive a particular communication is, i.e., how effective it is at changing attitudes. These factors are the source of the communication (who says it), the nature of the communication (how it is said), and the characteristics of the audience. All these factors can also be applied to print and broadcast media, not just face-to-face persuasion.

The first aspect of the source that the audience examines is credibility. People tend to believe people who appear to be experts or seem trustworthy. To the average person, it makes a lot of sense to be influenced by someone with these characteristics. Often, visual impressions are the only items a person can base impressions on, and these are what are used to infer credibility, whether of TV news anchors, an auto mechanic, or a teacher. Trustworthiness, on the other hand, can be improved by arguing there is nothing to lose, arguing against one's (apparent) self-interest, and appearing not to be trying to influence people or change their minds.

The concern for the nature of communication is the emotional approach vs. the reasonable (or logical) approach. Research results generally indicate that a shocking (emotional-based) approach is usually more effective in communication and persuasion than the logical approach.

As for the audience, individuals with low self-esteem are quicker to be convinced if the speaker appears credible or takes an emotional approach, while high self-esteem listeners are in higher conflict when presented with less-than-reliable information from a medium-credibility speaker. The speaker's prior experience with the audience is another crucial factor, as are educational level and previous contact with the issue being discussed.

Prejudice

Prejudice is an attitude. It is generally a negative attitude held toward a particular group and any member of that group. Prejudice is translated into behavior through discrimination, which refers to any action that results from prejudiced points of view. **Ethnocentrism** is a special form of prejudice where a person holds positive prejudices about her own ethnic group and negative prejudices about all other ethnic groups.

It is possible for individuals to be quite prejudiced and still not discriminate. Civil rights laws, for example, have reduced a great deal of the more obvious discrimination. However, some evidence exists that the prejudicial attitudes of Americans have been influenced by civil rights law. For instance, in 1964, most Americans were opposed to the Civil Rights Act, but today over 75 percent of the public favors integration.

When discrimination decreases and prejudice remains, discrimination may begin to take more subtle forms, such as not being included in informal discussions with other managers at work, being assigned the more routine tasks of a project, and being listened to through the filter of prejudiced attitudes— "he's not too bright," "she's too emotional," and so forth.

Although prejudice is a complex topic and difficult to analyze on an individual level, psychologists hypothesize that there are four basic causes of prejudice. The first cause of prejudice is **economic** and **political competition.** This view states that when any resource is limited, majority groups will vie for resources and thus form prejudices against the competing group for their own personal gain and advantage. Research has demonstrated a clear link between the level of discrimination and prejudice against a certain group in an area and the scarcity of jobs in that area.

The second causal factor of prejudice is **personality needs.** After World War II, researchers began to search for a prejudiced personality type. The major piece of research in this area, by Adorno et al., is titled *The Authoritarian Personality.* Adorno developed the F (fascist) Scale for authoritarianism. These researchers established a relationship between the strictness of parental upbringing and authoritarianism and a correlational relationship between authoritarianism, prejudice, and ethnocentrism. Yet they did not determine what causes prejudice, only what personality traits accompany it.

The third cause of prejudice is the **displacement of aggression.** This is referred to as a "scapegoat" theory of prejudice. Here, aggression (described further below) that cannot be otherwise expressed is displaced onto socially acceptable victims.

The fourth cause of prejudice is **conformity to preexisting prejudices** within the society or subgroup. Researchers note that while there seems to be a large difference between the amount of anti-black prejudice in the North and the South, neither group is distinguishable on the basis of how they score on the Authoritarian test. The problem appears to be caused by socially acceptable beliefs in each region. As Elliot Aronson has noted, historical events in the South set the stage for greater prejudice against blacks, but it is conformity which keeps it going.

There are four other factors which contribute to the construction and continuation of prejudice. People tend to be prejudiced against the group which is directly under them on the socio-economic scale. The four additional contributions are 1) people need to feel superior to someone, 2) people most strongly feel competition for jobs from the next lower level, 3) people from the lower socio-economic levels are more frustrated and therefore more aggressive (see below), and 4) a lack of education increases the likelihood that they will simplify their world by the consistent use of stereotyping.

There are ways of reducing prejudice. One unsuccessful manner of reducing prejudice is to provide information contrary to peoples' beliefs. Unfortunately, people tend to pay attention only to information which agrees with their beliefs.

However, if people of different backgrounds are brought together in **equal-status contact,** people tend to change their behavior and their attitudes towards other groups. Unfortunately, forced busing and desegregation efforts often bring people together in unequal status, defying their purpose. Finally, one very successful way to reduce prejudice is through **interdependence,** where all participants must work together with a mixed group. Social psychologists are currently trying to apply this method to educational settings.

Attributes and Stereotypes

An **attribute** is a perceived characteristic of some object or person. In attribution, people infer that some individual has certain characteristics. If a person infers that people possess certain characteristics because of their gender, race, or religion, that person is attributing a **stereotype** to that group. Stereotyping is not necessarily an intentional act of insult; very often it is merely used as a means of simplifying the complex world. However, if a stereotype narrows a person's views of actual interpersonal differences, prejudiced attitudes can result.

Attribution theory contends that individuals have a tendency to attribute a cause to any recently viewed behaviors. This attribution is essentially a specialized sort of stereotyping. When viewing an event, the observer uses the information available to her at the time to infer causality. Although there are many factors which affect what inference will be made, the major contributors are a person's beliefs, e.g., stereotypes or prejudices. The process of attribution based on a person's prejudices can be described as a "vicious circle." A person's prejudices affect her attributions, and her misdirected attributions then serve to reinforce and intensify her prejudice.

CONFORMITY AND OBEDIENCE

Conformity is a change in behavior or belief caused by real or imagined social pressure. For example, a teenager who goes to school in formal clothes will quickly observe that every other person her age is wearing blue jeans. No one may say a word about her dress, yet she observes that others are acting differently and may imagine that they are discussing her clothing. The next day, in blue jeans, she conforms. Conformity is generally divided into three subtypes: compliance, identification, and internalization.

Compliance is a change in external behavior, as opposed to a real attitude change, termed "private acceptance." Compliance is generally exhibited by individuals attempting to gain a reward or punishment. This behavior generally ceases once the reward or punishment is either not available or avoidable, respectively.

Identification results from the individual's desire to be like some other person, the person she is identifying with. Such behavior is self-satisfying, and does not require reward or threat of punishment. The individual loosely adopts the beliefs and opinions of the person she identifies with, a fact which differentiates identification from compliance.

Internalization occurs when the individual adopts the groups beliefs as his own. This process is a deeply rooted social response based on the desire to be right. The reward here is intrinsic. Identification is usually the method which introduces a belief to an individual, but once it is internalized it becomes an independent belief, and is highly resistant to change.

The most famous psychological demonstration of conformity was a series of experiments by Solomon Asch. Asch asked subjects to choose which of three lines on a card was the same length as line X, a line on a separate card. Each subject was on a panel with other "subjects" (Asch's confederates) who all initially gave the same wrong answer. Approximately 35% of the real subjects chose to give the obviously incorrect, but conforming, response. Since there were no explicit rewards or punishments, the reason for conformity could be that in the face of such "overwhelming" opposition the subjects doubted their own perceptions or agreed with the confederates to gain group acceptance (or avoid group rejection). Asch and his colleagues have repeated this study many times, varying the conditions in attempts to determine what variables play a causal role in decreasing or increasing conformity.

Obedience also involves conforming to others' expectations. Yet in obedience, an authority's demands are clearly expressed; the individual must consciously choose whether or not to obey. The study of obedience became especially important after World War II, when psychologists were eager to investigate just how and why the Nazis committed their death-camp atrocities.

While investigating obedience, Stanley Milgram discovered that the average middle-class American male would, under the direction of a legitimate authority figure, give severe shocks to other people in an experimental setting. Briefly, in his experiments two men were told that they would be taking part in an experiment on the effects of punishment on learning. One man was chosen as the learner (who was actually a confederate in the experiment), the other as the teacher. The learner was taken into an adjoining room and strapped into a chair. The experimenter read the instructions to the learner about a word-list he was to learn so that the teacher-subject could hear. The teacher was placed in front of a generator which could administer shocks from 15 to 450 volts to the learner. Under the shock levels were descriptions of the effects of the shock from "slight shock" to "danger, severe shock." The learning session would begin: the first time the learner would give an incorrect answer, a mild shock was given, and with each subsequent wrong answer stronger and stronger shocks were administered. Even amidst cries from the learner of "Let me out, I've got a heart condition," the teacher would continue administering the shock, though more and more reluctantly.

Out of the 40 males who took part in the initial experiments, 26 or 65% went all the way to the maximum shock of 450 volts. This alarming finding has been replicated many times. It demonstrates how much ordinary people will comply with the orders of a legitimate authority even to the point of committing cruel and harmful actions. On a television interview, Milgram stated that he would have no trouble staffing a Nazi-style concentration camp with guards from any middle-sized American town. This is not due to American anti-Semitism, but because of the evidence of his experiments regarding the power of legitimate authorities to evoke obedience.

GROUP DYNAMICS

People tend to act differently when they are in a group. A few of the differences are outlined above in the Asch experiment. In general, a group's primary purpose is to achieve some definite goal. To accomplish the goal, the group establishes **positions,** or places, where people fit into a group's hierarchy. Individuals themselves choose to fill **roles,** the set of different behaviors an individual displays in connection with a given social position. There are certain behaviors associated with the role of mother, employer, student, secretary, and teacher, for example. Most people have many roles which must be filled each day. However, people who occupy the same type of position may play very different roles. Three different roles are possible in any given position in a group. The **task-oriented** role requires that a person be concerned directly with accomplishing the goal of the group. The **maintenance** role requires that the individual playing it be more concerned with the group morale. The final type of role is the **self-oriented** role; the person who takes this role cares mainly for herself, and may even attempt to undermine the group's goals if they interfere with her personal desires or needs.

If a group is large enough—say, the size of New York City—social influence may move the person away from socially acceptable behavior. **Deindividuation** is a state where a person feels a lessened sense of personal identity and a decreased concern about what people think of him. This state, which probably results from feelings of anonymity, lessened responsibility and arousal, can lead to anti-social behavior. Philip Zimbardo once left an apparently abandoned car with the license plates removed and the hood raised in two cities, New York and Palo Alto (pop. 100,000). In New York, within 10 minutes a man, woman, and a nine-year- old child came by and immediately began to remove parts of the car. Within 24 hours, the car was completely ransacked. The vandals were not gangs, but most often well-dressed adults. In Palo Alto, the car remained untouched after 72 hours, except for one passerby who politely put the hood down when it began to rain. Zimbardo took this result as supporting the hypothesis that the anonymity of a large city gives rise to antisocial behavior. The chances of a person being recognized by someone in a city with a population of 8 million is much less than in a city with a population of 100,000.

Yet groups can also improve performance. In **social facilitation,** the mere presence of other people such as an audience or coworkers can increase individual performance. In the 1890s, Norman Triplett became interested in the fact that cyclists rode faster in groups than alone, while in the 1930s, John Dashiell discovered that though people respond more frequently in the presence of others, their rate of errors also increased. Robert Zajonc (1965) theorized that the presence of other people produces an increase in a person's arousal level (see Chapter 8) and enhances strong responses. However, if responses are poorly learned or weak, responses will suffer. This theory helps explain why stage fright may paralyze young actors and galvanize more experienced thespians into grand performance.

Altruism and Bystander Intervention

Altruism and the "bystander effect" are two opposite responses to situations where another person needs help. In **altruism,** a person will risk his own health or well-being to help another. Yet if a large group of people witnesses an event where someone desperately needs assistance, each individual person is less likely to intervene than if she were alone. This phenomenon is called the **bystander effect.**

Latane and Darley produced the most famous experiments on bystander intervention. In their study, male subjects heard someone fall, apparently uninjured, in the room next door. Whether subjects tried to help and how long they took to do so were the main dependent variables in the experiment. Subjects were placed in one of four conditions: alone, with a friend, with another subject who was a stranger, and with a confederate in the experiment who had been instructed to remain passive at the sounds of injury. In the alone situation, subjects responded to the need for help 91% of the time, while with the passive confederate, subjects responded only 7% of the time. With pairs of strangers, at least one of the subjects responded in 40% of the pairs, while in the group of two friends, at least one person intervened in 70% of the pairs. This finding can be explained through **social influence** or **diffusion of responsibility.** The former option suggests that people are susceptible to the apparent reactions of other people present. The subject may not feel the situation is serious or merely be concerned and confused by the confederate's passivity. In diffusion of responsibility, when other people are present, each person's total sense of responsibility (and justification for responding to emergencies) may diminish.

AGGRESSION

In animals, many types of aggression are specific to certain species and are clearly controlled by brain structures and hormone levels, such as maternal aggression in rats. In humans, sex steroid hormones called **androgens** have been conclusively linked to an increase in aggressive behavior. However, it is not clear whether high levels of androgens produce aggression, or high levels of aggression result in the production of testosterone; there is evidence for both conclusions. Mazur and Lamb (1980) found that men who lost tennis matches had lower levels of testosterone (an androgen) an hour later, while the men who won had higher levels.

According to social psychologists, three different **distinctions** should be used when discussing aggressive behavior. The first distinction is between **harmful and nonharmful behavior,** which is judged by the outcome of the behavior. The second distinction involves the **intent of the aggressor,** as hitting a person accidentally is not considered aggressive. Finally, there is a distinction between aggression necessary to achieve a goal (as in professional boxing), called **instrumental aggression,** and aggression which is an end in itself (as in common street fighting), called **hostile aggression.** Interpersonal aggression occurs most often between friends, relatives, and acquaintances, and is much less often associated with crime than most people think.

Many social psychologists believe that aggression is a learned behavior, like other behaviors. Albert Bandura's work on modeling, or learning through imitation, was designed to explain aggressive tendencies in children (see Chapter 6). Aggression, like attitudes, may also be conditioned (see Chapter 6). The frustration-aggression hypothesis states that frustration toward the accomplishment of some goal produces aggression. For example, if you are trying to buy a soda in a convenience store, but the clerk will not serve you because he is busy talking on the telephone, that clerk is frustrating you with regard to buying the soda. If the source of frustration is available and unthreatening, the aggression will be displaced onto that person: you may yell at the talkative clerk. Otherwise, the aggression will be displaced onto someone or something else, called a "scapegoat."

However, some psychologists believe that aggression is an inborn tendency. The only reason, according to these theories, that we are not involved in more wars than we currently are is that humans use their intelligence to vent their aggression, and therefore do not always express aggression physically. Konrad Lorenz applied Darwin's "survival of the fittest" theory to aggression, arguing that aggression is necessary for the continued existence of the species. However, he based his argument on the observation of animals, not humans. Others, including Freud, believe the catharsis theory. This theory states that aggression is a means of releasing inner tension. If this tension were to remain unreleased, mental illness would result. Research does not support this theory, though, and has actually shown the opposite to be true.

ORGANIZATIONAL PSYCHOLOGY

Organizational psychology studies human behavior in an industrial or organizational environment. It can be divided into two important subfields: **industrial psychology,** and **human factors psychology.** Human factors psychology is concerned specifically with how people receive information through their senses, store this information, and process it when making decisions.

The differences in these two areas is best understood by examining the jobs of industrial psychologists and human factors engineers. The industrial psychologist helps to improve safety programs and works with engineers on the human aspects of equipment design. She assists the office of public relations in its interactions with consumers and the local community. Industrial psychologists also engage in programs dealing with workers' mental health, and assist management in finding ways to reduce absenteeism and grievances. The industrial psychologist may draw up a plan for the executive development of newly hired college graduates on one day and discuss problems of aging employees the next.

The role of a human factors engineer, on the other hand, is concerned with contriving, designing and producing structures and machines useful to humans. He applies his knowledge of the mechanical, electrical, chemical, or other properties of matter to the task of creating all kinds of functional devices—safety pins and automobiles, mousetraps and missiles. Since the ultimate users of these machines are humans, human characteristics must be considered in their construction. Human muscular frailty dictated the need for and design of such devices as the lever, pulley, screw, and hand tools of all sorts (though these simple machines were not designed by human factors engineers). The L-shaped desk for the secretary was designed to bring an enlarged work space within easy reach. The task which confronts the human factors engineer is to describe humans' special abilities and limitations so that design engineers can effectively include the human operator in their man-made system. This requires knowledge about sensation and perception, psychomotor behavior, and cognitive processes as well as knowledge about the properties of the material world. It is because of the need for this special knowledge about human behavior that this type of engineer is also considered a psychologist.

REVIEW QUESTIONS

1. Social psychology draws on ideas from _____ and _____ .

2. True or False: Attitudes are sometimes learned through conditioning.

3. Which is generally more effective in persuasion: a logical rational approach or an emotional appeal?

4. When aggression is displaced onto a _____ , prejudice may develop.

5. Subjects were _____ likely to try to help in an ambiguous situation when a passive confederate was with them in the Latane-Darley experiment.

6. Is compliance a change in internal belief or external behavior?

7. Stanley Milgram's study of obedience was conducted with what subjects?

8. True or False: A person playing the "maintenance" role in a group is most concerned with accomplishing the group's goals.

9. Does "releasing" inner tension through aggression prevent mental illness?

10. The role of a _____ is to contrive design and produce structures and machines which take account of human characteristics.

ANSWER KEY

1. sociology and cultural anthropology

2. True

3. An emotional appeal

4. scapegoat

5. less

6. External behavior

7. White, middle-class American males

8. False

9. No

10. human factors engineer

Chapter 12

Abnormal Psychology

ABNORMAL BEHAVIOR: DEFINITIONS

Abnormal behavior is behavior that creates a problem for an individual or society. It is often referred to as maladaptive or pathological behavior. Abnormal behavior is what most people refer to when they use the term "mental illness." Abnormal psychology creates diagnoses for people who exhibit abnormal behavior, and provides treatments to help people to return to normal functioning.

Of course, this definition of abnormal behavior can be used to challenge the sanity of people who are not mentally ill but merely disagree with society's strictures. Artists, writers, scientists, labor union leaders, and other people who believe in changing society have been imprisoned against their will in mental hospitals in putatively advanced industrialized nations. It is important to consider the total environment and impact of a person's behavior before labelling it "abnormal." For instance, is singing loudly in a supermarket produce aisle abnormal? *Unusual* perhaps, but neither would it cause any harm. How about sitting mute in the middle of a cafeteria for 12 hours straight? Not necessarily, especially if you're a young student engaging in a sit-in to integrate a neighborhood eatery. What about standing in the middle of your nation's capitol, dousing yourself with gasoline, and setting yourself afire? Again, this is not inherently abnormal: during the Vietnam War, hundreds of Buddhist monks committed suicide in this way on the streets of Hanoi to protest the war. In the first case, the behavior is not abnormal because it does not interfere with the person's functioning in society. In the second case, the behavior may interfere with the person's functioning and local societal functioning (no one else will use the cafeteria), yet the person made a conscious decision to engage in this behavior. If you ask her a week or a month later, she would probably still be able to explain why she did this. In the third case, again, the monks made conscious decisions to perform acts which, in their culture, were regarded as effective means of protest which could help stop the devastation of their country. A Vietnamese Buddhist monk in the United States at the time could have made the same decision, yet Americans who did not understand the Vietnamese situation or the role of fire in Vietnamese culture could very well consider the monks' acts as abnormal behavior. Once labels are attached to a person, they are very hard to remove. There must be a thorough consideration of all relevant factors before a person's behavior is termed "abnormal."

On the other hand, there are certain mental illnesses which seem to be prevalent in only certain cultures. American women suffer from **anorexia nervosa,** a syndrome in which victims purposely starve themselves. This is virtually unknown in countries where there is no excess of food, or where women do not have to be thin to be considered beautiful. During the late 19th century, fainting spells and "hysteria" were much more common among Western women than today. Some social theorists believe that women became "hysterical" because they were expected to respond passively to stress, instead of expressing their frustration in some more active way. In Malaysia, there is a condition called "Amok," where victims suddenly start to run about attacking others and destroying property wantonly. Eventually, the victim either kills herself or enters a coma. When the victim awakes, she has no memory of her time running amok. Certain Canadian Indian tribes suffer from "windigo," an anxiety disorder in which victims become convinced that they will kill and eat a friend. Human minds are clearly "plastic," and able to adapt to different conditions. Even mental illness is quite subject to local mores.

Abnormal behavior is not a sign of artistic ability or special wisdom. It is simply a sign of abnormal behavior and perhaps a symptom of mental illness. Perhaps some schizophrenics see visions of heavenly beauty or grasp new knowledge that would benefit humanity. Yet the vast majority of mentally ill patients are simply ordinary people who would be happy to be able to control their moods and their minds, hold a steady job, and live with other people in the imperfect, bittersweet relationships that bring meaning to existence, instead of existing in their minds alone.

HISTORY OF ABNORMAL PSYCHOLOGY

There have always been two views of abnormal behavior. In earlier times, humans sometimes believed that abnormal behavior was caused by demons or evil spirits. Ancient skulls have been found with holes drilled in them, or been "trepanned," presumably to allow spirits to escape, in both European and South American native cultures. Early Chinese, Egyptians, and Greeks exorcised demons through prayer, f logging, and starvation. Yet in other cultures, people believed that people who exhibited abnormal behavior were blessed with an ability to see the future, or to speak to gods. They were supported by the community and consulted before important decisions were made. Certain African, North American, and European cultures held this view. Many modern theorists have suggested that this is a healthier view of abnormal behavior than current conceptions.

In Greece, a fifth-century-B.C. doctor named Hippocrates was one of the earliest proponents of the **somatogenic hypothesis,** which states that something wrong with the **soma** (physical body) disturbs thought and behavior. He also considered emotional and environmental stress to be causes of deviant behavior. Thus, deviant behavior became a matter for physicians as well as priests, and treatments became more entwined with physical health. Specifically, Hippocrates believed that the correct balance of the body's four "humors"—blood, black bile, yellow bile, and phlegm—was responsible for mental health. Too much of any "humor" would lead to a specific ailment.

In the European middle ages, the Christian church rejected Hippocrates's medical model. The devil was supposed to have possessed the bodies of "witches." Many of these "witches" were publicly executed. Later, in 1621, Robert Burton wrote *The Anatomy of Melancholy,* which turned attention back to medical models. This book led indirectly to the creation of asylums and encouraged a somewhat more humane, if not ideal, treatment for these people. Philippe Pinel was a vital figure in the movement towards humanitarian treatment of the mentally ill. In charge of an asylum during the French Revolution, he began to treat the "inmates" (for these asylums were little better than prisons) as sick human beings rather than beasts. He removed their chains, and they in turn became much more "manageable." When not treated as animals, Pinel's patients behaved like human beings. Pinel believed that the mentally ill should be treated with compassion and dignity, and he achieved some remarkable results.

More recently, Kraeplin (1883) distinguished between groups of symptoms (syndromes) in mentally ill individuals. He recognized two major groups of diseases: **dementia-praecox** (an early term for schizophrenia) and the **manic-depressive psychosis.** These distinctions were the predecessors of our current classification system.

In the 18th, 19th, and 20th centuries an alternative hypothesis called the **psychogenic theory** developed. This viewpoint attributed mental disorders to mental malfunctions. The pioneering work of Sigmund Freud and other early 20th century psychoanalysts came out of this theory.

Many contemporary psychologists (specifically, behaviorists and biologists) feel that scientific tests should be used to determine the true causes of, and the effectiveness of, cures for abnormal behavior. They point out that it is difficult, if not impossible, to test psychogenic theories this way. For example, how can Freud's assertion that everyone goes through an Oedipal conflict (see Chapter 9) be judged through experimentation? This question is currently the focus of a lively continuing debate.

MODELS OF ABNORMAL BEHAVIOR

The four predominant models or definitions of abnormal behavior are the **statistical, medical, psychoanalytic,** and the **social learning** models. The **statistical model** has to do with how often "normal" and "abnormal" characteristics occur in the population. By definition, a low frequency of occurrence of a certain characteristic within the general population results in that characteristic being termed "abnormal." This is at most a partial description of abnormal behavior. The **medical** or **organic model** is more useful. The critical assumption here is that abnormal behavior is like a disease. This model considers both somatogenic (originating in the body) and psychogenic (originating in the mind) causes. These causes could occur internally due to some disease or defect (systemic or infectious) or could be caused by some external injury (traumatic). Psychoanalytic theory can be considered an example of a psychogenic disease model. There are both **systemic** and **traumatic** disease components in Freudian theory. Systemic causes are exemplified by an innately weak "instinct," while traumatic components would include the varied and individually specific effects of external experiences on people. The fourth major model, the **social learning model,** is closely related to behaviorism. Here, the crucial assumption is that abnormal behavior is learned the same way as most other human behavior. In this model the importance of biological and genetic factors is minimized, so that the learning model is primarily psychogenic. Though some extreme behaviorists do not refer to any internal states or mental processes at all, other learning model theorists do use a "mediational approach" and do consider intervening mental and emotional processes. This viewpoint is closer to a disease model of mental illness.

There are no overwhelming and conclusive data in support of any one model. It is unlikely that any one of the above models will ever be able to fully account for all abnormal behaviors since people's experiences are so complex. Perhaps all these models are partially correct, and more research and careful synthesis are needed.

TYPES OF DISORDERS

Anxiety Disorders

In the **anxiety disorders,** some form of anxiety is either the predominant disturbance in the clinical disorder, or anxiety is experienced if the individual tries to resist giving in to her symptoms. According to the fourth edition of the Diagnostic and Statistical Manual of the American Psychiatric Association (DSM IV), there are five types of anxiety disorders: **panic disorder, generalized anxiety disorder, phobic disorder, obsessive-compulsive disorder,** and **stress disorder.**

The chief features of **panic disorders** are recurrent panic attacks followed by at least one month of persistent concern about having another panic attack. The panic attacks take place at times when there is no marked physical exertion or life-threatening situation. The patient may feel as if she is out of control or about to die, or she may have premonitions of an impending disaster. There are many physiological correlates such as rapid heart rate, irregular breathing, excessive sweating, choking, dizziness, or trembling.

Chronic, generalized, and persistent anxiety characterizes a **generalized anxiety disorder.** In order for the diagnosis of generalized anxiety disorder to be made, there must be evidence of at least three of the following six symptoms: (1) restlessness or feeling on edge, motor tension; (2) being easily fatigued; (3) difficulty concentrating or mind going blank; (4) irritability; (5) muscle tension; (6) sleep disturbance (difficulty falling or staying asleep, or restless unsatisfying sleep).

Phobic disorders are characterized by strong, irrational fears of specific objects or situations. For example, when a person is extremely fearful of heights, closed spaces, snakes or spiders, provided there is no objective danger, the label phobia is likely to be applied to her avoidance and fear. A person suffering from a phobic neurosis knows what she is afraid of and almost always recognizes that her fear is irrational, but she cannot account for her fear or control it. Two common phobias, both of which are discussed in some detail in DSM IV, are agoraphobia—fear of public places and open spaces—and social phobia—fear of social situations.

Although they are separate symptoms, **obsessive and compulsive** reactions often occur together as an anxiety disorder. Obsessions are persistent, often unreasonable thoughts which cannot be dispelled. A person may become obsessed with the idea that she will swear, make obscene gestures, or even commit murder. A compulsion is a persistent act which is repeated over and over, such as washing one's hands dozens of times a day, or touching a doorknob every few minutes. Virtually any behavior can be viewed as a compulsion if the individual reports an irresistible urge to perform it and experiences considerable distress if prevented from doing so.

Stress disorders, which are also characterized as anxiety disorders, are precipitated by exposure to an extreme traumatic event. The person may have experienced, witnessed, or have been confronted with an event that was life-threatening, involving serious harm to self or others, or was perceived as such. Some common symptoms found in Posttraumatic Stress Disorder (PTSD) and Acute Stress Disorder include sleep difficulties, dissociative episodes, intrusive recollections of the event, and flashbacks (a dissociative reexperiencing of the event).

Affective Disorders

Affective disorders are characterized by a disturbance of mood. **Mood** is defined as a prolonged emotion which colors the whole psychic life and generally involves either depression or elation. In the DSM IV, nearly all of the subtypes of affective disorders are divided according to two nosological (medical classification) dimensions, each having three divisions.

The first **nosological dimension** has to do with the predominant mood displayed by the patient. In affective disorders, mood tends to be at one extreme or the other. The patient may be **depressed,** or **manic,** or she may exhibit bipolar symptoms—that is, she may alternate between extremes of depression and mania. Symptoms of depression include loss of energy, loss of interest or pleasure in sexual activities, feelings of self-reproach, and recurrent thoughts of death or suicide. Some manic symptoms are hyperactivity, decreased need for sleep, loquacity (talkativeness), inflated self-esteem, and excessive involvement in activities without regard to their painful consequences (e.g., buying sprees, foolish business investments, sexual indiscretions, reckless driving). Another symptom of mania is the "flight of ideas," which refers to rapid shifts in conversation from one subject to another based on superficial associations.

These disorders can also be classified on a **second nosological dimension** that has to do with the onset of the patient's disorder. This dimension is divided into **episodic, chronic,** and **atypical** affective disorders. **Episodic** affective disorders feature an episode of the illness with a prominent, persistent mood disturbance that is clearly distinguished from prior functioning. The onset of the disorder is distinct. **Chronic** affective disorders imply a long-standing (at least two years) illness with either sustained or intermittent disturbance in mood. Chronic disorders usually begin in early adult life without a clear onset or cause. Generally, these mood disturbances are more prolonged but not so severe as those manifested in episodic disorders. Normal periods may last a few days to a few weeks; a diagnosis of chronic affective disorder is not made if there has been a normal period of two months or more. **Atypical** disorders is a category for individuals who are neither episodic nor chronic. An example of an atypical affective disorder is an illness which fulfills the criteria for a chronic depressive disorder, except that there have been intermittent periods of normal mood lasting more than two months.

Somatoform Disorders

Somatoform disorders are physical disorders which have psychological causes. The victim does not have conscious control over the disorder. However, psychological counseling often cures these illnesses. In **hypochondria,** a person is obsessed with his body's physical function. A hypochondriac may read a report on an illness in a newspaper health column, and report to a doctor that he suffers these symptoms. These people constantly complain about symptoms, though a physician seldom finds a physical cause. In **conversion reactions,** certain bodily functions are impaired, though the bodily organs themselves are sound. Patients with conversion disorders have reported symptoms such as paralysis, blindness, seizures, and anesthesia (loss of feeling), all without any sign of a physiological cause. However, despite the fact that there are no physical causes for these symptoms, in conversion disorder these symptoms are not under the patient's voluntary control. Conversion disorder frequently has a symbolic content. For example, researchers in California discovered that an alarming number of recent older female immigrants from Cambodia suffer conversion blindness.

These women, who witnessed the horrors of the Pol Pot regime in the 1970s, have reacted to these sights by becoming blind.

Personality Disorders

A **personality disorder** is a persistent abnormal pattern of behavior which usually develops by adolescence. In these disorders, the behavior is so abnormal as to cause suffering to the patient or others. These disorders include **paranoid personality disorder,** where a person is suspicious and mistrustful of all others, **asocial personality disorder,** where the victim cannot maintain lasting or meaningful social relationships, and **antisocial personality syndrome,** also known as sociopathy, as well as **narcissistic disorder,** which is characterized by extreme self-love and neglect of others.

An antisocial personality is an individual who is basically unsocialized, in that the person has no regard for other people, whose behavior repeatedly brings her into conflict with society. These people are often "con artists," and are skilled at manipulating others. According to H. Cleckly, the following characteristics distinguish antisocial personality disorder: average or superior intelligence, absence of irrationality or other common symptoms of psychosis, no sense of responsibility, disregard for the truth, no sense of shame, antisocial behavior without apparent regret, inability to learn from experience, general poverty of affect, lack of genuine insight, little response to special consideration or kindness, no history of sincere suicide attempts, unrestrained and unconventional sex life, and the onset of sociopathic characteristics no later than the early twenties. One of the most important aspects of sociopathy is the lack of emotional response from the individual after committing an antisocial act. This lack of shame or guilt can be linked to the sociopath's inability to learn from experience, particularly to avoid punishment. Because the sociopath does not become emotionally aroused easily, she is less likely to suffer from and change her antisocial ways. Many sociopaths have a history of repeated legal or social offenses. Sociopaths have little or no regard for social values and norms, are incapable of significant loyalty to individuals or groups, and tend to be selfish.

Schizophrenia: Symptoms

Schizophrenia is not a "split personality" syndrome: it is a group of disorders involving a breakdown of the thinking process, disengagement from reality, and flattened affect (emotion). About one percent of the U.S.

population will suffer from schizophrenia at some point in their lives. The rate of illness varies from country to country; Ireland has the highest rate of diagnoses. Schizophrenics' disordered behavior can be organized into disturbances in several major areas: cognition, perception and attention, affect or emotion, motor behavior, and contact with reality. Usually a patient diagnosed with schizophrenia will exhibit only some of these disturbances.

The classic, common schizophrenic symptom is **auditory hallucination.** Most schizophrenics hear voices, which may tell them to do things, or music. Another common symptom is the cognitive disorder of **delusions,** or beliefs contrary to reality which are firmly held despite contradictory evidence. Typically, schizophrenics have delusions of persecution, grandeur, or control. A person with delusions of persecution believes that others are plotting against him. In delusions of grandeur, a person believes that he is an especially important individual, such as a famous movie star or Jesus Christ. Delusions of control involve the person's believing that he is being controlled by some outside force, such as alien beings or radar waves. These delusions may be transient, or a highly organized focus of the person's life.

Schizophrenics also commonly suffer a disorder of cognition called **thought disorder.** Usually a schizophrenic will speak incoherently, making references to ideas or images which are not connected. Often, he will use neologisms, or words made up by the speaker. Thought may also be disordered by loose associations. The individual may have problems sticking to one topic, often drifting off into a series of idiosyncratic associations. Another aspect of schizophrenics' associative problems is the use of **clang associations.** Here, the patient's speech may contain many words associated only by rhyme—for example, "How are you in your shoe on a pew, Doctor?"

Disorders of **perception** and **attention** (aside from hallucinations) suffered by schizophrenics include changes in the way their bodies feel. Parts of their body may seem too large or too small, or there may be numbness or tickling. Some schizophrenics remark that the world appears flat or colorless. Schizophrenics often have trouble attending to what is happening around them. For example, a schizophrenic may be unable to concentrate on television because he cannot watch the screen and listen to what is being said at the same time.

As for affect, schizophrenics frequently have **flat affect,** where virtually no stimulus can produce an emotional response. Others display **inappropriate affect,** where their responses do not fit the situation, or **ambivalent affect,** where a person or object simultaneously arouses both positive and negative emotions.

Motor symptoms of schizophrenia are obvious and bizarre. A schizophrenic may grimace or adopt strange facial expressions. The overall level of activity may be increased, with the patient running around and flailing his limbs wildly, or there may be catatonic immobility, where unusual postures are adopted and maintained for very long periods of time.

Finally, most schizophrenics have little or no grasp of reality. They tend to withdraw from contact with the world into their own thoughts and fantasies. Usually a schizophrenic becomes unable to distinguish between her own fictitious constructions of reality and what is really happening around her.

Schizophrenia: Types

Because of the wide variety of symptoms associated with schizophrenia, psychologists have found it helpful to distinguish among four main types of schizophrenia, as listed in DSM IV: **catatonic, paranoid, disorganized,** and **undifferentiated.** Disturbances in motor functions are the most obvious symptoms of the catatonic type of schizophrenia. A **catatonic schizophrenic** typically alternates between immobility and wild excitement, but often one or the other type of motor symptoms may predominate. In the excited state the catatonic may shout and talk continuously and incoherently, all the while pacing back and forth. The immobile state is characterized by physical rigidity, muteness, and unresponsiveness. Despite the severity of its symptoms, catatonia is more likely than other forms of schizophrenia to "cure itself" without other treatment.

Paranoid schizophrenia is diagnosed through the presence of numerous and systemized delusions, usually of persecution, but sometimes of grandeur or being controlled by an alien force. Auditory and visual hallucinations may accompany the delusions. Generally, paranoid schizophrenics are more alert and verbal than other schizophrenics, and tend to intellectualize.

Disorganized schizophrenics display a variety of bizarre symptoms. Hallucinations and delusions are plentiful and poorly organized. They may severely regress to childhood behavior which is marked by a pattern of silliness and absurdity. They often completely neglect their appearance, rarely bathing or combing their hair, and often they will deteriorate to the point that they become incontinent. Prominent features include disorganized speech and behavior, and flat or inappropriate affect.

The label **undifferentiated** applies to schizophrenics who do not exhibit a pattern of symptoms that fits the other subtypes. A patient may have highly organized delusions or motor disorders, but not to the extent that he/she is considered either a paranoid or a catatonic schizophrenic. This particular category has been criticized as being somewhat of a "wastebasket diagnosis," which is applied simply because a patient is difficult to categorize. The patient is simply "very crazy," but not in any systematic way.

Schizophrenia and Social Class

Studies have consistently shown that the lowest social classes have the highest rates of schizophrenia. However, the correlation between social class and schizophrenia does not show a progressively higher rate of schizophrenia as the social class becomes lower. There is a marked gap between the number of schizophrenics in the lowest socioeconomic class and those in others. Many studies found that the rate of schizophrenia was twice as high in the lowest social class as the next-to-lowest.

One explanation is that being in a low social class itself may cause schizophrenia. The degrading treatment that these people receive, their low level of education, their poor environment, and their lack of opportunity combine to make membership in the lowest social class stressful enough to bring out schizophrenia in many victims. Another hypothesis is that the problems associated with schizophrenia force the schizophrenic to become a member of the lowest class. The schizophrenics' impairments reduce their earning abilities to such an extent that they have no choice but to live in poverty. In addition, entering a low social class often provides the schizophrenic with a welcome escape from social pressures and intense social relationships. There is empirical evidence for both of these hypotheses.

Heredity and Schizophrenia

According to several twin studies (see Chapter 10), if one identical twin has schizophrenia, the other twin is significantly more likely to develop schizophrenic symptoms than the general population. For identical twins, the rate of concordance (the same diagnosis) was around 40%. However, the discordance rate was higher (60%). If schizophrenia were solely the result of genetic factors, the concordance rate would be 100%. Yet these findings support the view that certain individuals are more prone to develop schizophrenia than others if placed under extreme stress. However, given a more favorable life situation, the individual's inherent vulnerability may never be expressed.

Psychosexual Disorders

Many psychological illnesses result from focusing sexual attention on inappropriate objects. One commonly described, but in reality rare, example of this is the development of **fetishes,** a sexual interest in some body part or inanimate object, such as a pair of boots. Use, contact, or thoughts about these objects are a source of sexual excitation for the individual and can become a dominant force in the individual's life. For example, a man may be so enthralled with women's feet that he takes a job as a shoe salesman even though he could qualify for a better position. The attraction is involuntary and irresistible. Intimate objects like underwear, shoes, and gloves are common sources of arousal for fetishists. Most often, these objects are kissed, fondled, tasted or smelled, and used in conjunction with masturbation.

In the past, **homosexuality** was considered a psychosexual disorder. In fact, homosexuality is not a psychological disorder, any more than heterosexuality or bisexuality. Just how a person develops a sexual preference for one gender or another simply is not known. Additionally, homosexual acts are not abnormal behavior. According to the Kinsey report, 37 percent of men and 13 percent of women have experienced homosexual orgasm after adolescence. There may, of course, be extra stress in a homosexual person's life due to discrimination and harassment or discomfort with his or her homosexuality. If a person has marked or persistent distress about his or her sexual orientation or about other people's attitudes towards that sexual orientation, then that person may be considered to have a mental disorder. However, an individual who is comfortable with being gay, lesbian, or bisexual will have no greater likelihood of mental concerns than anyone else.

Dissociative Disorders

In **dissociative disorders,** a portion of the mind "splits off" from the mainstream of consciousness, producing behavior that is incompatible with the rest of the personality. This topic has provoked hot debate in the psychological community. Many researchers do not believe that these states exist but say they are the product of overactive imagination. DSM IV lists five categories of dissociative disorders: **dissociative amnesia, dissociative fugue, dissociative identity disorder, depersonalization disorder,** and dissociative disorder not otherwise specified.

Dissociative amnesia involves loss of memory for a period of time, when the amnesiac cannot remember any personal details of his or her life yet retains knowledge of how to function in the world. This amnesia begins suddenly, usually following severe psychological stress, such as physical injury or death, or being abandoned by a spouse. In some instances, the stress is due to the unacceptability of certain acts, such as engaging in an extramarital affair.

Dissociative fugue is similar to dissociative amnesia. In a fugue state, a person suddenly travels away from her customary surroundings, and cannot recall her prior identity. Frequently a person with this disorder will move to a new place and start an entirely new life. This new identity will usually be more gregarious and uninhibited than her prior personality, which is typically quiet and very ordinary. Like amnesia, a fugue is usually produced by psychological stress. Marital quarrels, personal rejections, wars, and natural disaster are common examples. These fugues are usually brief, lasting hours or days, though in rare cases a fugue will continue for months.

Dissociative identity disorder, or the presence of separate and distinct personalities in one person, is the most dramatic type of dissociative disorder. Generally, a person with dissociative identity disorder has been severely abused as a child. To protect her sanity while still loving her parents, the child "cuts off" a portion of herself in order to keep the rest of her personality safe from the abuse. The individual personalities in this disorder are generally quite different from one another. For example, the personality of a quiet bachelor may alternate with that of a singles-bar Don Juan. Transition from one personality to another is sudden and frequently associated with psychosocial stress. Usually the more persistent or primary personality will remain unaware of the secondary personalities, while the latter is often fully aware of the thoughts and actions of the former.

Depersonalization is an alternate perception or experience of the self so that the feeling of one's own reality is temporarily lost. Individuals with this disorder have feelings of being mechanical or dream-like, or of not being in control of their actions. They may feel that their extremities have changed in size, or that they are seeing themselves from a distance. A diagnosis is made if at least six episodes lasting 30 minutes or more occur within six weeks. The category of other dissociative disorders is used for people who appear to have a dissociative disorder but do not satisfy any of the above criteria.

DSM IV

The American Psychiatric Association has developed a classification system of mental illnesses known as the Diagnostic and Statistical Manual **(DSM).** The most recent edition is the DSM IV. This book has 16 different categories of mental illness, and five different **axes of classification.** The first two axes have to do with diagnostic categories in the DSM IV. Axis I concerns every mental illness except for personality disorders, which are classified on Axis II. Axis III describes medical disorders which are not mental illnesses, such as high blood pressure or a broken leg. In Axis IV, the caregiver can describe the stress in a patient's recent life, and how severe it is, on a range from "none" to "catastrophic." Catastrophic stressors would involve war experience, several deaths in the family, or a natural disaster. There seems to be a high correlation between stress and the incidence of mental illness. Axis V describes the patient's highest level of functioning in the previous year. Of course, a patient's prognosis is quite closely related to how well that patient was functioning before the onset of illness. The range goes from superior, where a person is unusually effective in many activities and relationships, to grossly impaired, where the person cannot function, down to the level of basic hygiene, without assistance.

REVIEW QUESTIONS

1. Does the term "abnormal behavior" always imply mental illness?

2. In the statistical model of abnormal behavior, abnormality is measured in terms of deviation from _____ .

3. True or False: In anxiety disorders, panic attacks generally take place at times when there is marked physical exertion or life-threatening situation.

4. Obsessions are persistent, often unreasonable _____ .

5. True or False: People suffering affective disorders may alternate between extremes of depression and mania.

6. Somatoform disorders are _____ disorders which have _____ causes.

7. Are people who suffer antisocial personality disorder good at "conning" people?

8. The "classic" schizophrenic symptom is _____ _____ .

9. True or False: Dissociative disorders are more common than schizophrenia.

10. There seems to be a high correlation among these three items: DSM IV's Axis IV, _____ , and the incidence of mental illness.

ANSWER KEY

1. No

2. the mean rate of that behavior

3. False

4. thoughts

5. True

6. physical, psychological

7. Yes

8. aural hallucinations

9. False

10. stress

Chapter 13

Treatment of Psychological Disorders

A modern therapist must cope with a variety of problems. Some illnesses, such as schizophrenia, are made worse by the environment; others, such as post-traumatic stress syndrome, the existential crises faced by survivors of concentration camps, or reactions of victims of child abuse, are brought on by environments which have disappeared. Others seem to have a biological basis. Fortunately, therapists have a variety of tools at their disposal.

APPROACHES

All approaches to treatment of mental illness are designed to help a patient achieve an effective and satisfactory adjustment to life. There are two interesting facts about therapy which any patient should know. The first is that about two-thirds of adults who undergo psychotherapy show marked improvement or recover within two years, regardless of the type of therapy. The second fact is that the recovery rate of untreated patients is also about two-thirds. However, these figures may be misleading, since it is difficult to measure the degree of improvement in psychological cases. There is no consistent, valid criteria for evaluating improvement. There is also evidence that while untreated patients show moderate improvement over time, patients who have undergone therapy tend to show marked improvement or a marked change for the worse. In addition, certain therapies seem to work better for certain disorders. For example, behavior therapy works well for phobic reactions; depressive patients respond best to electroconvulsive therapy; and highly educated, mildly disturbed neurotic patients respond best to traditional psychoanalysis.

There are many different approaches to therapy, the major ones being psychodynamic, behavioral, cognitive, biological, or humanistic.

Psychodynamic Approaches

Psychodynamic or insight-oriented therapies usually operate within the framework of Freudian theory and methods, i.e., psychoanalysis. According to Freud, instead of dealing with inner conflicts, the patient represses the conflicts into the unconscious and is made helpless by his own defenses. Psychoanalytic theory holds that these repressed inner conflicts are revealed in the unconscious through dreams and pathological symptoms. The goal in this type of therapy is to reconstruct the patient's personality by uncovering the underlying causes for the patient's maladaptive symptoms. The material of the unconscious mind must be brought into the conscious mind so that it no longer serves as a source of anxiety and confusion for the patient.

To accomplish this goal, Freudian psychoanalysts use a technique called **free association.** In this process, which Freud developed with Breuer, the patient says anything that comes to mind, no matter how trivial or unimportant it may seem. Because unconscious material is always seeking expression, this technique is thought to encourage the expression of repressed material. The therapist directs the flow of associations to the source of the pathology. In addition to this method of freeing repressed conflicts, Freud also developed a system for **interpreting dreams** (see Chapter 5) as a tool for "entering" the repressed areas of the patient's unconscious mind.

A third aspect of psychodynamic therapy is **transference.** This term is the name Freud gave to the patient's tendency to react to the therapist with the same childhood emotions she experiences towards her parents or other important figures. One of the main roles of the therapist, therefore, is to serve as a transference object. Generally, the patient resists recalling painful or guilty memories, and it is the therapist's role to help the patient overcome this resistance. In expressing and reliving his past, the patient transfers to the analyst the hostilities, affections, resentment, and guilt he formerly felt toward his parents. Thus, transference brings the problems into the open where they can be analyzed in a rational manner.

The resolution of the transference neurosis is one of the most important parts of the cure in classical psychoanalysis. Analysts must be able to maintain a stance of compassionate neutrality and not introduce their own personality or transference onto the patient. Partly for this reason, all therapists trained as psychoanalysts must undergo psychoanalytic treatment themselves before they begin to practice.

Behavior Therapy

Behavior therapy, also called behavior modification, is an attempt to study and change abnormal behavior by using methods drawn from experimental psychology. There are four basic techniques in behavior therapy; **countercon-ditioning,** which is used in systematic desensitization and aversive conditioning, **operant conditioning, modeling,** and **cognitive restructuring.**

In **counterconditioning,** an undesired response to a stimulus is eliminated by creating a new response to that stimulus. For example, a child who is afraid of the dark might be fed her favorite foods in the dark. The fear (undesired response) produced by darkness (stimulus) might be dispelled by the positive feelings (new response) associated with eating. Repeated associations of darkness with positive feelings would most likely cure the child of her phobia. In systematic desensitization, invented by Joseph Wolpe, a deeply relaxed person is asked to imagine or experience a series of anxiety-provoking situations along a continuum. For example, a person who is afraid of taking tests will first be told to imagine that the teacher is telling the class about an upcoming test; then she will be told to think of herself taking the test; then she will sit in the testing room quietly; and finally, she would take the actual test. The relaxation serves to inhibit an anxiety that might otherwise be produced by the imagined scenes. The imagined scene can be viewed as the stimulus; the anxiety is the undesired response, and relaxation is the new response. The ability to tolerate stressful imagery is generally followed by a reduction of anxiety in similar real-life situations.

Another variant of counterconditioning is **aversive conditioning,** which attempts to attach negative feelings to stimuli that are considered inappropriately attractive. Imagine that a smoker wishes to be less attracted to the sight and smell of cigarettes. To reduce the attraction, a therapist might give him repeated electric shocks as pictures of cigarettes are presented. The goal of such therapy would be to make cigarettes (stimulus) elicit anxiety (new response) instead of feelings of attraction (undesired response).

Operant conditioning, also known as behavior shaping, was described in Chapter 6. The principles are very straightforward: desirable behaviors are rewarded, and undesirable behaviors are punished. The results of these programs are quite encouraging, especially among children with behavior problems. Another technique of behavioral psychotherapy, called modeling, is also described in Chapter 6. Here, clients learn by observing and imitating the behavior of others.

Cognitive Therapy

Cognitive therapy attempts to directly manipulate the client's thinking and reasoning processes. The best example of a cognitive restructuring procedure is rational-emotive therapy, developed by Albert Ellis. **Rational-emotive** therapy assumes that people cognitively interpret what is happening around them. Sometimes these interpretations can cause emotional turmoil, and a therapist's attention should be focused on these interpretations, these internal beliefs, and not on historical causes. One example of an internal belief which may lead to distress is the idea that a person must be thoroughly competent in everything she does. A person who believes this will view every error she makes as a catastrophe. A rational-emotive therapist would help such a client by first making her aware of her irrational structure, then guiding her towards a belief in realistic goals.

Biological Therapies

Many different and sometimes bizarre medical treatments have been developed for mental illness. **Psychosurgery,** the most drastic form of physical therapy, was pioneered in the 1930s by Moniz and Freeman. This treatment consists of various surgical procedures including the slicing, puncturing, or removal of certain areas of the prefrontal lobes of the brain. The theory underlying this approach was that severing the nerve connections with the thalamus, then believed to be the controlling center for the emotions, would relieve severe emotional disturbance. In certain cases, this procedure turned unmanageable patients into more docile creatures. But in the majority of cases, patients were left with irreversible brain damage. Many were turned into listless, lifeless, insensitive human beings. Thus, psychosurgery has been restricted for use with a limited number of patients. It has been found to be effective in reducing the extreme pain associated with certain forms of terminal cancer.

In the 1930s it was also believed that schizophrenia and convulsions could not exist in the same body. Therefore, theorists reasoned that it might be therapeutic to induce convulsions in schizophrenic patients. For some years the drug metrazol was used to induce convulsions in patients. The drug had the disadvantage of causing extreme fear and unpredictably strong seizures. In the 1940s, psychologists began to use electroconvulsive shock treatment (ECT) because it caused immediate unconsciousness. There was no time for fear reactions, and doses could be controlled so that extreme convulsions could be avoided.

ECT involves the passage of a 100-volt electric current across electrodes placed at the patient's temples. The current causes immediate unconsciousness and is followed by what appears to be a mild epileptic seizure. Today, before administering the shock, the patient is usually given a muscle relaxant to reduce the severity of the convulsions during the seizure. ECT drastically reduces the amount of oxygen in the brain due to the electroshock which depletes the supply of oxygen and glucose.

These ECT-induced convulsions are ineffective for schizophrenic patients. However, they are quite useful in the treatment of depressive patients. The usual procedure consists of 10 to 14 treatments spread over several weeks. The aftereffects of the treatments can include temporary loss of memory, disorientation, and confusion. These effects usually disappear within a month or two after the treatments but are one of the reasons patients resist this type of therapy.

ECT is one of the most effective and speediest treatments used today for depressive patients. It is more effective than antidepressant drugs which generally require at least two weeks before their effects can be seen. However, there is no valid scientific explanation for ECT's effects, which are ultimately only temporary. ECT has been likened to fixing a computer software problem by dropping it off a building. One theory is that the temporary improvement may be due to the mobilization of resources against a real threat to existence.

The most common biological therapy is the use of psychoactive drugs. **Pharmacological therapy** began with the introduction of chlorpromazine, also called Thorazine, in 1952. This synthetic drug was first used to control violent symptoms in psychotic patients. Before drugs were introduced into therapy, patients were commonly controlled through physical restraint. Aside from some barbiturate use, many patients were also controlled with pre-frontal lobotomies, electro-convulsive shocks, and insulin-shock therapy. The introduction of drugs into mental hospitals revolutionized clinical psychology.

The most commonly used drugs in clinical practice are **antidepressants.** These drugs can reverse a state of depression in a mentally ill person, yet have no effect on normal people. These drugs were discovered in 1952, with the advent of a drug called iproniazid. At the time, iproniazid was used to treat tuberculosis. After iproniazid was found to elevate mood, further research concentrated on how this drug functioned. It was finally classified as an MAO (monoamine oxidase) inhibitor, which prevented certain neurotransmitters from functioning in the brain. Although some MAO inhibitors are still used, most depression is treated with safer, more effective drugs called tricyclic antidepressants. These drugs inhibit the activity of certain neurotransmitters called catecholamines. This research with MAO inhibitors led to the catecholamine hypothesis of affective disorders, which states that different forms of psychological disorders are due to chemical imbalances in the brain.

Also used to treat mental illness are the **antipsychotic** drugs. Also referred to as tranquilizers, these drugs control symptoms of acute psychotic disorders. Their overall effect is to lower the patient's motor activity and sensitivity to both internal and external activity. They also reduce the occurrence of delusions and hallucinations. The side effects of these drugs include low blood pressure, drowsiness, and blurred vision. However, the psychotic symptoms are usually far more serious than the drugs' side effects.

The three basic classes of antipsychotic drugs are **phenothiazines, thioxanthines,** and **butyrophenones.** Phenothiazines, which include chlorpromazine, are the oldest psychopharmaceuticals, and the standard against which all other similar drugs are compared for safety and effectiveness. Phenothiazines have mainly been used to treat acute schizophrenics. This type of drug is also used to "maintain" people once they are released from mental hospitals. Extensive research by state hospitals and the federal government indicates a very high level of effectiveness. Thioxanthines and butyrophenones are basically derivatives of phenothiazine, and are used for the same purposes.

For anxiety disorders, psychiatrists generally prescribe minor **tranquilizers,** or anti-anxiety drugs. **Sedatives** such as barbiturates and alcohol have been used to control the level of anxiety in the past, but a class of drugs known as meprobamates was found to be more effective. Meprobamates were initially introduced under the trade names Miltown and Equanil. Their popularity was widespread compared to the use of previous types of barbiturates. This popularity ended when far more effective anxiety control agents called benzodiazepines were introduced. They include chlordiazepoxide (Librium) and diazepam (Valium). The major problem with this class of drugs is overuse, and they are often abused. This area of treatment is also plagued by insufficient knowledge about the drugs' effects on different forms of anxiety.

Humanistic Therapy

Humanistic therapies emphasize people's positive, constructive capacities instead of their mental illness. Chief among these therapies is Carl Rogers's client-centered therapy. Rogers contends that people who enter therapy have an incongruence between their ideal self and their real self. This causes them to feel anxious and to act defensively. The goal of therapy is to have the client freely explore his thoughts and establish a realistic self-image that is congruent with his real self, the self that is disguised by a set of parental or socially imposed values that have no inherent relation to the client's needs. Since the client is in his normal environment and cannot explore his thoughts freely without criticism from others, it is necessary to enter into a therapeutic environment.

The Rogerian therapist has the responsibility of viewing the client with unconditional positive regard and of being genuine in his acceptance of the client regardless of what the client says or does. A client who says "I just throttled a puppy," must be greeted with a smile. The therapeutic environment must be as unthreatening as possible, and the client must feel free to explore his inner self without fear of judgment. This unthreatening environment theoretically allows the client to actually experience the feelings that were denied to awareness because they were so threatening to the structure of the client's self-image. The client often finds his behavior changing in a constructive fashion as a result of this new freedom.

Rogerian therapy expresses a faith in the positive side of human nature, and a belief that there is a potential for every human being to lead a happy life. The therapist's view is extremely distant from the client's view of life, because the client is at a low point in his emotional life. He must draw strength from the therapist to explore his mind and establish his own values. The therapist is supposed to inspire the patient's confidence. At the same time, the therapist should not advise or suggest solutions—this would be counter to the theory of Rogerian therapy. This is why the theory is called **non-directive:** the therapist does not direct the client in any way. The client is at the center of the process; she does the thinking, talking, and solving. The therapist provides the environment in which the client can work. The results of successful therapy for the client are openness to experience, absence of defensiveness, accurate awareness, unconditional self-regard, and harmonious relations with others.

The basic factor distinguishing client-centered therapy from other therapies is that client-centered therapy does not view human nature as self-destructive, defensive, or irrational. Client-centered therapy views humans as possessing an innate capacity and motivation towards positive self-fulfillment, termed self-actualization. Consistent with this optimistic view is Rogers's belief that all behavior is selected with the self-fulfillment goal in mind, and that although some behavior choices might prove to be self-damaging, the intention is always positive.

TYPES OF THERAPY

Most of the treatments described above are used in individual therapy, where the therapist concentrates solely on one client. In **group therapy** a professional treats a number of patients simultaneously. Group therapy has gained acceptance not only because of its economic advantages but also because many therapists regard it as uniquely appropriate for treating some psychological problems. From many therapists' point of view, group therapy is a far more efficient use of professional time than one-to-one therapies since it provides a way to treat more clients.

Proponents of group therapy feel that groups have many other advantages. First of all, the group member has an opportunity to explore his or her interactions in a group and how they differ from the way he or she would like to behave with other people. The social pressures in a group can aid the therapist. For example, if a therapist tells a client that her behavior is childish, the message may be rejected; however, if three or four other people agree with the therapist, the person concerned may find it much more difficult to reject the observation. Also, clients in group therapy learn to articulate their problems, listen, and give support to others. Group therapy provides an opportunity for clients to gain insights vicariously when attention is focused on another participant. In addition, many clients are comforted by the knowledge that others have problems like theirs.

One type of group therapy is **family therapy.** Here, the family is viewed as a patient in itself, and the members of the family are treated together. This approach is based on the theory that the individual is a product of his environment and that to produce change within the individual, the environment must be altered. The therapist's orientation determines the techniques and approach that are used in the family therapy sessions. This might involve diverse aims such as uncovering the power structure in the family or improving the communications system. Most people working with the family approach to therapy agree that the aim of the sessions is to promote differentiation, individuation, and growth for each family member. The problems within a family system in Western culture usually arise because the family members are too close or too emotionally involved with each other. The therapist attempts to help each member as a separate unit who can stand alone. This process is called **progressive segregation.**

Family therapy developed from the **general systems theory** originated by Ludwig von Bertalanffy. General systems theory sees humans as autonomous, creative organisms living in an open system. Human behavior is regulated by family systems. In this view, the whole is more than the sum of the parts. The individual is a responsible participant in her family structure who has a capacity for growth and a potential for change. She must contribute to the improvement of the total system. General systems theory also stresses that humans live in a symbolic world of thought and language. Family systems therapy reflects this orientation by stressing communications improvement. Through studying communication systems, the therapist helps the family members see the subtle communication signals (verbal and nonverbal) that regulate their behavior, and learn how to adopt new, more growth-oriented behaviors.

Another type of group therapy takes place in **encounter groups.** In these groups, open expression of emotions is encouraged. Popular in the 1970s, encounter groups usually include fairly normal individuals. These groups are supposed to allow individuals to undergo personal growth through direct confrontation. Groups generally include one or more leaders and eight to 15 people. The leaders generally are also participants in the group. Groups differ in emphasis and may have religious or dramatic functions as well as therapeutic uses. The most common purpose is to help people remove barriers to their feelings and emotional expression. The leader may be confrontational and cajole members to face their feelings. Alternatively, Carl Rogers's encounter groups typically feature a passive leader, much like the therapist in his client-centered therapy, where the leader tries to reflect and clarify members' feelings.

Encounter groups are most famous for their exercises. These activities include the trust exercise, where a person falls backwards into the group's arms, or the blind walk, where one of each pair of participants walks blindfolded, holding onto the sighted member's hand. Members of encounter groups also touch each other a great deal more than people do in everyday America. Perhaps this relief from cold, sterile urban life is one of encounter groups' greatest attractions.

REVIEW QUESTIONS

1. The recovery rates for treated and untreated patients are _____ .

2. True or False: The goal of psychodynamic therapy is to uncover the underlying causes of the patient's maladaptive symptoms.

3. An existential neurosis is characterized by _____ from society and self.

4. True or False: In rational-emotive therapy, a therapist's attention should be focused on historical causes of symptoms.

5. Electroconvulsive therapy is most effective in treating _____ .

6. Under what circumstances will a Rogerian therapist show disapproval towards her client?

7. The most commonly used drugs in psychotherapy are _____ .

8. The social pressures in group therapy often _____ therapists achieve their goals.

9. True or False: Most people working with family therapy see the family itself as a single patient.

10. What disorders do most members of encounter groups suffer from?

ANSWER KEY

1. about the same, 65 percent

2. True

3. alienation

4. False
5. depression

6. None whatsoever

7. antidepressants

8. help

9. True

10. None

ADVANCED PLACEMENT EXAMINATION IN
PSYCHOLOGY

Test 1

ADVANCED PLACEMENT
PSYCHOLOGY TEST 1
SECTION I

TIME: 70 Minutes
100 Questions

DIRECTIONS: Choose the best answer for each question and mark the letter of your selection on the corresponding answer sheet.

1. The retina

    (A) is the round opening in the center of the eye through which light passes.

    (B) is the photosensitive curtain of nerve cells located at the back of the eye.

    (C) bends and focuses light rays.

    (D) protects the internal parts of the eye.

    (E) is the muscle holding the pupil in place.

2. Which of the following is the most widely accepted significance level for demonstrating significance in experimental results?

    (A) .5   (B) .05

    (C) .55   (D) 5.0

    (E) .10

3. In auditory sensation, pitch

    (A) is the only variable by which we distinguish sounds.

    (B) is closely related to the loudness of sound.

    (C) is closely related to the frequency of sound.

    (D) is closely related to the intensity of sound.

    (E) is measured in decibels.

4.   Ivan P. Pavlov is famous for his research on

   (A)   teaching machines.   (B)   perceptual learning.

   (C)   forward conditioning.   —(D)   classical conditioning.

   (E)   backward conditioning.

5.   A stimulus that elicits a response before the experimental manipulation is a (an)

   (A)   response stimulus (RS).

   (B)   unconditioned stimulus (UCS).

   (C)   generalized stimulus (GS).

   (D)   conditioned stimulus (CS).

   (E)   specific stimulus (SS).

6.   Erikson proposed that trust or mistrust develops during the

   (A)   muscular-anal stage.

   (B)   locomotor-genital stage.

   (C)   latency stage.

   (D)   oral-sensory stage.

   (E)   maturity stage.

7.   One effect of anxiety on learning is

   (A)   the removal of mental blocks.

   (B)   a reduction in performance on difficult tasks.

   (C)   a reduction in the ability to discriminate clearly.

   (D)   more interference with familiar material than with new material.

   —(E)   reduction in the ability to perform any task.

8.   According to Carl Jung's personality theory, the terms "anima" and "animus" refer to

   (A)   the collective unconscious.

   (B)   the personal unconscious.

   (C)   feminine and masculine archetypes.

(D)   the shadow archetypes.

(E)   the animal instincts in man's unconscious.

9.   Intelligence tests are not considered reliable

(A)   at any age.   (B)   before seven years of age.

(C)   before puberty.   (D)   before 20 years of age.

(E)   none of the above

10.   Physiologically, emotional responses take place

(A)   in the brain.

(B)   in the autonomic nervous system (ANS).

(C)   in the muscles and internal organs.

(D)   in the sympathetic nervous system.

(E)   in all of the above

11.   A "positively skewed" distribution is

(A)   a distribution that has a few extremely high values.

(B)   a distribution that has a few extremely low values.

(C)   a flat distribution, with a wide dispersion of values.

(D)   a distribution that is very peaked and leptokurtic.

(E)   a distribution that is both flat and leptokurtic.

12.   A few extreme scores in a distribution

(A)   will affect the value of the median more than that of the mean.

(B)   will affect the value of the mean more than that of the median.

(C)   will affect the values of the mean and median equally.

(D)   will affect the value of the mode more than that of the median.

(E)   will affect neither the value of the mean nor the median.

13.   A psychologist wants to observe language development. He studies five children over a 10-year period. This psychologist is performing

(A)   longitudinal study.   (B)   case study.

(C)   factor analysis.   (D)   laboratory study.

(E)   durational study.

14. By obtaining two scores for one subject with just one test, a researcher achieves

    (A) test-retest reliability.   (B) alternate reliability.

    (C) split-half reliability.   (D) parallel reliability.

    (E) scorer reliability.

15. The major affective disorders are characterized by

    (A) extreme and inappropriate emotional responses.

    (B) severe depression.

    (C) withdrawal and emotional distortion.

    (D) chronic experience of depression.

    (E) delusional emotional experiences.

16. Which of the following problems would require divergent thinking?

    (A) adding a column of numbers

    (B) deciding whether to turn left or right at an intersection while driving a car

    (C) choosing the best move in a card game

    (D) repairing a broken typewriter

    (E) (A) and (D)

17. In perceptual research, backward masking refers to

    (A) inhibition of the detection of simple figures in the presence of emotional stimuli.

    (B) an interfering stimulus that closely precedes presentation of the target stimulus.

    (C) an interfering stimulus presented shortly after the target stimulus.

    (D) a longer lasting interfering stimulus that is presented simultaneously with the brief target stimulus.

    (E) none of the above

18. In sensory systems, a minimum difference between two stimuli is required before we can distinguish between them. This minimum threshold, which can be measured, is called the *Just noticible difference*

    (A) interstimulus difference (ISD).

    (B) differential threshold (DL).

    (C) signal detectability threshold (TSD).

    (D) comparison stimulus threshold (CST).

    (E) subdifferential threshold (SDL).

19. In perceiving the distance a sound has traveled, a person depends heavily upon

    (A) loudness and intensity.　　(B) resonance.

    (C) brightness and hue.　　(D) saturation.

    (E) frequency.

20. When light changes from bright to dim the iris of the eye

    (A) dilates.　　(B) constricts.

    (C) remains the same.　　(D) changes in color.

    (E) thickens.

21. Organization theory uses theories of reinforcement to increase worker efficiency and satisfaction. According to reinforcement theory, the best time to reward a worker is

    (A) at the end of the year in the form of a bonus.

    (B) never.

    (C) when he first begins work in the company.

    (D) immediately before a task is performed.

    (E) immediately after a task has been performed.

22. In drug research, a control group, consisting of subjects administered a "fake" drug with no active ingredients, is usually included. This "fake" drug is known as a

    (A) phoneme.　　(B) null drug.

    (C) blind drug.　　(D) null, dependent variable.

    (E) none of the above

23. According to Freud, a developmental halt due to frustration and anxiety is referred to as

    (A) depression.   (B) fixation.

    (C) regression.   (D) neurosis.

    (E) learned helplessness.

24. *The Interpretation of Dreams* was written by

    (A) Carl Jung.   (B) Sigmund Freud.

    (C) Ernest Jones.   (D) Alfred Adler.

    (E) Carl Rogers.

25. Modeling is a technique used in

    (A) behavior therapy.   (B) logotherapy.

    (C) client-centered therapy. (D) psychoanalysis.

    (E) rational-emotive therapy.

26. Freud believed that the primary driving force in an individual's life was

    (A) the superego.   (B) psychosexual development.

    (C) sexual urge.   (D) bodily functions.

    (E) domination.

27. "The aim of all life is death." This quote from Sigmund Freud's work refers to

    (A) Thanatos.   (B) Eros.

    (C) the struggle between Eros and Thanatos.

    (D) the death instinct.

    (E) reproduction, a pun on death as sexual orgasm.

28. A between-subjects design is less efficient than a within-subjects design because

    (A) it has more subjects.   (B) it has less validity.

    (C) it is less reliable.   (D) it is not counterbalanced.

    (E) it must deal with differences among subjects.

29. As an approach to personality research Gordon Allport favored

    (A) nomothetic studies.   (B) nonparametric studies.

    (C) ideographic studies.   (D) case conference studies.

    (E) cross-cultural studies.

30. The simplest measure of variability is the

    (A) standard deviation.   (B) Z-score.

    (C) variance.   (D) range.

    (E) chi-square.

31. Transference neurosis is an aspect of the therapeutic process most common in

    (A) logotherapy.   (B) implosive therapy.

    (C) psychoanalysis.   (D) client-centered therapy.

    (E) none of the above

32. The general-adaptation syndrome can lead to bodily damage when

    (A) psychosomatic diseases fail to protect one from stress.

    (B) adaptive physiological responses fail.

    (C) the adrenal glands return to normal size before adaptive responses occur.

    (D) one is unable to reduce stress which results in chronic bodily arousal.

    (E) the resistance stage sets in.

33. The arousal theory, stating that emotion precedes overt behavior and consists mainly of a general state of arousal or activation, is called the

    (A) Cannon-Bard theory.   (B) James-Lange theory.

    (C) general-adaptation theory.   (D) Premack principle.

    (E) paired-arousal theory.

34. In which form of conditioning is the conditioned stimulus (CS) presented after the unconditioned stimulus (UCS)?

    (A) higher-order conditioning   (B) forward conditioning

    (C) backward conditioning   (D) second-order conditioning

    (E) delayed conditioning

35. According to Carl Rogers, the structure of the personality is based upon

    (A) introversion and extroversion.

    (B) being and non-being.

    (C) the organism and the self.

    (D) the will to meaning and the will to power.

    (E) expectations and reality.

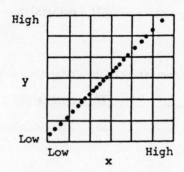

36. Which of the following choices best describes the correlation pictured above?

    (A) correlation = +1.00   (B) correlation = –1.00

    (C) correlation = 0.00   (D) correlation = –0.45

    (E) correlation = +0.45

37. Compute the range of the following set of numbers: 5, 692, 415, 17, 63, 200, 145.

    (A) 145   (B) 220

    (C) 687   (D) 5

    (E) 692

38. The greatest concentration of cones occurs in the

    (A) pupil.   (B) blind spot.

    (C) optic nerve.   (D) fovea.

    (E) ganglion.

39. Receptor cells that are very sensitive to color are the

    (A) ganglion cells.   (B) rods.

    (C) cones.   (D) bipolar cells.

    (E) chromatic cells.

40. According to Alfred Adler, man is striving for

    (A) self-actualization.   (B) power.

    (C) superiority and goals.   (D) leadership.

    (E) distinction.

41. The colored portion of the eye is called the

    (A) lens.   (B) cornea.

    (C) pupil.   (D) iris.

    (E) retina.

42. The role of imitation in social learning was first systematically observed by

    (A) Miller and Dollard.   (B) Bandura and Walters.

    (C) Stanley Milgram.   (D) B.F. Skinner.

    (E) J.B. Watson.

43. In our society, money is an example of a

    (A) primary reinforcer.

    (B) secondary (conditioned) reinforcer.

    (C) socio/reinforcer.

    (D) negative reinforcer.

    (E) simple operant.

44. An important function of rehearsal in verbal learning is

    (A) mediation.

    (B) transference of material from short-term to long-term memory.

    (C) acclimation to the meaning of the material.

    (D) both (A) and (B)

    (E) all of the above

45. Which of the following correlation values is the best predictor for a relationship between x and y?

    (A) .70   (B) +.60

    (C) +.50   (D) .10

    (E) +7.0

46. A measure of variability based upon the differences between each score and the mean is the

    (A) standard deviation.   (B) sampling error.

    (C) Z-score.   (D) range.

    (E) t-score.

47. A platykurtic curve is

    (A) flat.   (B) peaked.

    (C) positively skewed.   (D) negatively skewed.

    (E) hyperbolic.

48. Correlational studies

    (A) indicate causality.

    (B) are more valid than laboratory studies.

    (C) involve manipulations of independent variables.

    (D) indicate some relationship between two variables.

    (E) all of the above

49. The general Graduate Record Examination is an example of a (an)

    (A) projective test.   (B) cross-cultural test.

    (C) achievement test.   (D) aptitude test.

    (E) intelligence test.

50. The Thematic Apperception Test is an example of a (an)

    (A) intelligence test.   (B) projective test.

    (C) cross-cultural test.   (D) aptitude test.

    (E) achievement test.

51. Stanley Milgram, in his landmark study on obedience to authority, found that when subjects were asked to shock a confederate in increasing amounts in order to teach him a word-matching task,

    (A) 65% of the subjects administered shocks throughout the experiment and gave the maximum 450-volt shock.

    (B) 75% of the subjects refused to participate in the experiment.

    (C) 30% of the subjects administered shocks throughout the experiment and gave the maximum 450-volt shock.

    (D) people of low intelligence were more likely to apply the maximum 450-volt shock.

    (E) both (A) and (D)

52. Someone who repeatedly washes his hands even when they are not dirty may be said to be suffering from

    (A) learned helplessness.   (B) a conversion reaction.

    (C) an obsession.   (D) a phobia.

    (E) a compulsion.

53. Electroconvulsive shock therapy (ECT) has been demonstrated to be effective in the treatment of

    (A) severe depression.   (B) symptoms of schizophrenia.

    (C) manic episodes.   (D) OCD.

    (E) all of the above

54. In the DSM IV, a paranoid disorder is classified as a(n)

    (A) adjustment disorder.   (B) personality disorder.

    (C) psychotic disorder.   (D) dissociative disorder.

    (E) both (B) and (C).

55. An inability to recall one's prior identity and a sudden desire to travel away from one's customary surroundings are the essential features of

    (A) conversion disorder.   (B) dissociative amnesia.

    (C) dissociative fugue.   (D) dissociative identity disorder.

    (E) both (A) and (C).

56. A psychologist is studying the relationship between verbal learning and mode of presentation. Upon analyzing the data, the psychologist finds a correlation of +1.50. On the basis of this correlation, he would conclude that there is a

    (A) strong positive correlation.

    (B) strong negative correlation.

    (C) computational error.

    (D) low negative correlation.

    (E) low positive correlation.

57. The reinforcement schedule that produces the highest rates of performance is a

    (A) fixed-interval schedule.   (B) variable-interval schedule.

    (C) fixed-ratio schedule.   (D) variable-ratio schedule.

    (E) none of the above

58. Second-order conditioning is an important phenomenon because it demonstrates how an originally neutral CS used in the first-order conditioning can assume the properties of a (an)

    (A) first-order conditioning stimulus.

    (B) instrumental stimulus.

    (C) reinforcer.

    (D) positive reward.

    (E) negative reward.

59. Each score in a distribution has been multiplied by 5. The standard deviation is

    (A) increased by 5.

    (B) increased by 10.

    (C) unchanged from the original value.

    (D) divided by 5.

    (E) increased to 5 times its original value.

60. One type of test validity is

    (A) the extent to which a test measures a theoretical construct.

    (B) the degree of thoroughness in a test.

    (C) the extent to which repetitions of a test result in the same score.

    (D) the degree to which subjects find a test valid.

    (E) the effectiveness of a test.

61. According to the Diagnostic and Statistical Manual IV, which of the following is not a psychotic disorder?

    (A) Brief Psychotic Disorder,   (B) Delusional Disorder.
         with Postpartum Onset.

    (C) Folie à Deux.   (D) Bipolar II Disorder, Most Recent
         (Shared Psychotic Disorder)   Episode.

    (E) Schizoaffective Disorder.

62. Alcohol shares features with:

    (A) anxiolytics.   (B) amphetamines.

    (C) hypnotics.   (D) nicotine.

    (E) A and C

QUESTIONS 63–65 refer to the following passage:

Many psychologists believe that aggression is a behavior which is learned through operant conditioning, in which rewards and punishments shape a person's behavior. Modeling, or vicarious conditioning, is also thought to contribute to the development of aggressive behavior. In contrast with this predominant school of thought is the school that believes that aggression is an inborn tendency, and that because humans use their intelligence to aggress, they have never developed natural controls on aggression against their own species, as have other animals.

63. The belief that aggression is learned is held by

    (A) social learning theorists.   (B) phenomenological theorists.

    (C) psychodynamic theorists.   (D) experimental theorists.

    (E) all of the above

64. Which of the following statements is false?

    (A) If a child is rewarded for random, aggressive behavior, chances are good that the behavior will be repeated.

    (B) If a child is punished for acting aggressively, the likelihood of that behavior recurring is lessened.

    (C) If aggression is reinforced irregularly, the aggressive behavior is gradually discouraged.

    (D) both (B) and (C)

    (E) none of the above

65. The approach in which it is believed that aggression is an inborn tendency has been most supported by the work of

    (A) Sigmund Freud.   (B) Konrad Lorenz.

    (C) Carl Rogers.   (D) Albert Bandura.

    (E) B.F. Skinner.

66. The short-term memory can hold how many items at one time?

    (A) Seven items, plus or minus two

    (B) 10 items, plus or minus two

    (C) 10 items, plus or minus five

    (D) Five items

    (E) none of the above

67. The highest level in Maslow's hierarchical model of motivation is

    (A) esteem and self-esteem.   (B) love and belonging.

    (C) self-satisfaction.   (D) self-actualization.

    (E) interpersonal union.

68. Approach-avoidance conflicts are difficult to resolve because

    (A) the positive and negative aspects of a situation are equally strong.

    (B) a single goal possesses both positive and negative aspects.

    (C) one must choose the lesser of two evils.

    (D) they produce cognitive dissonance.

    (E) all of the above

69. The first systematic study of operant conditioning was performed in 1938 by

    (A) E.L. Thorndike.   (B) B.F. Skinner.

    (C) Miller and Dollard.   (D) A. Bandura.

    (E) I. Pavlov.

70. The reinforcement schedule that yields the lowest performance is the

    (A) fixed-ratio schedule.

    (B) variable-ratio schedule.

    (C) fixed-interval schedule.

    (D) variable-interval schedule.

    (E) intermittent reinforcement schedule.

QUESTIONS 71–72 refer to the following diagrams:

(A)

(B)

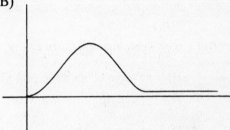

(C)

(D)

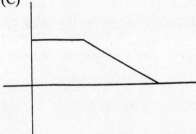
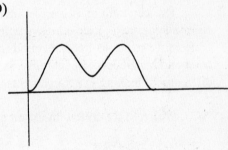

(E)

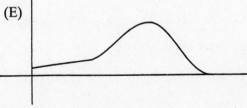

71. Which graph represents a platykurtic distribution?

72. In which graph is the mean greater than the mode and the median?

73. All of the following are human factors and components of the work cycle except

    (A) perceptual processes.   (B) problem solving.

    (C) communication processes.   (D) recall processes.

    (E) muscular (motor) processes.

74. Extreme scores in a distribution most dramatically affect the

    (A) t-score.   (B) mode.

    (C) mean.   (D) median.

    (E) Z-score.

75. During the premoral stage described by Kohlberg's moral development theory, children

    (A) think bad behavior is punished and good behavior is not punished.

    (B) have no conception of good or bad behavior.

    (C) are amoral.

    (D) are uncooperative.

    (E) conform to authority figures.

The cerebellum is greatly involved in planning movements as well as in coordinating them. It develops new motor programs which enable slow and deliberate movements to become rapid and automatic after practice. Damage to the cerebellum can lead to inability to perform rapid alternating movements and difficulty in making eye movements.

76. Which of the following is not controlled by the cerebellum?

    (A) speaking   (B) writing

    (C) playing the piano   (D) walking

    (E) playing basketball

77. A "normal" average I.Q. score is

    (A) 85.   (B) 100.

    (C) 115.   (D) 110.

    (E) none of the above

78. Extinction of a conditioned response occurs when

    (A) the CS is presented without the UCS several times.

    (B) the UCS is presented without the CS several times.

    (C) the CS is presented for more than five seconds before the start of the UCS.

    (D) the CS terminates before the onset of the UCS.

    (E) the CS begins after the UCS is terminated.

QUESTIONS 79–81 refer to the following diagram:

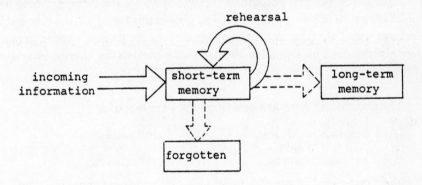

79. In the process of verbal learning, rehearsal

    (A) aids retention of items in short-term memory.

    (B) aids retention of sensory representations in short-term memory.

    (C) facilitates the transfer of material from short-term to long-term memory.

    (D) both (A) and (C)

    (E) all of the above

80. Which of the following is not a factor that influences the learning of a list?

    (A) position of the items   (B) frequency of the items

    (C) similarity of the items   (D) concreteness

    (E) all are factors that influence learning

81. Which is/are the most important factor(s) in rehearsal?

    (A) individual presentation rate

    (B) number of trials

    (C) time spent learning

    (D) both (A) and (C)

    (E) both (B) and (C)

QUESTIONS 82–83 refer to the following passage:

A person desperately needs to be cured of a phobia. The therapy chosen for him involves the use of learning principles. The goal of this therapy is the elimination of the patient's specific fear, rather than alteration of the patient's entire personality pattern. In the case of a phobia, the approach most often chosen is systematic desensitization.

82. The therapeutic approach described above is that of a

    (A) humanistic therapist.   (B) logotherapist.

    (C) behavior therapist.   (D) psychoanalyst.

    (E) gestalt therapist.

83. Systematic desensitization is a (an) _____ technique.

    (A) cognitive restructuring   (B) operant

    (C) counterconditioning   (D) aversive

    (E) counterbalancing

An experiment was performed in which a pigeon was placed in a Skinner box. The pigeon had been trained to peck a key in order to receive grain. Another pigeon was placed in the box during an extinction period (when grain was not being given for pecking) and the trained pigeon attacked the newcomer by pecking at his head, throat, and eyes.

84. Which of the following theorists have performed this experiment?

    (A) Skinner   (B) Burner

    (C) Hull   (D) Dollard

    (E) Guthrie

85. According to Allport, the ego is better termed the

    (A) proprium.   (B) functional autonomy.

    (C) collective conscious.   (D) mediator.

    (E) ego functions.

86. According to Erikson, a child four to six years of age is in which stage of development?

    (A) latency stage   (B) muscular-anal stage

    (C) locomotor-genital stage   (D) oral-sensory stage

    (E) locomotor-sensory stage

87. In Jungian theory, the "shadow" represents

    (A) unconscious drives.   (B) the animus.

    (C) the anima.   (D) the persona.

    (E) motivational drives.

88. The founder of client-centered therapy is

    (A) Victor Frankl.   (B) Carl Rogers.

    (C) Sigmund Freud.   (D) Carl Jung.

    (E) Alfred Adler.

89. Which of the following does not describe a true relationship between environmental factors and the stability of the I.Q.?

    (A) There is an increasing stability of I.Q. with age.

    (B) Prerequisite learning skills contribute to the stability of I.Q.

    (C) Changes in family structure have no effect on I.Q.

    (D) Emotional stability has a beneficial effect on I.Q.

    (E) Parental concern over the child's welfare has a stabilizing effect on I.Q.

90. The capacity of a test to measure what is set out to measure is called its

    (A) standardization.   (B) reliability.

    (C) objectivity level.   (D) validity.

    (E) concurrence.

QUESTIONS 91–93 refer to the following paragraph:

A classical experiment in conformity research done by Muzafer Sherif involved the effects of group judgments on "the autokinetic phenomenon." A light projected on the wall appears to move although this movement is actually due to the movement of the subject's eyes. It was found that individual's judgments of the rate of movement of the light were influenced very much by the opinions of others. Even when the group was no longer present, the individual estimates were still in agreement with previous group opinions.

91. The fact that the subjects still agreed with the confederate group although they were no longer present shows that

    (A) compliance took place.

    (B) private acceptance took place.

    (C) internalization has occurred.

    (D) both (A) and (B)

    (E) all of the above

92. Which of the following statements is false?

    (A) The more authoritarian a person, the less he or she will conform.

    (B) "External" personalities are more likely to conform than "internals."

    (C) People with low self-esteem are likely to conform.

    (D) If a group is not unanimous there is a large decrease in conformity.

    (E) People with greater intelligence conform less than those with low intelligence.

93. A person who publicly supports an opinion that he does not privately accept will often change his opinion so that it will agree with the publicly expressed one. This occurs as a result of

    (A) compliance.   (B) internalization.

    (C) dissonance.   (D) deindividuation.

    (E) hypocrisy.

QUESTIONS 94–95 refer to this distribution of SAT scores.

94. What percent of the SAT scores fall between 500 and 600?

(A) 50%   (B) 68%

(C) 14%   (D) 34%

(E) 98%

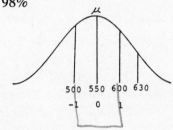

95. In this distribution,

(A) the mean is greater than the mode.

(B) the mean is greater than the median.

(C) the mode, median and mean are equal.

(D) the mode and median are equal and higher than the mean.

(E) the mean and mode are equal and higher than the median.

96. The ethologist who spent several years studying the problem-solving abilities of chimpanzees was

(A) Margaret Mead.   (B) Wolfgang Kohler.

(C) Joy Adamson.   (D) Aldous Huxley.

(E) Erik Erikson.

97. The fundamental attribution error is a tendency in humans to

(A) blame people for situationally induced behavior.

(B) engage in sexist stereotypes.

(C) emphasize dispositional factors in determining people's behavior.

(D) accept placebo effects.

(E) emphasize I.Q. and race when forming opinions.

98. The fact that a blind infant would smile for the first time at about the same age as a sighted infant is evidence that smiling is

   (A) learned.

   (B) imitative behavior.

   (C) congenital.

   (D) nurtured behavior.

   (E) innate.

99. According to Piaget, a person who cannot consistently use abstract logic has not reached the stage of

   (A) concrete operations.

   (B) preoperational development.

   (C) formal operations.

   (D) initiative vs. guilt.

   (E) extrovert vs. introvert.

100. The drug that has been a successful treatment for some cases of Bipolar Disorder is

   (A) thorazine.

   (B) valium.

   (C) seconal.

   (D) lithium carbonate.

   (E) chlorpromazine.

ADVANCED PLACEMENT PSYCHOLOGY TEST 1

SECTION II

TIME: 50 Minutes
         2 Essays

DIRECTIONS: In this portion of the test, you will write on both essay questions. We suggest you allow slightly under 25 minutes per essay. Read the question carefully, and then write a response in essay form.

Essay 1: What is classical conditioning? Include a brief explanation of the principal terms used to describe a simple classical conditioning experiment (CS, UCS, CR and UCR).

Essay 2: What is the difference between I.Q. (intelligence quotient) and intelligence?

TEST 1

ANSWER KEY

1.	(B)	26.	(C)	51.	(A)	76.	(D)
2.	(B)	27.	(C)	52.	(E)	77.	(B)
3.	(C)	28.	(E)	53.	(E)	78.	(A)
4.	(D)	29.	(C)	54.	(E)	79.	(E)
5.	(B)	30.	(D)	55.	(C)	80.	(E)
6.	(D)	31.	(C)	56.	(C)	81.	(C)
7.	(B)	32.	(D)	57.	(D)	82.	(C)
8.	(C)	33.	(A)	58.	(C)	83.	(C)
9.	(B)	34.	(C)	59.	(E)	84.	(D)
10.	(E)	35.	(C)	60.	(A)	85.	(A)
11.	(A)	36.	(A)	61.	(D)	86.	(C)
12.	(B)	37.	(C)	62.	(E)	87.	(A)
13.	(A)	38.	(D)	63.	(A)	88.	(B)
14.	(C)	39.	(C)	64.	(C)	89.	(C)
15.	(A)	40.	(C)	65.	(B)	90.	(D)
16.	(C)	41.	(D)	66.	(A)	91.	(D)
17.	(C)	42.	(A)	67.	(D)	92.	(A)
18.	(B)	43.	(B)	68.	(B)	93.	(C)
19.	(A)	44.	(B)	69.	(B)	94.	(B)
20.	(A)	45.	(A)	70.	(C)	95.	(C)
21.	(E)	46.	(A)	71.	(A)	96.	(B)
22.	(E)	47.	(A)	72.	(B)	97.	(A)
23.	(B)	48.	(D)	73.	(C)	98.	(E)
24.	(B)	49.	(D)	74.	(C)	99.	(C)
25.	(A)	50.	(B)	75.	(A)	100.	(D)

DETAILED EXPLANATIONS
OF ANSWERS

AP PSYCHOLOGY TEST 1
SECTION I

1.   **(B)**   The retina is composed of photoreceptor nerve cells (rods and cones) which form a photosensitive curtain at the back of the eye. Over 120 million photoreceptor cells are found in the retina of each eye.

2.   **(B)**   The appropriate significance level is .05. This is the usual cut-off point for determining the significant difference between two means. At the .05 level the difference between the means is considered so great that it is unlikely that it could have occurred by chance. A p value of .05 means that the results obtained could have occurred by chance in only five out of 100 replications of the experiment.

3.   **(C)**   Pitch is closely related to the frequency of the stimulus. Sound is basically vibrations of particles in the air. These vibrations are wavelike and are called soundwaves. The frequency of a vibration is a measure of how many times it goes up and down in a single period of time. We generally experience high frequency waves as high pitched tones. Waves with low frequencies correspond to low pitched tones; therefore, pitch is closely related to the frequency of sound.

4.   **(D)**   Ivan P. Pavlov (1849-1936) virtually discovered the phenomena of classical conditioning and was the first to investigate it systematically. In Pavlov's experiments with the salivating response of his dogs, he established the basic methodology and terminology still used today in classical conditioning experiments. Pavlov referred to food as the unconditional stimulus (UCS) because it naturally and consistently elicited salivation, which he called the unconditioned response (UCR). Pavlov later taught dogs to salivate to light. This was accomplished by presenting the light just prior to presenting the food. After a series of such pairings, the dogs would salivate in response to the light. In this case, the light was a conditioned stimulus (CS) and the salivation in response to the light was a conditioned response (CR). Hence, Pavlov's research elucidated the process of classical conditioning.

5.   **(B)**   In classical conditioning the stimulus that elicits a response before any conditioning begins is called the unconditioned stimulus. It reliably elicits the unconditioned response (UCR) before the experiment. During the experimental manipulation the unconditioned stimulus (UCS) is paired with a conditioned stimulus (CS) that originally does not elicit a response. After several such pairings

the subject will elicit a conditioned response (CR) to the conditioned stimulus (CS) that is very similar to the unconditioned response (UCR). After this conditioned response (CR) is learned, the unconditioned stimulus (UCS) may be removed, but the subject will keep responding to the conditioned stimulus (CS).

6. **(D)** The oral-sensory stage is the first stage in Erikson's developmental theory. During the oral-sensory stage, the basic crisis centers on the development of either trust or mistrust. If these needs are consistently satisfied and if the infant receives love, he will develop a sense of trust, not only in others, but in himself and his ability to handle his needs. If these needs are not met and the infant lacks love, attention, and stimulation, he will develop a sense of mistrust. Erikson believes that the development of a healthy personality is contingent upon the formation of trust at this early stage.

7. **(B)** Anxiety is an emotional state characterized by non-specific fears and various autonomic symptoms. The effect of anxiety is different for different learning tasks. One major finding is that anxiety does not hinder the learning of simple tasks, such as discrimination learning, but does hinder the learning of more complicated, less familiar tasks.

8. **(C)** The "anima" is Jung's theoretical construct of the female image. He believed that the "anima" is the projected image of the female throughout history in man's unconscious. This internalized female image is based on man's real experiences with women, particularly his mother, sister or other family members and on the collective experience of men throughout history. In contrast to the "anima," both the "anima" and the "animus" are archetypes in Jung's theory of the collective unconscious.

9. **(B)** In general, humans do not have the life experience, cognitive, verbal and motor skills required to complete an I.Q. test before the age of seven. Few people question the reliability of I.Q. tests. The validity of these tests has been questioned.

10. **(E)** Arousal is a total physiological response to a situation. During arousal, the EEG pattern in the brain changes. The autonomic nervous system (ANS) becomes more active during arousal states. The sympathetic part of the ANS increases heart rate, blood pressure, and distributes more blood to the exterior muscles. It also causes changes in the muscles and internal organs by causing blood to be pumped away from internal organs and muscles. It then rushes toward exterior muscles in the trunk and limbs. The entire body prepares for action when in an aroused state. The results of lie detector tests are not admissible in a court of law because they are only 65% reliable.

11. **(A)** To state that a distribution is positively skewed is an attempt to describe the curve form of that frequency distribution. A few extreme higher values form a positively skewed graph.

12. **(B)** Since the median is the single middle score in a distribution, it is not affected by a few extreme scores, unless it is one of those extreme scores. Then it would not be a representative median. In contrast, the mean is an average of all the scores in a distribution; therefore, it would always be affected by extreme scores.

13. **(A)** A longitudinal study is an extended examination of the same subject or subjects over a (usually long) period of time. This approach is particularly useful in examining the stability of a behavior characteristic over time, or the development of a behavior over time.

14. **(C)** In split-half reliability the correlation between the two scores is the reliability coefficient. Usually, the examiner uses scores on odd and even items as two scores. This procedure is preferred to comparing scores from the first and second half of the test due to practice effects and fatigue. The split-half reliability coefficient is often called the coefficient of internal consistency because the comparison of two scores on a test indicates whether the test has an underlying consistency.

15. **(A)** Affective disorders are characterized by a disturbance of mood accompanied by related symptoms. Mood is defined as a prolonged emotional state which colors the whole psychic life and generally involves either depression or elation. In affective disorders, mood tends to be at one extreme or the other. The patient may be depressed, or he may be manic, or he may exhibit bipolar symptoms, an alternation between depression and mania.

16. **(C)** In choosing the best move in a card game, one must be able to generate a number of possible solutions; therefore, divergent thinking is the process being utilized. Divergent thinking requires flexibility, fluency of ideas, and originality.

17. **(C)** The backward masking effect can be achieved in experiments by flashing a letter on a screen and following the letter image (target stimulus) with a flash of bright light (interfering stimulus). The effect the light flash has on the letter image is to "erase" it from one's perception. The backward masking effect demonstrates that the brief life of memory codes can be easily erased by input that is specific to the given sense modality.

18. **(B)** The concept of a differential threshold (DL) is basic to understanding sensory systems. The differential threshold is not considered constant, even for a specific sensory system. For example, if you are in a room with one person talking, you will definitely notice when a second person begins talking. That additional sound energy will be above the DL. If you are in a room where 20 people are talking, you may not notice if one other person begins to speak. In this case the DL is higher; a greater amount of sound energy is needed in order for the addition to be noticed. In general, the greater the intensity of the original stimulus, the greater is the differential threshold.

19. **(A)** The loudness of a sound is closely related to the intensity of the physical stimulus. Intensity is a measure of the amount of physical energy a stimulus sends to our senses, in this case our auditory system. We experience a high intensity sound as being loud. Hence, in perceiving the distance of a sound, loudness and intensity are important factors. In addition to these factors, previous psychological and physical experience with the sound is of great importance.

20. **(A)** The iris responds to dimmer light by dilating. This adjusts the amount of light entering the eye through the pupil. When the light dims, the iris opens more to allow more light in. Conversely, when the light becomes brighter, the iris constricts to reduce the amount of light entering the pupil.

21. **(E)** Reinforcement theory has proven that reinforcement is most effective if it occurs immediately after a task has been performed. End-of-the-year bonuses or quarterly reviews may not be as effective as immediate bonuses. Investigation of optimal schedules of reinforcement is ongoing and diverse; both negative and positive reinforcement schedules have been shown to be quite effective on worker productivity and satisfaction.

22. **(E)** A "fake" drug is known as a placebo. A placebo is used to control the effects caused by the simple ingestion of a pill or injection of a drug. It is also used as a baseline measure against which the effects of the other drugs are compared. In order to demonstrate that a drug is effective, one must show that it had a greater effect on the subject than the placebo.

23. **(B)** According to Freud, fixation results from abnormal personality development. Freud stated that a person feels a certain amount of frustration and anxiety as he passes from one stage of development to the next. If that frustration and anxiety become too great, development may halt, the person becoming fixated at the stage he is trying to grow out of. For example, an overly dependent child is thought to be fixated. Development has ceased at an early stage preventing the child from growing up and becoming independent.

24. **(B)** *The Interpretation of Dreams* was one of Sigmund Freud's most famous books, dealing with psychoanalytic and personality theory.

25. **(A)** In modeling, an individual learns by observing and then imitating the behavior of others. For example, to rid a client of a dog phobia, the therapist exposes the client to both live and filmed displays of people interacting fearlessly with dogs. The client then imitates this behavior, eventually overcoming his fear of dogs. As a number of research programs have shown, this kind of learning helps people acquire new resources in a relatively short time.

26. **(C)** Freud believed that the primary driving force in an individual's life is the sexual urge (the libido). His theory of motivational development was particularly

concerned with sexual gratification, as it changed in relation to the child's body. His theory of personality constructs (the id, ego and superego) also deals with the sexual urge, as it confronts the constraints of the outer world.

27. **(C)** Late in his life, Freud proposed that the aim of all life was death, and that human behavior was the outcome of a struggle between Thanatos (the death instinct) and Eros (the life instinct). Freud contended that the goal of all instincts was a return to inorganic matter, to death and the end of all stimulation.

28. **(E)** A between-subjects design deals with differences among people, and this decreases efficiency. It is a conservative form of design, but this conservatism does afford at least one advantage. There is no chance of one treatment level affecting another treatment level because the same person never receives both treatments. A tradeoff is thus made between confused subject differences and confused treatment levels.

29. **(C)** Ideographic study involves selecting methods of study that will not blur or conceal the uniqueness of the individual subject. The ideographic approach emphasizes the importance of individual traits in determining behavior, and thus recommends study of the individual as the most effective approach to understanding behavior. Since Allport did not believe in the validity of general principles of behavior, he preferred to use the ideographic method. Allport was the first psychologist to stress the ideographic approach.

30. **(D)** The range is the simplest measure of variation since it gives the limits within which all the elements of a distribution are confined. The range of a set of scores is the difference between the highest and lowest score in a set of scores. For example if you have the scores 18, 12, 23, 30, 34, then 12 is the lowest score and 34 is the highest score. The difference between the highest and lowest score is 22. Hence, the range is 22.

31. **(C)** The resolution of the transference neurosis is one of the most important parts of the cure in classical psychoanalysis. For it to occur successfully, the analyst must be able to maintain the stance of compassionate neutrality. Transference neurosis refers specifically to displaced and usually intense and inappropriate reactions of the patient to the analyst.

32. **(D)** General-adaptation syndrome describes the three stages the body passes through in its reaction to stress: the alarm reaction, the stage of resistance, and the stage of exhaustion. The syndrome can ultimately lead to bodily damage during the final stage of exhaustion. At this point, prolonged stress and the resulting physical arousal exhausts the body's resources. This is caused in part by a depletion of the adrenal hormones. When this occurs, disorders such as rheumatism and arthritis can develop. Ultimately, death may result from prolonged exhaustion.

33. **(A)** The Cannon-Bard theory argues that if "we see a bear, we experience fear, and then we run." Cannon and Bard considered the thalamus the "seat of the emotions." An emotion-producing stimulus first stimulates the thalamus, which then discharges impulses to the lower brain area, which in turn activates the cerebral cortex and the autonomic nervous system. This produces a general state of arousal which is experienced as an emotion. The observable behavior—in this case, running—shortly follows the emotion.

34. **(C)** In backward conditioning, the CS is presented after the UCS. Backward conditioning is not very effective, if at all. In a classical conditioning experiment, backward conditioning would take place if a light (CS) would be turned on shortly after the food (UCS) was delivered to the dog. This particular procedure has shown that no response is conditioned even though there exists a temporal contiguity between the CS and UCS.

35. **(C)** Rogers's personality constructs are the organism and the self. The organism is conceived to be the locus of experience; experience includes everything available to the awareness and all that occurs within the organism. The self or self-concept refers to the organized and consistent set of perceptions that are self-referential, i.e., that refer to "I" or "me." It also includes the perceptions of the relationships between the self and the rest of the world. In addition to the self, there is an ideal self which represents what the individual aspires to be.

36. **(A)** The figure depicts a perfect, positive correlation. Note that all the observations fall on the same straight line. This is a perfect "linear relation." Since this is a positive correlation, X increases as Y increases by a proportionate amount.

37. **(C)** The range of a set of numbers is defined as the highest score minus the lowest score, in this case, $692 - 5 = 687$. The range is the quickest and least informative measure of variability. The best measure to use is the standard deviation.

38. **(D)** Cones are located primarily in the fovea. There are about 6 to 7 million cones in each eye. Cones require a large amount of light energy to respond to a stimulus.

39. **(C)** Cones respond differentially to different color wavelengths, providing us not only with color perception but also an ability to sense fine gradations of color.

40. **(C)** To Adler, the goal of behavior is to compensate for a subjectively perceived sense of inferiority by achieving superiority. Therefore, an individual cannot fully comprehend his or her life without understanding the goal for which he or she is striving.

41. **(D)** The colored portion of the eye is called the iris. It is the tissue that surrounds the pupil and regulates its size. By contracting or dilating, the iris adjusts the amount of light entering the eye.

42. **(A)** Experiments with children, in which they were rewarded for imitating a model, formed the basis of Miller and Dollard's conclusions concerning learning from model imitation. They concluded that imitation of social behavior probably derives strength from the fact that conformist behavior is rewarded in many situations, whereas nonconformist behavior often results in punishment.

43. **(B)** Conditioned, or secondary, reinforcement occurs when the reinforcing stimulus is not inherently pleasing or reinforcing, but becomes so through association with other pleasant or reinforcing stimuli. Money is an example of a secondary (conditioned) reinforcer. Coins and paper currency are not in themselves pleasing, but the things they buy are pleasing. Therefore, an association is made between money and inherently pleasing primary reinforcers, such as food and drink. Hence, the term "conditioned reinforcer" is used.

44. **(B)** Rehearsal serves two functions. It allows items in short-term memory to be retained. Also, it appears to facilitate material from the short-term to long-term memory. In transference of most contents, rehearsal is necessary for learning.

45. **(A)** The correlation of −.70 is the best predictor. Correlations can have any value between −1.0 and +1.0. As the absolute value of the correlation approaches 1.0, the prediction based on the correlation becomes more accurate. A negative correlation shows an inverse relationship between x and y: as x goes up, y goes down, and vice versa. A positive correlation shows a direct relationship between x and y: as x goes up, y goes up, and vice versa.

46. **(A)** By definition, the standard deviation is

$$\sqrt{\sum_i \frac{(x_i - \bar{x})^2}{n}}, \text{ where } \bar{x} = \frac{\Sigma x_i}{n}.$$

The standard deviation gives a feeling for how far away from the mean we can expect an observation to be.

47. **(A)** A platykurtic curve is marked by flatness, indicating a wide dispersion of measurements. It is possible for this kind of curve to be positively or negatively skewed, but skewness in itself does not determine a platykurtic curve. A curve that is peaked is called leptokurtic.

48. **(D)** Correlations are indicative of a relationship between two variables. The higher the absolute value of the correlation, the stronger the relationship between the variables. Correlation measures how well the existence of a variable or some aspect of a variable is predictive of another variable. Unfortunately, correlation tells us nothing about which of the two variables has an effect on the other. Many times, it is a third variable that is affecting both variables together.

49. **(D)**   Aptitude tests serve to predict subsequent performance, e.g., to determine if an individual will profit from an education at a particular college. Examiners usually apply the term "aptitude" to tests which measure the effects of learning under uncontrolled or unknown conditions. In addition, people who take aptitude tests do not usually have a uniform prior experience. All the people taking the Graduate Record Examination have attended college, but not the same college, and they have not all studied the same subjects.

50. **(B)**   The Thematic Apperception Test (TAT) was designed by Murray and Morgan in 1935 to determine an individual's major themes of concern by having him respond freely to vague and ambiguous pictures presented on TAT cards. Theoretically, the themes expressed in the responses reflect the subjects' concerns, i.e., the subject projects his concerns onto the TAT pictures.

51. **(A)**   In spite of the confederate's "desperate" screams and complaints of a heart condition, most of the subjects reluctantly complied with the orders of the experimenter—a "legitimate authority"—and eventually applied the maximum shock. Although intelligence of the subject had no effect on compliance, the status of the experimenter showed a strong effect. From this experiment, Milgram concluded that the atrocities that happened in Nazi Germany could have occurred anywhere, even in small-town America, because of people's tendency to obey authority.

52. **(E)**   Repeated hand-washing is a symptom of obsessive-compulsive disorder. In obsessive-compulsive disorder, both obsessions and compulsions need not exist simultaneously to warrant diagnosis. Repeated hand-washing is termed compulsive if the person feels compelled to perform the behavior, and the action interferes with more appropriate behavior. As opposed to a compulsion, an obsession is a recurring thought, rather than an action, which a person cannot control or stop. This disorder is grouped with other anxiety disorders.

53. **(E)**   Electroconvulsive therapy (ECT) is a safe and effective treatment of patients with major depressive disorder, manic episodes, and other serious mental disorders. Many clinicians and researchers believe that because of bad press ECT is underused. Currently about 50,000 to 100,000 patients receive ECT annually in the United States. ECT works by affecting both pre-and post-synaptic receptors.

54. **(E)**   Paranoia is found in both Axis I and Axis II in the DSM IV. Paranoid Personality Disorder can be distinguished from Delusional Disorder, Persecutory Type, Schizophrenia, Paranoid Type, and Mood Disorder with Psychotic Features because these disorders are characterized by episodes of psychotic symptoms (DSM IV, p. 636). Paranoia, whether in a personality disorder or a psychotic disorder, revolves around feelings of suspiciousness and distrust. A person with Paranoid Personality may read hidden meanings into benign events. A person with Schizophrenia, Paranoid Type is likely to have delusions of grandiosity or persecution, or both.

55.   **(C)**   Frequently, a person experiencing a dissociative fugue will move to a new geographic location and try to start an entirely new life. During a fugue, individuals generally appear to be without psychopathology. Most fugues do not involve the formation of a new identity. However, if a new identity is formed, the emerging identity will usually be more gregarious and uninhibited than the prior personality. Like amnesia, a fugue is usually precipitated by psychosocial stress. The duration of most fugues is brief—hours or days—although in rare cases a fugue will last many months.

56.   **(C)**   The strongest possible correlations are +1.0 and −1.0. These are perfect correlations. Any correlation higher than +1.0 or lower than −1.0 is erroneous, and the data should be analyzed again.

57.   **(D)**   With the highest rates of performance, the variable-ratio schedule elicits consistently high rates even after prolonged discontinuance of the reinforcement. In fact, once an operant learning response has been established with a variable-ratio reinforcement schedule, it is difficult to extinguish the response.

58.   **(C)**   In secondary reinforcement, a neutral stimulus is paired with the conditioned stimulus, after that conditioned stimulus can reliably elicit the conditioned response. When this is accomplished, the new or second conditioned stimulus will elicit the conditioned response even though it was never directly paired with the unconditioned stimulus. In this manner, the original, neutral CS comes to work as a reinforcer for the second-order conditioning response.

59.   **(E)**   The standard deviation (sd), increases by the same multiple as each of its scores. In this case it is the multiple 5.

60.   **(A)**   The extent to which a test measures a theoretical construct is called construct validity. A psychological construct is a term that represents a set of consistent data about persons. The degree to which a test extracts information about the psychological construct is the degree to which it possesses construct validity, and therefore, the degree to which it is a valid measure of that construct.

61.   **(D)**   A psychotic disorder is a severe mental disorder in which thinking and emotion are so impaired that the individual is seriously out of contact with reality and is unable to meet the demands of daily life. In this case, the Bipolar II Disorder with Psychotic Features is primarily a disorder of mood, not thought.

62.   **(E)**   Alcohol reduces anxiety (anxiolytic) and acts as a depressant, often causing sleepiness (hypnotic).

63. **(A)** The social learning theory of aggression holds that most aggression is learned through operant conditioning. Therefore, aggression results only after certain actions are reinforced by rewards and discouraged by punishments. Modeling is another form of social learning that contributes to the development of aggressive behavior.

64. **(C)** According to the social learning theory of aggression, if a child is rewarded for random aggressive behavior, it is highly probable that the behavior will occur again. On the other hand, if a child is punished for acting aggressively, the likelihood of that behavior occurring again is reduced. It has been found that the schedule of reinforcement is particularly important in the learning of aggressive responses. For example, if aggression is reinforced irregularly, the aggressive behavior will tend to last longer than if the reinforcement is continuous.

65. **(B)** The belief that aggression is an inborn tendency in all animals, including man, has been most supported by the work of Konrad Lorenz.

66. **(A)** Short-term memory (STM) is very limited in its capacity. It can only hold about seven items (plus or minus two items) of information at a time. This brief memory span requires deliberate rehearsal to prevent a specific memory from decaying over time.

67. **(D)** Maslow's Hierarchy of Needs has five levels. These are: physiological needs, safety and security, love and belonging, esteem and self-esteem, and self-actualization. As one type of need is satisfied, the next higher in the hierarchy becomes the dominant motivating factor. According to Maslow, few people achieve the highest stage in the motivation hierarchy.

68. **(B)** In an approach-avoidance conflict situation, one is both attracted to and repelled by the same goal. For example, one may want to go to college, but may also be fearful of the typical college work load.

69. **(B)** Skinner developed an apparatus consisting of a small enclosure with a lever device and a food receptacle. A hungry rat was placed in the box, and in time usually pressed the lever by chance, and automatically received food (a reward). After some time, most of the rats learned to make this response (lever-pressing) as soon as they entered the box. This learning was termed operant conditioning because the animal had to perform an operation to get a reward.

70. **(C)** In the fixed-interval schedule, reinforcement is given after a fixed period of time, no matter how much work is done. This schedule has the lowest yield in terms of performance. However, just before the reinforcement is given, activity increases.

71. **(A)** A platykurtic distribution is very flat, indicating a wide dispersion of measurements.

72. **(B)** In a positively skewed distribution the mean is greater than both the median and the mode. In any skewed distribution the mean is affected most and pulled in the direction of the skew.

73. **(C)** In analyzing the human input into any task, four psychological functions are usually distinguished. These are: perceptual processes, recall processes, problem-solving processes, and muscular processes. These components are considered when forming a step-by-step description of a task in a work cycle.

74. **(C)** Extreme scores most dramatically affect the mean because the mean is essentially an average of a set of scores. The inclusion of extreme scores changes their average and might, therefore, be a less desirable measure of central tendency.

75. **(A)** According to Kohlberg, the premoral stage is the first level of moral behavior. During the early stage of this level, children have a good-bad conception of behavior. For the early premoral child, moral behavior is based on the subjective consequences.

76. **(D)** The cerebellum controls the ballistic movements of speaking, writing, playing an instrument, and performing most athletic skills. The basal ganglia control the slower, more gradual movements that are modified by sensory feedback while the movement is still occurring. The basal ganglia are involved with postures and movements of the body as a whole.

77. **(B)** A "normal" I.Q. score is considered to be about 100, while 98% of the people who take I.Q. tests fall in the range between 60 and 140. Someone who scores above 140 is considered a genius.

78. **(A)** Extinction occurs when the conditioned stimulus is repeatedly presented without the unconditioned stimulus. The strength of the response elicited by the CS and its ability to elicit the CR at all, gradually decreases as the CS continues to be presented alone. The CR strength eventually declines to at least the level present before conditioning began.

79. **(E)** In verbal learning, rehearsal allows items in short-term memory to be retained and it also facilitates transference of material from short-term to long-term memory. Short-term memory holds the trace of an experience for only a limited amount of time. If there is no rehearsal, the items will be forgotten rapidly.

80. **(E)** Characteristics of verbal materials that influence how effectively they are learned include position in the list, similarity in appearance, meaning or category, frequency, and concreteness. The type and amount of past learning a person has done also affects his rate of acquisition of new material.

81. **(C)** The time spent learning is the important factor in rehearsal. The individual presentation rate and the number of trials are not as important.

82. **(C)** Behavior therapy attacks symptoms of behavioral disorders through the use of learning principles. There is no probing of the unconscious or any attempt to change the entire personality. There are four methods of behavior therapy: counterconditioning, operant conditioning, modeling, and cognitive restructuring.

83. **(C)** Three of the most frequently used counterconditioning techniques are systematic desensitization, assertive training, and aversive conditioning. Assertive training is used for people who cannot express positive or negative feelings to others. Aversive conditioning tries to attach negative feelings to stimuli that are considered inappropriately attractive.

84. **(D)** Dollard, along with Doob and Miller, is a social learning theorist who proposed the frustration-aggression hypothesis. In this experiment, the absence of grain elicits frustration and aggression, which is taken out on the innocent pigeon.

85. **(A)** Allport believed that terms like "ego" or "self" should be used as adjectives. He decided to rename the ego functions of the personality the "proprium" or "propriate functions." These functions include bodily sense, self-identity, self-esteem, rational thinking and cognitive style. The proprium is considered to develop with time; it is not innate.

86. **(C)** The third stage of Erikson's theory of psychosocial development is called the locomotor-genital stage, lasting from age four to six. This period is characterized by the formation of initiative or guilt, the development of fine motor skills, and an increase in language development and curiosity.

87. **(A)** The "shadow" represents the repressed unconscious drives and desires of the personal unconscious. Because it is believed to be found in all people, often referred to as a person's "dark side," it is considered part of the collective unconscious.

88. **(B)** Carl Rogers developed client-centered therapy based on his theories of the self-actualizing potential in man. He felt that the patient in therapy should bear responsibility for his own self-actualization and wellness. In client-centered therapy, the therapist is nondirective, while the patient is responsible for working out his own problems.

89. **(C)** Changes in family structure such as divorce, loss of parents, adoption, and severe or prolonged illness of a family member all have a negative effect on the child's intellectual development. In general, these changes disrupt the stability of the child's intelligence quotient by acting as stressors in the child's life.

90. **(D)** Test validity is generally defined as the capacity of a test to measure what it sets out to measure. In terms of test construction, content validity is built into the test; an analysis of the subject matter or content of the test must be undertaken before the construction of test items. Criterion-related validity must also be established. To do this, one must correlate the test with some objective criterion that is an appropriate measure of the trait or ability that the test is supposed to be measuring.

91. **(D)** Compliance refers to a change in external behavior, while private acceptance refers to a change in attitude. In the presence of a group, the subjects conform with their beliefs outwardly; that is, they show compliance. The fact that they continued to do so in the group's absence shows that private acceptance also took place. Internalization is a very strong social response based on a desire to be "right." Once a belief is internalized it is highly resistant to change.

92. **(A)** Authoritarian persons prove to be greatly influenced by authority figures, and, the more authoritarian a person is, the more he or she will conform. "External" personalities feel their lives are controlled by factors outside their control, while "internals" feel life is in their control. "Externals" tend to conform more than "internals." It has been found that a large decrease in conformity results if even one person in a group disagrees. Tests have shown that conformity varies inversely with intelligence.

93. **(C)** When there is an inconsistency between actions and attitudes, psychological distress occurs. This is known as cognitive dissonance. In order to rid oneself of this dissonance, a person often changes his opinion or attitude so that it is in agreement with his actions.

94. **(B)** In a normal distribution 68% of the population falls within ±1 standard deviation of the mean. 95% falls within ±2 standard deviations of the mean, and 99.5% falls within ±3 standard deviations of the mean.

95. **(C)** This is a normal distribution, in which the mode, median, and mean are always equal.

96. **(B)** Kohler spent years studying the problem-solving behavior of chimps. He observed that the animals often exhibited "insight," i.e., the sudden solution to a problem without the use of trial and error learning.

97. **(A)** We tend to take credit for our successes. We blame others or situational variables for our errors and mistakes. However, we don't extend that consideration to others. When people make mistakes, we hold them totally responsible and discount any situational variables that may have influenced them.

98. **(E)** Since the blind baby has never seen a smile it can't be imitating it. Likewise, it cannot be a learned or nurtured behavior. Smiling when we are pleased

or content must therefore be an innate (inborn) characteristic in humans. Congenital refers to factors being present at birth. Smiling usually doesn't occur for the first few months.

99.   **(C)**   The stage of formal operations is noted for the ability of the individual to deal with abstract problems and concepts. It usually begins around puberty but research shows that some people never develop these skills, and continue to function at the level of concrete operations for life.

100.   **(D)**   A small quantity of lithium (a white powdered metal) is essential for human functioning. Some people who suffer from Bipolar Disorder have a lithium deficiency; their bodies don't retain the metal. Lack of lithium produces the mood swings observed. Treatment consists of taking lithium carbonate capsules to maintain the body's lithium levels.

SECTION II

Here are examples of good essay answers:

Essay 1:   Pavlovian, classical (because of Pavlov's now classic experiments) or, the term preferred by many today, respondent conditioning is a simple form of learning in which a subject is conditioned to respond to a new stimulus with an innate or a previously acquired response. In Pavlov's experiments with the salivating response of his dogs he established the basic methodology and terminology still used today in classical conditioning experiments. He knew dogs would salivate when they tasted food. Pavlov referred to the food as the unconditioned stimulus (UCS) because it naturally and consistently elicited salivation, which he called the unconditioned response (UCR).

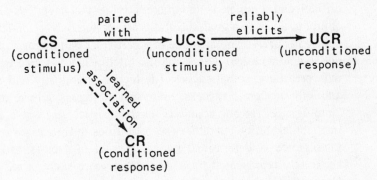

Diagram of classical conditioning.

Pavlov later taught dogs to salivate to light. This was accomplished by presenting a light just prior to presenting the food. After a series of such pairings, the dog would salivate to the light even before food was presented. In this case, the light was a conditioned stimulus (CS) and the salivation to the light was a conditioned response (CR). Pavlov found that he could condition many neutral stimuli to elicit a particular response by repeatedly pairing the neutral stimulus with an UCS.

In classical conditioning, then, the conditioned stimulus (CS) which elicits no response at first, and the unconditioned stimulus (UCS), which consistently evokes a particular response, are presented together to the subject for a number of trials. After some time, the unconditioned stimulus (UCS) can be removed and conditioned stimulus (CS) will elicit a response similar to the unconditioned response (UCR). The subject learns to respond to a stimulus in a way he had not responded before. The subject has been respondently or classically conditioned.

Essay 2:   Psychologists do not agree on a definition of intelligence. Almost all do agree, however, that it is a psychological construct, i.e., intelligence is a trait that is inferred on the basis of behavioral observation. Some people are observed to learn more quickly, seem to be better at tasks which require abstract conceptualization, read faster and retain more information, have better memories, are capable of expressing their ideas more comprehensively, etc. These people are referred to as intelligent.

In addition to the characteristics observed above, the various definitions of intelligence stress that intelligence is an ability or capacity to profit from experience, learn new information, adjust to new situations, to deal "effectively" with the environment, to succeed in activities that are difficult and complex, to undertake activities that have "social value," the ability to adapt to a goal, the ability to act purposively under stress, the ability to survive and advance in a particular culture, and the ability to understand and deal with symbols. Intelligence has also been equated with creativity, social success (defined economically and politically), and with academic success. Many psychologists believe that the trait "intelligence" is not a unitary characteristic, i.e., not a generalized intellectual ability, but rather a set of abilities and processes and therefore intelligence is determined by a large set of factors and cannot be accurately represented by a single test score such as an intelligence quotient (IQ).

Intelligence is not the same as IQ. IQ is best seen as a score on an intelligence test. However, though the IQ is popularly equated with intelligence, it can be either an accurate or an inaccurate indicator of intelligence, depending on one's definition of intelligence. If intelligence is equated with academic achievement, then the IQ is a good way to measure intelligence since the IQ tests are usually validated against criteria of academic achievement. However, if intelligence is viewed as equal to economic/political success and with the carrying out of goals that have social value, then the IQ does not reflect intelligence at all.

IQ tests mostly measure verbal skills. Intelligence is not necessarily synonymous to verbal skills. If it is presumed that intelligence is an innate generalized intellectual ability, it does not follow that the ability is going to be reflected by an IQ score. After all, many innately intelligent people have not had the opportunity to learn or to fully develop their verbal skills, especially if they do not live in the Western Hemisphere.

The IQ is presented as an expression of an individual's intellectual ability level at a given point in time, in relation to his chronological age. Various IQ tests differ in content and thus the meaning of IQ scores on different tests is not necessarily the same. It must be remembered that IQ tests are most useful and accurate as a reflection of prior educational achievement and as a predictor of subsequent educational performance because the tests are validated against the criteria of academic achievement.

In 1904 Alfred Binet was asked by the French government to construct a test that would distinguish between normal children and children with severe learning disabilities. Binet conceived of intelligence as the relationship of mental ability and chronological age.

Binet believed that children developed specific abilities at specific ages. Thus, at age nine, the average child may develop the ability to learn certain arithmetic functions. If a child is capable of learning these arithmetic functions at age six, then he is considered to be more intelligent than the child who could not learn them until the age of nine. The mental age of a child is determined according to what test level he could pass. If the highest test level that a child could pass was the test level that all average nine-year-olds passed and no average eight-year-olds passed then the child was presumed to have a mental age of nine.

For each age up to 15 years, there is a set of characteristic abilities that develop in the normal child. If they develop earlier than average, the child is more intelligent than the average child; if the abilities develop later, then the child is considered to be of below average intelligence. The IQ for children (but not adults) was computed by dividing the mental age (M.A.) by the chronological age (C.A.) and multiplying the quotient by 100 in order to eliminate decimals.

$$I.Q. = \frac{M.A.}{C.A.} \times 100$$

A boy with a mental age of eight and chronological age of five has an IQ of 160:

$$I.Q. = \frac{M.A.}{C.A.} \times 100 = \frac{8}{5} \times 100 = 160.$$

An IQ of 160 is considerably above average.

IQs are currently computed on the basis of standard scores. The scores are so arranged that the mean IQ for the adult population is 100 and the standard deviation is 16 (therefore, 68% of the population is considered to have IQs between 84 and 116).

IQ and intelligence should not be confused. The IQ is a test score that has predictive value with respect to academic achievement. Intelligence is a psychological construct that is useful in describing an individual's behavior. The IQ is representative of intelligence only when one believes that the abilities, processes, and characteristics of which intelligence consists are adequately represented on the IQ test.

ADVANCED PLACEMENT EXAMINATION IN
PSYCHOLOGY

Test 2

ADVANCED PLACEMENT
PSYCHOLOGY TEST 2
SECTION I

TIME: 70 Minutes
100 Questions

DIRECTIONS: Choose the best answer for each question and mark the letter of your selection on the corresponding answer sheet.

1.   According to Carl Rogers, the structure of personality is based on

   (A)   ego and superego.

   (B)   organism and self.

   (C)   conscious and collective unconscious.

   (D)   inferiority and superiority.

   (E)   introversion and extroversion.

2.   The theory that we all experience a series of psychosocial crises throughout our lives was proposed by

   (A)   Freud.   (B)   Adler.

   (C)   Sheldon.   (D)   Erikson.

   (E)   Jung.

3.   All of the following choices are advantages of field research except that

   (A)   "real people" are studied.

   (B)   reactions of subjects are more natural.

   (C)   it has more impact than lab studies.

   (D)   behavior is not influenced by the psychologist.

   (E)   there is an appropriate control involved.

4. In a cross-sectional study, the researcher examines

    (A) subjects over extended periods of time.

    (B) different subjects at different developmental levels.

    (C) different cultural groups for comparison.

    (D) the dynamics of relationships with family members.

    (E) both (A) and (B)

5. The psychological point of view which emphasizes unconscious motivation as a factor in human behavior is

    (A) client-centered therapy.

    (B) gestalt psychology or field theory.

    (C) psychoanalysis.

    (D) stimulus-response or S-R psychology.

    (E) rational-emotive therapy.

6. What is the value of the median for the numbers: 34, 29, 26, 37, 31 and 34?

    (A) 31   (B) 34

    (C) 30.1   (D) 32.5

    (E) 5.5

7. Find the range of the sample composed of the observations: 33, 53, 35, 37, 49.

    (A) 37   (B) 5

    (C) 10   (D) 4

    (E) 20

QUESTIONS 8–9 refer to the following graphs:

(A)   (B)

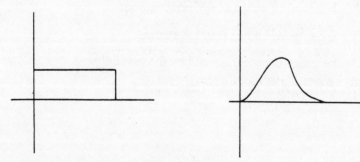

(C)   (D)

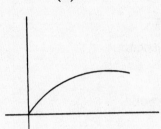 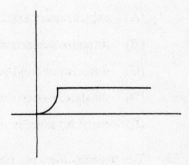

(E)

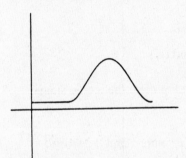

8.   Which curve represents an ogive?

9.   In which graph does each score occur with the same frequency?

10.   An approving comment made by a boss to his employee is an example of

     (A)   generalized reinforcement.   (B)   conditioned reinforcement.

     (C)   primary reinforcement.   (D)   social reinforcement.

     (E)   positive reinforcement.

11.   Neurons are unique among cells in that they

     (A)   cannot conduct impulses.

     (B)   cannot reproduce.

     (C)   have a nucleus containing genetic material.

     (D)   are surrounded by a membrane.

     (E)   all of the above

12. According to Carl Rogers, human motivation is based on the need to

    (A) express one's sexuality and aggressive nature.

    (B) actualize and enhance the self through experiences.

    (C) find meaning in life.

    (D) struggle between being and non-being in the world.

    (E) strive for affection and approval from others.

13. Which of the following best describes the major function(s) of the spinal cord?

    (A) acts as a messenger to the brain

    (B) filters sensory impulses

    (C) directs simple actions independent of brain

    (D) (A) and (B)   (E) (A) and (C)

14. According to Bruner's theory of cognitive development, the iconic stage is

    (A) concerned with language development.

    (B) concerned with the use of visual images to understand the world.

    (C) concerned with the use of action to understand the world.

    (D) concerned with symbolism in the understanding of the world.

    (E) representative of egocentric activity.

15. The opponent-process theory of color perception was proposed by

    (A) E. Hering.   (B) H. Helmholtz.

    (C) C. L. Franklin.   (D) E. Land.

    (E) D. Premack.

16. The region at the base of the brain which is highly involved in most emotional and physiological motivation is the

    (A) medulla.   (B) rhinencephalon.

    (C) pituitary gland.   (D) hypothalamus.

    (E) actomyosin.

17. The sensitivity of the eye to light varies with

    (A) wavelength.   (B) the eye's state of adaptation.

    (C) the region of the retina.

    (D) the contraction or dilation of the iris.

    (E) all of the above

18. The type of validity which measures the extent to which a test measures a theoretical construct is

    (A) content validity.   (B) face validity.

    (C) synthetic validity.   (D) criterion validity.

    (E) construct validity.

QUESTIONS 19–20 refer to the following paragraph:

Suppose you are playing Monopoly with a group of children. These children understand the basic instructions and will play by the rules. They are not capable of hypothetical transactions dealing with mortgages, loans and special pacts with other players.

19. According to Piaget, these children are in which stage of cognitive development?

    (A) sensorimotor stage

    (B) formal operations stage

    (C) preconceptual preoperational stage

    (D) concrete operational stage

    (E) intuitive preoperational stage

20. What are the probable ages of these children?

    (A) 8-13   (B) 4-7

    (C) 2-4   (D) 7-11

    (E) 5-10

21. The Language Acquisition Device was proposed by

    (A) Piaget.   (B) Bruner.

    (C) Kohler.   (D) Chomsky.

    (E) Mednick.

22. When we say that our visual system is 50% crossed, we mean that

    (A) half of the information from the right visual field is perceived by the left retina.

    (B) half of the fibers from the optic nerve cross over to the opposite side of the brain.

    (C) half of the visual image strikes the left side of the retina, and the other half strikes the right side of the retina.

    (D) half of the visual image is inverted in the retina.

    (E) none of the above

23. In which form of schizophrenia would you most likely see delusions of grandeur or persecution?

    (A) undifferentiated type   (B) residual type

    (C) disorganized type   (D) catatonic type

    (E) paranoid type

24. All of the following are characteristics of Antisocial Personality Disorder except

    (A) absence of irrationality or symptoms of psychosis.

    (B) disregard for the truth.

    (C) no sense of shame.

    (D) a history of suicide attempts.

    (E) onset no later than teenage years.

25. Echoic code is to auditory system as iconic code is to

    (A) tactile experience.   (B) visual system.

    (C) sensory system.   (D) olfactory system.

    (E) none of the above

26. The Theory of Selective Attention was proposed by

    (A) Selfridge.   (B) Bruner.

    (C) Broadbent.   (D) Lockhart and Craik.

    (E) Tolman.

27. Those items that are most likely to be forgotten are those

    (A) items that are "concrete."

    (B) items with the least digits/letters.

    (C) at the beginning of a long list.

    (D) at the middle of a long list.

    (E) at the end of a long list.

28. A model in which the internal representation of a pattern is structurally similar to the stimulus pattern is called a

    (A) visual feature model.   (B) constructive model.

    (C) template matching model.   (D) specific feature model.

    (E) pandemonium model.

29. Which of the following best describes correlational analysis?

    (A) a measure of association between two variables

    (B) a measure of linear association between two characteristics

    (C) a measure of causation between X and Y

    (D) a measure of causation of X on Y

    (E) a measure of causation of Y on X

30. Spinal nerves belong to the

    (A) peripheral nervous system.

    (B) central nervous system.

    (C) antagonistic nervous system.

    (D) residual nervous system.

    (E) none of the above

31. A person who has more difficulty hearing high pitched tones than low pitched tones probably has

    (A) nerve deafness.   (B) conduction deafness.

    (C) functional deafness.   (D) tone specific deafness.

    (E) tonotopic deafness.

32. Abraham Maslow is a chief proponent of the _____ school of human behavior.

    (A) behaviorist   (B) structuralist

    (C) humanist   (D) functionalist

    (E) existentialist

33. When the difference between two means is shown to be significant

    (A) the null hypothesis is rejected.

    (B) the null hypothesis is disproved.

    (C) the alternative hypothesis is disproved.

    (D) the independent variable is proved.

    (E) both (A) and (B)

34. Conjunctive, disjunctive, and relational concepts refer to

    (A) simple concepts.   (B) complex concepts.

    (C) precepts.   (D) imagery concepts.

    (E) symbols.

QUESTIONS 35-37 refer to the following passage:

Most American psychologists favor the component process theory of cognitive development. The theory is based on the assumption that a child's cognition develops as he reaches certain levels of competence in various cognitive skills. As the child gains cognitive abilities, they are integrated into a general cognitive ability. The component process is concerned with problem solving. The degree of success achieved is used as an index for measuring cognitive ability. Before a child is fully competent to solve problems, he must be able to use the following five mental processes: encoding, memory, evaluation, deduction, and mediation.

35. The component process theory, probably developed out of a tradition of _____ research.

    (A) cognition   (B) emotion

    (C) motivation   (D) behavioral

    (E) information processing

36. This theory of cognitive development assumes that cognitive ability will be reflected in _____ .

    (A) cognition   (B) encoding

    (C) deduction   (D) performance

    (E) memory

37. This theory deemphasizes the importance of _____ in the cognitive development of the child.

    (A) language   (B) thinking

    (C) emotion   (D) performance

    (E) using indexes

38. A man walking to work counts the number of stop signs he sees on the street. As he arrives at the entrance to his office, he fears that he has miscounted and that his children will die unless he counts the signs correctly. He runs back home and starts recounting the stop signs as he walks. This man would be diagnosed as having a(an)

    (A) systematic reaction.

    (B) social phobia.

    (C) obsessive-compulsive disorder.

    (D) dissociative fugue.   (E) factitious disorder.

39. The ego, in contrast to the id,

    (A) mediates between wish-fulfilling desires and the outer reality.

    (B) is composed of only wish-fulfilling desires.

    (C) mediates between reality and internal rules.

    (D) cannot mediate with the superego.

    (E) is innate, not learned.

40. A diagnosis of substance dependence can be applied to every class of substances except

    (A) cannabis.   (B) nicotine.

    (C) inhalants.   (D) caffeine.

    (E) phencyclidine.

41. Stanley Schacter (1959), in his studies on the human affiliative need, found that

    (A) highly fearful people are much more likely to affiliate than less fearful people.

    (B) first-born children are more likely to affiliate than later-born children.

    (C) when given a choice, highly fearful people preferred to affiliate only with those who were in the same experimental condition.

    (D) people affiliate to reduce fear.

    (E) all of the above

42. The Thematic Apperception Test supposedly reflects

    (A) how one organizes ambiguous stimuli.

    (B) one's overall level of introversion-extroversion.

    (C) interpersonal conflicts and needs.

    (D) one's relative ranking on several trait scales.

    (E) one's possible latent psychosis.

43. Cross-sectional studies differ from longitudinal studies in that the former

    (A) are more time consuming and expensive.

    (B) are not susceptible to changing generational experiences.

    (C) are more susceptible to changing generational experiences.

    (D) use data from samples of varying age levels.

    (E) are less efficient than the latter.

44. Which of the following psychoanalytic theorists proposed the need to move toward people, move against people, and move away from people?

    (A) Sullivan   (B) Horney

    (C) Fromm   (D) Anderson

    (E) Adler

45. The repeated presentation of the CS without the UCS results in

    (A) spontaneous recovery.   (B) inhibition.

    (C) extinction.   (D) higher-order conditioning.

    (E) negative reinforcement.

46. The classic social psychology experiments that demonstrated that most people would perform acts in direct contradiction to their morals and beliefs, if a legitimate authority figure accepted responsibility for those acts, was performed by

    (A) B.F. Skinner.   (B) Sigmund Freud.

    (C) Stanley Milgram.   (D) Leon Festinger.

    (E) Rollo May.

47. In psychology, the concept of motivation was first described in terms of instinctive behavior. On whose theory was this concept largely based?

    (A) Hume   (B) Descartes

    (C) James   (D) Darwin

    (E) Freud

48. An EPSP causes the nerve cell to

    (A) polarize.   (B) contract.

    (C) become more negative. (D) become less negative.

    (E) none of the above

49. The pituitary gland secretes which of the following hormones?

    (A) TSH (thyroid stimulating hormone)

    (B) ACTH (adrenocorticotrophic hormone)

    (C) FSH (follicle stimulating hormone)

    (D) LH (luteinizing hormone)

    (E) all of the above

50. Problems that have more than one correct solution require

    (A) divergent thinking.   (B) symbolic thought.

    (C) disjunctive thinking. (D) convergent thinking.

    (E) complex concepts.

51. A frequency-distribution will often approach the normal distribution as

    (A) the number of scores included gets very large.

    (B) the number of scores included gets very small.

    (C) more variables are included in the frequency distribution.

    (D) certain scores are eliminated from the distribution.

    (E) the distribution normalizes in shape.

52. According to Freud, memories and drives that can be easily recalled but are not within consciousness at the moment are in the

    (A) personal unconscious.   (B) collective unconscious.

    (C) unconscious.   (D) preconscious.

    (E) ego.

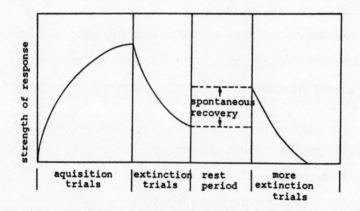

53. According to the above diagram, which of the following best describes the occurrence of spontaneous recovery?

    (A) New learning takes place during the rest period.

    (B) CR reappears in weaker form than before extinction was begun.

    (C) CR reappears in full strength.

    (D) There is memory of learning.

    (E) (A) and (C)

54. Because the id seeks to gratify its desires without delay, it operates on the

    (A) satisfaction principle.   (B) pleasure principle.

    (C) ego.   (D) superego.

    (E) unconscious desires.

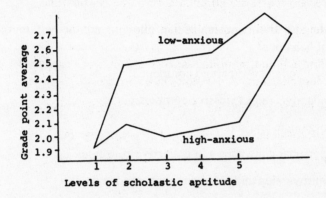

Levels of scholastic aptitude

55. According to the above diagram, which of the following statements is true?

    (A) Levels of scholastic aptitude are not related to grade point average.

    (B) Low-anxiety students have higher grade point averages and higher scholastic aptitudes.

    (C) High anxiety students have higher grade point averages and higher scholastic aptitudes.

    (D) (A) and (B)   (E) (A) and (C)

56. In classical conditioning, the response that automatically occurs whenever the unconditioned stimulus is presented without any training is called a(an)

    (A) behavioral response.   (B) unconditioned response.

    (C) preconditioned response. (D) unlearned response.

    (E) instinctive response.

57. Social learning theory was first proposed by

    (A) Bandura and Walters.

    (B) B.F. Skinner.

    (C) Miller and Dollard.

    (D) J.B. Watson.

    (E) Carl Rogers.

58. Which of the following psychologists places special emphasis on the need for positive regard and the need for self-regard?

(A) Maslow   (B) Rogers.

(C) Adler   (D) Sheldon

(E) Frankl

59. According to Allport, which of the following are the two important components of behavior?

(A) ego body and superego components

(B) adaptive and expressive components

(C) organism and self

(D) personal conscious and collective conscious

(E) introversion and extroversion components

60. In contrast to the cones,

(A) rods function mainly in night vision.

(B) rods are concentrated in the fovea.

(C) rods produce color images, as well as black and white images.

(D) rods are connected to bipolar cells in a one-to-one ratio.

(E) rods are unimportant to night vision.

61. The behavioral modification technique which uses repeated exposure to aversive stimuli or disturbing scenes to extinguish the emotional responses associated with those stimuli is

(A) systematic desensitization.   (B) implosive therapy.

(C) reciprocal inhibition.   (D) token economy system.

(E) negative reinforcement.

62. The opponent-process theory of color vision

    (A) proposed that there were three types of color receptors in the eye.

    (B) stated that there are only two kinds of color receptors in the eye.

    (C) was proposed by B. Young.

    (D) explains color vision by the process of mixing the light of different colors.

    (E) contradicted psychophysics theory about the perception of color thresholds.

63. According to Freud, the main function of dreams is

    (A) to bridge the unconscious with the conscious mind.

    (B) the assimilation of conscious memories into the unconscious.

    (C) the release of unconscious materials into preconscious.

    (D) wish fulfillment of the individual.

    (E) release of sexual and social tensions.

64. Which of the following is true of a normal distribution?

    (A) It has two modes.

    (B) It has one mode.

    (C) It has a skewed curve.

    (D) The mode and the mean are equal.

    (E) (B) and (D)

65. Alfred Binet is famous for developing the first

    (A) item analysis.   (B) adult intelligence test.

    (C) projective test.   (D) fixed alternative test.

    (E) child intelligence test.

66. For this series of observations find the mean, median, and mode (in that order)

    500, 600, 800, 800, 900, 900, 900, 900, 900, 1000, 1100.

    (A) 845.45, 600, 900   (B) 845.45, 900, 900

    (C) 845.45, 900, 850   (D) 854.54, 600, 900

    (E) 854.54, 900, 850

67. The Milgram experiments indicate that

    (A) reward and punishment increases compliance.

    (B) pressure from legitimate authorities in a situation increases compliance.

    (C) social pressure increases compliance.

    (D) justification increases compliance.

    (E) group pressure on individuals increases compliance toward group decisions.

68. Which of the following developmental periods is characterized by indifference to sexually related matters?

    (A) latency stage   (B) oral stage

    (C) anal stage   (D) tactile stage

    (E) phallic stage

69. The "Oedipus Complex" is to the "Electra Complex" as

    (A) girl is to boy.   (B) girl is to mother.

    (C) id is to ego.   (D) boy is to father.

    (E) boy is to girl.

QUESTIONS 70-72 are based on this paragraph.

A woman visits a psychologist for the following problem. She is extremely afraid of pigeons, and is overcome with fear and anxiety every time she sees a pigeon. She tells the psychologist that her fear is irrational and she cannot control it. She first remembers being afraid of pigeons at age eight when she fell off her bicycle in the street and landed on a dead pigeon. Her fear is growing more intense and earlier that week a pigeon flew past her and sent her huddling in a doorway crying with fear.

70. The most probable diagnosis of this woman's case is

    (A) conversion disorder.   (B) dissociative disorder.

    (C) posttraumatic stress disorder.(D) specific phobia.

    (E) obsessive-compulsive disorder.

71. The most likely treatment prescribed for this disorder is

    (A) aversion therapy.   (B) token economy techniques.

    (C) systematic desensitization.   (D) modeling techniques.

    (E) client-centered therapy.

72. Within a learning theory paradigm, the origin of this disorder could be explained by stating that fear associated with falling from the bike was the UCS and that the bird lying in the street was the

    (A) US.   (B) CR.

    (C) UCR.   (D) CS.

    (E) SS.

73. The "persona" is the mask of conscious intentions behind which an individual hides. This personality construct was proposed by

    (A) A. Bandura.   (B) G. Allport.

    (C) C. Rogers.   (D) C. Jung.

    (E) S. Schachter.

74. Of the following tests, the most suitable for determining the I.Q. of most 12-year-olds is the

    (A) Raven Progressive Matrices.

    (B) WAIS.   (C) WISC.

    (D) WPPSI.   (E) Bayley Scales.

75. The double-blind technique refers to a method of experimentation

    (A) where neither the experimental nor control group knows the purpose of the study.

    (B) often used in perceptual research.

    (C) where there are two control groups.

    (D) where neither the subject nor the experimenter knows whether the subject is in the experimental or control group.

    (E) involving the absence of sight in both eyes.

76. Which of the following is not characteristic of a Major Depressive Disorder?

    (A) diminished ability to think and concentrate

    (B) considerable stress tolerance

    (C) tendency to feel guilty

    (D) psychomotor agitation or retardation

    (E) feelings of hopelessness

QUESTIONS 77-79 refer to parts of the brain pictured in this diagram.

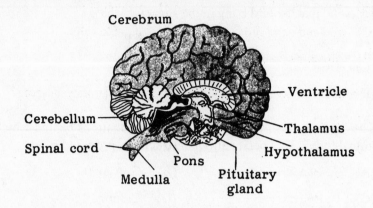

77. The part of the brain which regulates and coordinates muscle movement is the

    (A) cerebellum.   (B) pons.

    (C) ventricle.   (D) medulla.

    (E) thalamus.

78. The fourth ventricle is located in the

    (A) hypothalamus.   (B) medulla.

    (C) spinal cord.   (D) pons.

    (E) ventricle.

79. The part of the brain which coordinates muscle movements on the two sides
    of the body is the

    (A) thalamus.   (B) hypothalamus.

    (C) medulla.   (D) cerebellum.

    (E) pons.

80. Which of the following acts as a relay station for information coming from the
    mid and hindbrains and going to the cortex?

    (A) parietal lobe   (B) spinal cord

    (C) pons   (D) cerebellum

    (E) thalamus

81. All of the following are cells of the retina except

    (A) ganglion cells.   (B) bipolar cells.

    (C) rod and cone cells.   (D) granule cells.

    (E) amacrine cells.

82. How many stages are there in the general-adaptation syndrome?

    (A) 1   (B) 2

    (C) 3   (D) 4

    (E) 5

83. The Skinner box is used for studies of

    (A) chaining behavior.   (B) forward conditioning.

    (C) classical conditioning.   (D) operant conditioning.

    (E) second-order conditioning.

84. Perhaps the oldest systematic theory of human development was developed by Sigmund Freud. It assumes that development is made up of which of the following components?

    (A) instinctive, psychosexual, maturative

    (B) sensorimotor, preoperational, concrete operational

    (C) compensation, reversibility, identity

    (D) dynamic, sequential, structural

    (E) enactive, iconic, symbolic

QUESTIONS 85-86 refer to the passage below.

In a study, subjects watched a person in an unpleasant situation. The person was hooked up to an array of electrical apparati. Upon hearing a buzzer, the person feigned pain which the subjects watched. The physiological responses of the subjects witnessing this behavior were recorded. After the subjects watched the person "suffer" a few times, the subjects demonstrated an increased emotional response when the buzzer sounded.

85. The study shows the effects of

    (A) vicarious conditioning.   (B) operant conditioning.

    (C) conditioned empathy.   (D) perceptual conditioning.

    (E) none of the above

86. This study presents the modeling theory of _____ disorders.

    (A) anxiety   (B) phobic

    (C) depressive   (D) affective

    (E) compulsive

87. Which of the following choices identifies the synaptic boutons which contain neurotransmitters?

    (A) 1   (B) 2

    (C) 3   (D) 4

    (E) 5

88. Which of the following choices identifies the dendrites, neural fibers that receive electrical impulses?

    (A) 1   (B) 2

    (C) 3   (D) 4

    (E) 5

89. The phenomenon of backward masking provides evidence for

    (A) long-term memory.   (B) short-term memory.

    (C) latent inhibition.   (D) information processing.

    (E) iconic coding.

90. Material in long-term memory

    (A) may be lost if the person is interrupted while retrieving it.

    (B) is hypothesized to involve ongoing electrical processes in the brain rather than changes in the brain cells.

    (C) includes all memory that is not currently active.

    (D) may include information that never passed through short-term memory.

    (E) both (A) and (C)

91. Which of the following chemicals is responsible for the transmission of an impulse between neurons?

    (A) actomyosin   (B) acetylcholine

    (C) acetylcholinesterase (D) luteinizing hormone

    (E) (A) and (C)

92. Which of the following are not innervated by the autonomic nervous system?

    (A) leg muscles   (B) pupillary muscles

    (C) adrenal glands   (D) pituitary glands

    (E) heart muscles

93. Intelligence tests measure

    (A) innate ability.   (B) performance.

    (C) educational level.   (D) (A) and (B)

    (E) (A) and (C)

94. Which of the following is not a projective test?

    (A) TAT   (B) DAP

    (C) Rorschach   (D) Rosenweig P-F

    (E) WAIS

95. Which of the following theorists stressed the "proprium" or conscious ego functions as being most influential in behavior?

    (A) Allport   (B) Horney

    (C) Adler   (D) Rogers

    (E) Jung

96. Second-order conditioning is an important phenomenon because it demonstrates how an originally neutral CS can assume properties of

    (A) first-order conditioning.   (B) instrumental stimuli.

    (C) a reinforcer.   (D) a positive reward.

    (E) a negative reward.

97. In 1915, Cannon and Bard sharply criticized the James-Lange theory on emotion by showing that

    (A) there were not different physiological patterns for different emotions.

    (B) there were different physiological patterns for different emotions.

    (C) the hypothalamus was not the "seat of emotions."

    (D) we experience the emotion after perceiving the physiological change.

    (E) both (A) and (C)

98.   The vibrations of the eardrum are transmitted to the inner ear by the

    (A)   cochlea.   (B)   malleus, incus, and stapes.

    (C)   basilar membrane.   (D)   hair cells.

    (E)   all of the above

99.   A significant correlation means that

    (A)   a high correlation is more likely to exist between significant variables.

    (B)   the likelihood of getting a correlation that large is very probable.

    (C)   a relationship is likely to exist between two variables in the general population.

    (D)   none of the above   (E)   (A) and (C)

100. Graphically presented material in which a bar represents the number of cases in an interval of measurement is a (an)

    (A)   polygon.   (B)   histogram.

    (C)   cumulative frequency.   (D)   interval.

    (E)   standard norm.

ADVANCED PLACEMENT
PSYCHOLOGY TEST 2
SECTION II

TIME: 50 Minutes
             2 Essays

DIRECTIONS: In this portion of the test, you will write on both essay questions. We suggest you allow slightly under 25 minutes per essay. Read the question carefully, and then write a response in essay form.

Essay 1:   Outline and explain some of the variables that increase or decrease conformity.

Essay 2:   Contrast Jungian and Freudian theories. Particularly discuss their different versions of the unconscious mind.

TEST 2

ANSWER KEY

1.	(B)	26.	(C)	51.	(A)	76.	(B)
2.	(D)	27.	(D)	52.	(D)	77.	(A)
3.	(E)	28.	(C)	53.	(B)	78.	(B)
4.	(B)	29.	(B)	54.	(B)	79.	(E)
5.	(C)	30.	(A)	55.	(B)	80.	(E)
6.	(D)	31.	(A)	56.	(B)	81.	(D)
7.	(E)	32.	(C)	57.	(C)	82.	(C)
8.	(D)	33.	(A)	58.	(B)	83.	(D)
9.	(A)	34.	(B)	59.	(B)	84.	(D)
10.	(D)	35.	(E)	60.	(A)	85.	(A)
11.	(B)	36.	(D)	61.	(B)	86.	(B)
12.	(B)	37.	(C)	62.	(B)	87.	(D)
13.	(E)	38.	(C)	63.	(D)	88.	(A)
14.	(B)	39.	(A)	64.	(E)	89.	(E)
15.	(A)	40.	(D)	65.	(E)	90.	(C)
16.	(D)	41.	(E)	66.	(B)	91.	(B)
17.	(E)	42.	(C)	67.	(B)	92.	(A)
18.	(E)	43.	(D)	68.	(A)	93.	(B)
19.	(D)	44.	(B)	69.	(E)	94.	(E)
20.	(D)	45.	(C)	70.	(D)	95.	(A)
21.	(D)	46.	(C)	71.	(C)	96.	(C)
22.	(B)	47.	(D)	72.	(D)	97.	(A)
23.	(E)	48.	(D)	73.	(D)	98.	(B)
24.	(D)	49.	(E)	74.	(C)	99.	(C)
25.	(B)	50.	(A)	75.	(D)	100.	(B)

DETAILED EXPLANATIONS
OF ANSWERS

AP PSYCHOLOGY TEST 2
SECTION I

1.   **(B)**   According to Carl Rogers, the organism and the self are the two constructs of personality. The organism is conceived to be the locus of experience; experience includes everything available to awareness and all that occurs within the organism. The self or self-concept refers to the organized and consistent set of perceptions that are self-referential, i.e., that refer to "I" or "me." These two constructs interact to form the personality.

2.   **(D)**   Erikson determined that there were eight developmental crises in our lives that corresponded to the eight developmental periods. These crises in their developmental order are: (1) trust vs. mistrust, (2) autonomy vs. doubt and shame, (3) initiative vs. guilt, (4) industry vs. inferiority, (5) identity crisis, (6) intimacy vs. isolation, (7) crisis of child rearing, and (8) integrity vs. despair in old age.

3.   **(E)**   The issue of control in field research is problematic. Control is not an advantage of field studies because there isn't appropriate control involved in these types of studies. Control is a tradeoff for the other advantages in field research.

4.   **(B)**   A cross-sectional study is one in which different subjects at different developmental levels are compared. For example, a researcher could examine language development by comparing the linguistic ability of different groups of children at different stages of development.

5.   **(C)**   In psychoanalysis, the material of the unconscious mind needs to be brought into the conscious mind so that it no longer serves as a source of anxiety and confusion for the patient. By bringing the unconscious motivations into consciousness, the analyst seeks to reconstruct the patient's personality, to enable him to deal more effectively in relationships.

6.   **(D)**   The sample arranged in order is 26, 29, 31, 34, 34, 37. The number of observations is even and thus the median, or middle number, is chosen halfway between the third and fourth number. In this case the median is

$$\frac{31 + 34}{2} = 32.5$$

7. **(E)**   The range is a measure of dispersion of the sample and is defined to be the difference between the largest and smallest observations. In this example, the largest observation is 53 and the smallest is 33. The difference is $53 - 33 = 20$ and the range is 20.

8. **(D)**   An ogive is an S-shaped curve.

9. **(A)**   A rectangular distribution is one in which each score occurs with the same frequency.

10. **(D)**   Social reinforcement occurs when the reinforcer consists of feedback from individuals in one's environment. Approval from a boss is clearly an example of positive social reinforcement. Other examples of positive social reinforcement would be attention and affection, while examples of negative social reinforcement would be indifference or enmity.

11. **(B)**   Neurons are the basic structural and functional units of the nervous system. There are many types, each having a specific function. Despite their diversity, there are certain characteristics common to all neurons. They all conduct impulses and consist of a cell body, an axon and dendrites. They are different from all other types of cells in the body in that they cannot reproduce.

12. **(B)**   Carl Rogers' theory of human motivation is based on the assumption that the organism is a purely monistic dynamic system. This means that there is one universal, all encompassing drive. According to Rogers, the one drive is the desire to "actualize, maintain, and enhance the experiencing organism." The basic tendency is to grow and expand oneself. To actualize means to have a person's real self, or essence, emerge and replace any false aspects of his personality.

13. **(E)**   The spinal cord has two major functions. It acts as a messenger, relaying information from the body to the brain and back to the body. It also directs simple reflex actions without input from the brain.

14. **(B)**   The iconic mode is the second stage in Bruner's theory of cognitive development. In this stage, knowledge of the world is based heavily on images which stand for perceptual events. A picture, for example, may stand for an actual event. While the emphasis is usually on visual images, other sensory images are possible.

15. **(A)**   Ewald Hering (1878), a German physiologist, proposed that there were three different receptor types, each composed of a pair of opponent processes. He thought there was a white-black receptor, a red-green receptor, and a blue-yellow receptor. If one member of the opponent pairs was stimulated more than the other, that color was seen. If red was stimulated more than green, red was the color observed.

16.   **(D)**   The hypothalamus, located under the thalamus, is a collection of nuclei concerned with homeostatic regulations. Electrical stimulation of certain cells in the hypothalamus produces sensations of hunger, thirst, pain, pleasure, or sexual drives. These are all important emotional and physiological motivators of behavior.

17.   **(E)**   Several factors influence the sensitivity of the eye to light. The eyes are affected by the nature of light, which itself is a function of wavelength, intensity, and composition. The eye's state of adaptation varies with the surrounding stimuli and is subject to great variability. The region of the retina is directly associated with light sensitivity because it contains the rod and cone photoreceptor cells. The iris regulates the amount of light entering through the pupil.

18.   **(E)**   Construct validity is concerned with the degree to which a test measures a theoretical construct or an underlying trait. It also raises the question of what a test score reveals about an individual; will the test score help the examiner to understand the examinee by providing meaningful information about the individual's personality or intellectual characteristics? Meaningful information is essential to construct validity.

19.   **(D)**   Based on the description of the way these children understood the game rules, one could determine that they are in the concrete operational stage of development. This stage emphasizes concrete understanding of rules, and logical thinking as it relates to real concrete objects. Abstract and hypothetical thinking are largely undeveloped.

20.   **(D)**   The concrete operational stage lasts from ages seven to 11 years. This is the usual age span, but it may be shorter or longer in an individual child.

21.   **(D)**   Noam Chomsky believes that children are born with a certain "something," a certain genetic predisposition that enables them to learn grammar. Chomsky called this predisposition the Language Acquisition Device (LAD). It is believed to exist at birth. Chomsky used this concept to explain the relative ease with which normal children learn grammar.

22.   **(B)**   The retina sends visual information it receives from the environment to the brain through various nerve fibers. These fibers are known collectively as the optic nerve. There is a right and left optic nerve, one from each eye. These join in a region called the optic chiasm. At this point, half of the fibers of each optic nerve cross over to the opposite side of the brain. This is what we mean when we say our visual system is 50% crossed.

23. **(E)**   The paranoid schizophrenic is characterized by the presence of numerous and systematized delusions, usually of persecution or grandeur. They may sometimes have the delusion of being controlled by an alien force. Auditory and visual hallucinations may accompany the delusions. Generally, paranoid schizophrenics are more alert and verbal than other schizophrenics. They tend to intellectualize, building up an organized set of beliefs based on the wrong (paranoid) assumptions.

24. **(D)**   A history of suicide attempts is not characteristic of Antisocial Personality Disorder. A person with this disorder displays a pervasive pattern of disregarding social norms and violating the rights of others. This pattern needs to have been present since age 15 to be diagnosed.

25. **(B)**   Iconic coding represents a fleeting, visual experience that is of great importance in the study of information processing. In the visual realm, the iconic image is that which occurs during a single glance. Usually lasting about ⅟₁₅ of a second, iconic storage consists of a series of successive glances each representing a small section of a larger object.

26. **(C)**   The Theory of Selective Attention was proposed by Broadbent. Broadbent's approach also became known as the filter theory, because it generally hypothesized that certain sensory inputs are rejected, while others are "allowed in" for further processing. According to the theory, information passes through a selective filter which attends only to the important aspects of stimuli. This filtered information then passes through channels into a limited-capacity short-term memory bank where it is retained by the processing system.

27. **(D)**   Generally, the items that are forgotten are those in the middle of the list. This is because what is learned first usually interferes with what comes later (productive interference) and what is learned later usually interferes with what came earlier (retroactive interference). Thus, the items in the middle are most susceptible to being forgotten because they are subject to both kinds of interference.

28. **(C)**   Template-matching theories purport that each pattern is recognized by noting its similarity with a basic, internal model. It is considered a problematic theory due to its rigidity. For example, people recognize an "R" even if it is upside down, very small, or huge. The template theory would have to be expanded to include a new template for every possible size and orientation of the letter, to provide a viable explanation of the capabilities of the human, pattern-recognition system.

29. **(B)**   Correlational analysis measures the degree of linear association between two characteristics, X and Y. Correlation should not be confused with causation. Correlation is a mathematical technique for showing whether elements in two sets of data are linearly related to each other, while causality implies that one of the variables has a causal effect on the other.

30.   **(A)**   Spinal nerves belong to the peripheral nervous system (PNS). They arise as pairs at regular intervals from the spinal cord, branch, and run to various parts of the body to innervate them. In humans, there are 31 symmetrical pairs of spinal nerves.

31.   **(A)**   A person suffering from nerve deafness will have more difficulty hearing high pitched tones. This type of deafness results from damage to the auditory nervous system. Hair cells in the cochlea translate sound vibrations into electrical messages our brain can "understand." Specific hair cells respond to specific tones. If some are damaged, the vibrations of certain tones will not be properly translated into electrical messages.

32.   **(C)**   Maslow is a chief proponent of the humanist school of human behavior. His most popular theory concerns the hierarchical nature of man's motivational structure. He set forth a five-stage model in which the lower, most dominant needs control man's motivation until they are satisfied. The next needs then come into play. Maslow's theory, though popular and innovative, lacks empirical support. In this respect it is similar to other humanistic theories of behavior.

33.   **(A)**   A null hypothesis is analyzed in terms of its acceptance or rejection rather than in terms of its proof or disproof. The null hypothesis cannot be proved anymore than disproved because there always exists the possibility of Type I or Type II errors. A null hypothesis can only be accepted or rejected according to the level of significance of the results. A significant result means only that the difference obtained probably did not occur by chance.

34.   **(B)**   Concepts are symbols of connections between two or more objects, events, or ideas. They allow the mind to distinguish relations among objects and events. When multiple stimuli are considered simultaneously, a concept is complex. Conjunctive, disjunctive, and relational concepts all constitute complex concepts. Conjunctive concepts exist when the objects possess two or more common properties. Disjunctive concepts are based on entities in which only one property, or a combination of properties is necessary to fulfill the concept. Comparisons between two properties express a relational concept.

35.   **(E)**   The inclusion of encoding, memory, evaluation, deduction, and mediation indicate that the component process theory is based on work in information processing. Each of these areas is of interest to the psychologist studying information processing. The component process theory is an interesting assimilation of these concepts.

36.   **(D)**   This theory assumes that the knowledge and ability of the child to perform problem solving tasks will appear in the child's performance on objective indexes that test problem solving. This question taps into the debate of competence versus performance that is of concern to many areas of psychology.

37.   **(C)**   You will notice in the reading of the passage that there is no mention of the emotional effects and experience of the child on its cognitive development. This theory is limited to looking at the progressive problem-solving ability in the child. It does not examine the emotional or psychosocial development of the child.

38.   **(C)**   Although they are separate symptoms, obsession and compulsion often occur together as a neurotic reaction pattern. Obsessions are persistent, often unreasonable thoughts which cannot be banished. A person may become so obsessed with an idea that he will count stoplights, and cracks in the pavement, or will swear inappropriately or even commit murder as a defense mechanism against it. A compulsion is a persistent act which is committed over and over again. Virtually any behavior may be viewed as a compulsion if the individual reports an irresistible urge to perform the behavior. Obsessive-compulsive behavior prevents a person from thinking anxiety-provoking thoughts.

39.   **(A)**   The ego is the intermediary between the id and reality. It develops between the ages of eight months and 18 months, as the child acquires an understanding of what is possible in the outer world. The ego also distinguishes between long-range and short-range goals and decides which activities will be most profitable to the individual. The id and ego work together to determine the individual's goals.

40.   **(D)**   Substance dependence is one of the most pervasive and expensive disorders. Technically, caffeine is the only substance listed in the DSM IV that cannot lead to a diagnosis of substance dependence. A diagnosis of substance dependence requires obtaining a detailed history from the individual and, whenever possible, from additional sources.

41.   **(E)**   All of these are characteristics of affiliation. Schachter had two conditions in his experiment: High versus Low fear, in which he warned subjects that they were going to receive a shock that was either extremely painful or just a tickle. After announcing a 10-minute delay before the shocks, he gave subjects a questionnaire that indicated their desire to affiliate. High-fear subjects wanted to affiliate much more than the Low-fear subjects. He also found that first-born children affiliate more when fearful and that "misery only loves misery's company," that is, fearful subjects prefer to affiliate with others in the same situation.

42.   **(C)**   The Thematic Apperception Test was designed by Murray and Morgan in 1935, to determine the major themes of concern for a particular individual by allowing him to respond freely to the vague and ambiguous pictures presented on TAT cards. Theoretically, the themes expressed in the responses reflect the subject's present motivational, emotional, and conflicted condition.

43. **(D)**   A cross-sectional study is one in which different subjects at different developmental levels are compared. Instead of using a longitudinal approach, for example, a researcher could investigate language development with children of different developmental levels. The obvious advantage of a cross-sectional study over a longitudinal study is that it is much less time consuming. It is also less expensive.

44. **(B)**   Karen Horney, an analyst who broke from classical psychoanalysis, developed a theory concerning the neurotic needs of the individual. She identified 10 neurotic needs which fall under three general categories: 1) moving toward people, 2) moving away from people, 3) moving against people. She thought most people achieve an integration and balance of these forces, but the neurotic individual lacks this balance and integration.

45. **(C)**   Extinction of conditioned respondent behavior occurs when the CS is presented without the UCS a number of times. The magnitude of the response elicited by the CS and the percentage of presentations of the CS which elicits responses, gradually decreases as the CS continues to be presented without the UCS. If CS presentation continues without the UCS, the CR will decline to at least the level present before the classical conditioning was begun.

46. **(C)**   Milgram designed an experiment where a subject (the teacher) would give electric shocks to another human (the learner) whenever the learner gave the wrong answer on a word association task. Each shock was stronger than the one before. Although the shock apparatus was labelled "WARNING–INTENSE SHOCK," and the learner begged the teacher to stop, 63% of the subjects continued the experiment because the researcher told them that he would take full responsibility for the results.

47. **(D)**   The concept of instinctive human motivation was based on Darwin's evolutionary theory, which stressed the survival value of instinctive animal behaviors. Since Darwin claimed that humans were descendants of lower animals, psychologists such as McDougall and James used Darwin's theory in their studies on human motivation. Eventually the concept of instinct was abandoned and in its place came the concept of drive as the motivational force.

48. **(D)**   An EPSP is an excitatory postsynaptic potential, and refers to changes in a nerve cell's charge relative to the environment. An EPSP occurs when stimulation makes the nerve cell less negative, as would occur if the cell membrane now begins to allow positive charges to pass through. It is considered excitatory because if it is large enough, it may cause the nerve cell to become sufficiently positive in order to fire.

49. **(E)** The pituitary gland produces TSH, ACTH, FSH, and LH. TSH induces secretion of another hormone in the thyroid gland. ACTH stimulates the adrenal cortex to secrete cortisol. Both LH and FSH control the secretion of the sex hormones by the gonads. They also regulate the growth and development of sperm and ovum. Hence, the pituitary is in a sense a master gland that directs the hormone secretions to other glands and organs.

50. **(A)** Problems with more than one correct solution require divergent thinking. Divergent thinking produces several different solutions for a problem. This type of thinking requires flexibility, fluency of ideas, and originality. Divergent thinking is believed to be the basis for creativity.

51. **(A)** The normal distribution is the most important distribution in statistics. As the number of scores in a frequency distribution grows, the curve will approach the shape of the normal distribution curve. It is also important to note that every population which is normally distributed may be characterized by two population parameters: the mean and the variance.

52. **(D)** In Freud's system, three levels of consciousness were distinguished: the conscious, the preconscious, and the unconscious. In terms of this question, the preconscious is midway between the conscious and the unconscious. The preconscious contains memories and drives that can easily be recalled but are not within consciousness at the moment.

53. **(B)** Conditioned behavior can later reappear without additional conditioning, even though extinction had appeared to be successful. This is known as spontaneous recovery. If a rest interval follows the extinction of a CR, it will reappear spontaneously but in a weaker form. Then if conditioning is done again, using the same stimuli, the original response will be strengthened quickly.

54. **(B)** The pleasure principle might be translated as "if it feels good, do it." This principle is what guides the id to seek gratification of its desires and to avoid unpleasurable stimuli leading to pain. The id is basically an instinctive pleasure seeker.

55. **(B)** Based on the reading of the graph in the diagram, low-anxiety students have higher grade point averages and higher levels of scholastic aptitude than high-anxiety students. Notice the performance jump from level 1 to level 2 of scholastic aptitude. Usually, the more anxious a person is, the lower his performance level on a verbal learning task.

56. **(B)** Examples of unconditioned responses are salivation to food and adrenal gland responses to fear stimuli.

57.   **(C)**   Social learning theory, first described by Miller and Dollard, is an attempt to combine the principles of social analysis of behavior with principles of learning taken from the behavior scientist's animal laboratory. In this respect, Miller and Dollard took important steps in integrating these two previously separate areas of inquiry in psychology. Based on this theory, Bandura and Walters created another social learning theory that emphasized the role of "modeling" in the acquisition of behavior.

58.   **(B)**   Carl Rogers places special emphasis on the need for positive regard and the need for self-regard. He considers both to be learned needs. Positive regard refers to the positive assessment an individual receives from other people. The need for self-regard is established as a result of receiving positive regard from others.

59.   **(B)**   Allport stated that there are two components of behavior, adaptive and expressive. The adaptive component refers to the function of the act and the expressive component accounts for the individuality of an act. Allport was especially interested in the individual and the study of expressive behavior. Allport believed in a general unity underlying personality, and, therefore, he maintained that studying an individual's expressive behavior would lead to an understanding of the central aspects of his personality.

60.   **(A)**   Rods are more sensitive to light than cones, and thus will respond to very dim lights to which cones cannot respond. Due to this sensitivity, rods function mainly in night vision. They also produce only black and white images. This explains why, though we usually can see everything in a dark room, little appears in color.

61.   **(B)**   Implosive therapy is an effective technique in reducing the adversiveness of stimuli. Once the client understands the procedure, the therapist begins to describe scenes he knows will produce strong negative emotions. The idea is to emotionally "flood" the person by describing the stimuli vividly. The client is not permitted to avoid the imagined disturbing scene; he must withstand the repeated exposure if the therapist is to extinguish the associated emotional response. Therapy is concluded when the adversive images no longer produce negative emotional responses in the client.

62.   **(B)**   The opponent-process theory stated that there are only two kinds of receptors in the eye. Each receptor was thought to represent a pair of colors — one red-green, and one yellow-blue. The receptors were thought to respond to these colors in an "opponent" fashion. This means that they would be excited in response to one of the colors, and inhibited in response to the other color.

63.   **(D)**   Freud reasoned that the dream is a hallucinatory state that structures events not as they would be in reality, but as the dreamer wishes them to be. When unconscious desires conflict with conscious restraints, however, it is necessary for the "dream work" to pursue devious paths to express the wish.

64.   **(E)**   A normal distribution has a number of defining characteristics. It is represented by a bell-shaped curve, has one mode, and the mean, mode, and median are equal. This curve is the graphic representation of the normal probability distribution.

65.   **(E)**   In 1904 Alfred Binet was asked by the French government to construct a test that would distinguish between normal children and children with severe learning disabilities. Binet conceived of intelligence as the relationship of mental ability and chronological age. For each age up to 15 years, there is a set of characteristic abilities that develop in the normal child. If they developed earlier than average, the child is more intelligent than average; if the abilities develop later, then the child is considered to be of below average intelligence.

66.   **(B)**   The mean is the value obtained by adding all the measurements and dividing by the number of measurements.

$$\text{mean } (\bar{x}) = \frac{500 + 600 + 800 + 800 + 900 + 900 + 900 + 900 + 900 + 1000 + 1100}{11}$$

$$\bar{x} = \frac{9300}{11} = 845.45$$

The median is the observation in the middle. We have 11, so here it is the sixth, 900. The mode is the observation that appears most frequently. That is also 900, which has five appearances. All three of these numbers are measures of central tendency.

67.   **(B)**   In his studies on the nature of obedience, Stanley Milgram discovered that the average middle-class American male would, under direction of a legitimate authority figure, administer severe shocks to other individuals in an experimental setting. This alarming finding demonstrated the extent to which ordinary people would comply with the orders of a legitimate authority figure, even to the point of harming his fellow man.

68.   **(A)**   The latency stage lasts about five years, from ages six to 11. During this period the child's identification with the parent of his own sex becomes stronger. The child also incorporates more of the beliefs and values of his culture, hence, the superego is developing to a greater degree. The child comes to distinguish between acceptable and unacceptable behavior in his society. During this period children generally seek out more playmates of their own sex.

69.   **(E)**   The Oedipus Complex is to the Electra Complex as boy is to girl. In the Oedipal Complex, the boy wants his mother for himself and wants to be rid of the competing father, but he fears castration from the father. In order to deal with that fear, he represses it and identifies with his father. In the Electra Complex, the girl

desires the father and wants to be rid of the mother, but with time, her devaluation of her mother and her jealousy fade, as she develops the female behaviors of appealing to the father and desiring a baby as a substitute for the penis she is lacking.

70.   **(D)**   Phobic reactions are strong, irrational fears of specific objects or situations. For example, when a person is extremely fearful of birds, snakes, heights or closed places, provided that there is no objective danger, the label phobia is applied to the person's fear and avoidance. A person suffering from a specific phobia knows what he is afraid of and usually recognizes that his fear is irrational but cannot control it.

71.   **(C)**   Systematic desensitization is a behavioral procedure whereby the therapist reinforces a behavior which is in opposition to the behavior the patient wants to eliminate. The behavior reinforced is usually a relaxation response. In this problem, the patient would be asked to relax and continue relaxing as she imagined fearful situations with pigeons. Eventually, the previously anxiety-arousing stimulus is associated with relaxation and the behavior (fear of pigeons) ceases to be maladaptive.

72.   **(D)**   In terms of this example, falling off one's bicycle (UCS) reliably elicits fear and anxiety (UCR). The single pairing of the sight of a dead pigeon (CS), with the act of falling (UCS), created a conditioned response (CR) of fear and anxiety elicited upon seeing pigeons in future situations. The UCS of falling off the bicycle was no longer needed to be present to create the CR of fear and anxiety. Although this theory sounds like a good explanation for the occurrence of phobias, in many cases phobics have never had any early traumatic experiences with the phobic object.

73.   **(D)**   While all the choices list personality theorists, C. Jung proposed the "persona" as a basic personality element. He believed that an individual's persona is one aspect of the collective psyche—it comes into existence to mitigate an individual's realization of being part of the collective mass of humanity.

74.   **(C)**   The Wechsler Intelligence Scale for Children (WISC) would be the most appropriate choice for the majority of 12-year-olds. The WISC is normally administered to children from the ages of 6½ – 16½. There are subscales which measure mathematical ability, vocabulary, problem solving and digit span problems.

75.   **(D)**   The double-blind technique is most often used in drug research. This method ensures that neither the experimenter nor the subject can affect the results; thus, biases are reduced.

76. **(B)** Considerable stress tolerance is not characteristic of a major depressive episode. In fact, severely depressed people generally have a considerable intolerance to stressful situations. A rigid conscience, feelings of guilt, hopelessness, and less energy are all characteristics of a major depressive episode.

77. **(A)** The cerebellum is made up of a central part and two hemispheres extending sideways. The size of the cerebellum in different animals is roughly correlated with the amount of muscular activity. The cerebellum coordinates muscle contraction. Injury to the cerebellum results in the inability to coordinate muscle movements, although the muscles can still move.

78. **(B)** The medulla is connected to the spinal cord and is the most posterior part of the brain. Here the central canal of the spinal cord (spinal lumen) enlarges to form a fluid-filled cavity called the fourth ventricle. The medulla also has numerous nerve tracts which bring impulses to and from the brain.

79. **(E)** The pons is an area of the hindbrain containing a large number of nerve fibers which pass through it and make connections between the two hemispheres of the cerebellum, thus coordinating muscle movements on the two sides of the body. The pons also contains the nerve centers that aid in the regulation of breathing.

80. **(E)** The thalamus, a part of the forebrain located just above the midbrain, functions mainly as a major relay station of the brain. Information from sensory receptors which travels through the spinal cord, or information coming from the forebrain and midbrain usually arrives at the thalamus and is then relayed to the appropriate areas in the cortex.

81. **(D)** Granule cells are in the cerebellum, not in the retina. The retina is composed of three cell layers—a transparent layer of ganglion cells, transparent bipolar cells, and rod and cone receptor cells. The ends of the bipolar cells are interconnected through amacrine cells. The receptor cell layer is located on the side of the retina away from the light. Light must travel through the rest of the retina before reaching the light-sensitive rods and cones.

82. **(C)** There are three stages in the general adaptation syndrome. The first stage is the alarm reaction, which is the initial reaction to stress. This reaction consists of bodily reactions including increased heart rate and blood pressure. The second stage is the stage of resistance. Here the body recovers from the initial stress and attempts to endure. The third stage is exhaustion and the body is no longer able to tolerate any further stress.

83. **(D)** Operant conditioning is a learning process in which the frequency of a specific response is shaped and maintained by the consequences of the response. For the specific demonstration of such a process, Skinner developed an apparatus designed to give a signal (to respond) and a method for delivering the reinforcement. This device is nicknamed the "Skinner box."

84. **(D)** Freud viewed humans as passive organisms whose psychological development is initiated and maintained through "intrapsychic" events, that is, internal events. The dynamic component includes the expression of the basic instincts. The sequential component includes the five psychosexual stages: oral, anal, phallic, latency and genital. The structural component includes the concept of the id, ego and superego. Although abstract and absent of the study of observational behavior, Freud's theory is a major force in developmental psychology.

85. **(A)** This study, done by Bandura and Rosenthal, demonstrated the effects of vicarious conditioning, which is observing a model. In this study, the subjects learned that the buzzer was aversive by watching someone else (model) being "shocked," as the buzzer rang. The subjects learned the aversion to the buzzer so well that they responded physiologically to the buzzer sound.

86. **(B)** The modeling theory of phobic disorders assumes that phobic responses may be learned through the imitation of others. The learning of phobic reactions through modeling is generally referred to as vicarious conditioning. Vicarious conditioning can take place through both observation and verbal instruction. In this study, the phobic reaction conditioned was fear in response to a buzzer, and the conditioning took place through observation.

87. **(D)** Synaptic boutons, also called axonic terminals, is the end tip of the axon. They almost make contact with the dendrites of another neuron. The neurotransmitters produced in the boutons travel across the synaptic cleft to interact with the membrane of the receiving cell, changing the membrane permeability.

88. **(A)** Dendrites are numerous in the neuron. They receive information either from other neurons or directly from the environment, and then divert the electrical impulses (information) toward the cell body of the neuron. Action potentials are not generated along the dendrites.

89. **(E)** In the backward masking procedure, a letter is flashed on a screen. After the letter is flashed, there is a brief period of time during which the impression can be completely erased by the flash of a bright light. This time period is about 5 seconds, but during this time, the image can be read as though the stimulus was still present. This backward masking effect demonstrates that the brief life of memory codes can be easily erased by input that is specific to the given sense modality.

90. **(C)** Long-term memory is complex and possesses a virtually limitless capacity. It is therefore difficult for theorists to study. Long-term memory can be slow and difficult. Past events that relate to a current situation have to be searched for out of billions of stored items. It usually requires effort to put new information into long-term memory. Material that is in long-term memory can be brought into active memory and will not be lost if it is interrupted.

91. **(B)** Nerves of the parasympathetic system secrete a neurotransmitter called acetylcholine. Acetylcholine is the transmitter chemical for synapses between neurons of the peripheral nervous system outside the autonomic system.

92. **(A)** The leg muscles are innervated by the somatic nervous system. The other choices are innervated by the autonomic nervous system. The somatic nervous system includes the sensory nerves that bring all sensory information into the central nervous system, plus the motor nerves that control the activity of the skeletal muscles. The autonomic system directs the activity of smooth and cardiac muscles and of glands.

93. **(B)** All intelligence tests, and psychological tests in general, measure the performance or behavior of the subject. From the measure of performance, we infer the knowledge and ability, as well as predict future performance, of the subject. It is important to consider that factors such as motivation can affect the performance on tests by either enhancing it or deterring it.

94. **(E)** The WAIS is an intellectual test for adults. The other choices are all projective tests that attempt to identify unconscious desires, conflicts, and impulses. The subject "projects" into the stimulus material his needs and attitudes. In all these tests (TAT, DAP, Rorschach, and Rosenweig P-F), it is assumed that when a person's mind is free to wander, it will "fix" on those issues that are important.

95. **(A)** Allport claimed that in order to understand an individual, it is necessary to know what his conscious intentions are; he stressed ego functioning, also called the proprium, as being the most influential in behavior. Allport focuses on the current thoughts and goals of the individual. He regarded the past as insignificant in the assessment of an individual's behavior.

96. **(C)** Second-order conditioning is based on secondary reinforcement. In second-order conditioning, a neutral stimulus is paired with the conditioned stimulus, after that conditioned stimulus can reliably elicit the conditioned response. When this is accomplished, the new or second-conditioned stimulus will elicit the conditioned response even though it was never paired directly with the unconditioned stimulus.

97. **(A)** The James-Lange theory proposed that we first experience a specific, psychological state in reaction to some stimulus and then perceive an emotion on this state. For example, we see a huge bear running towards us, we run and then we feel afraid, because we see that we are running. Cannon and Bard compiled evidence that showed that there are not specific, physiological patterns for different emotions. They proposed that we see the bear, we experience fear, and then we run. They thought it was stimulus stimulation of the hypothalamus that created the emotion.

98. **(B)** Otherwise known as the hammer, anvil, and stirrup, these three bones (ossicles) of the middle ear are responsible for transmitting the vibrations of the eardrum to the inner ear, where they are transformed into nerve signals. These nerve signals are sent to the brain and are interpreted as sound.

99. **(C)** A significant correlation whether positive or negative, describes the relationship between two variables in such a way that change in one is associated with change in the other. A positive correlation indicates that the two variables change in the same direction. A negative correlation indicates that the two variables change in opposite directions.

100. **(B)** A histogram is a graphic representation of a frequency distribution in which the cases falling in each score category are represented by a bar whose size is proportional to the number of cases. Since each bar is the full width of the score category, the bars make a continuous "pile" showing the form of the frequency distribution.

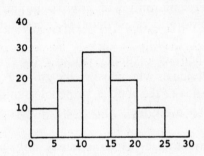

SECTION II

Here are examples of good essay answers:

Essay 1:   One of the factors which is causal in controlling conformity is whether or not the opinion of the majority is unanimous. If the subject is presented with one ally, his probability of conforming to the majority is sharply curtailed. In situations where the confederate "subjects" are unanimous in their judgments, there need not be a large number to elicit conformity from the actual subjects. As few as three other people can elicit conformity from a subject and the amount of this conformity remains consistently the same up to 16 other people. A method which is frequently used to decrease conformity is having the subject make some form of commitment to his initial judgment. Psychologists testing this have found that conformity with prior commitment drops to about 6% from a 25% conformity rate without prior commitment.

Another factor which is causal in the amount of conformity is the kind of individuals who make up the group. A group which consists of experts, friends of the subject, or people similar to the subject (i.e., other students) is most likely to increase subject conformity.

The final factor which is causal in the amount of conformity exhibited by subjects is the self-esteem of the subjects themselves. As might be expected, individuals with low self-esteem are much more likely to conform in a given situation than individuals with high self-esteem in the same situation.

Essay 2:   Due partly to his published acknowledgment that Freud's ideas had been useful in his own clinical work, early in his career Carl Jung became Freud's handpicked successor. Jung had especially found the concept of the unconscious valuable in his experimental work. At first Jung agreed with Freud as to what was to be found in the unconscious mental processes of his subjects — repressed, unacceptable infantile sexual and aggressive strivings.

As Jung continued his explorations of the unconscious, he found it more and more difficult to accept that sexual motives were the chief motivator of human behavior. Freud's principal concept that a pleasure drive rooted in an individual's childhood sexual experience was the base of all behavior caused Jung great consternation. Jung felt that the concept of sexuality should be reserved for extreme forms of libido only and that the more generalized expressions of what Freud called libido or sexual drive should be considered in a different framework for better understanding.

The more Jung worked, the more he opposed this point in Freud's conceptual analysis. As his powers of personal perception increased and his professional judgment matured, he discovered forces and content within the unconscious quite unlike anything Freud had ever referred to. Jung's reference point moved from the personal conflict over unacceptable sexual and aggressive motives to transpersonal, universal symbols of the human race's life experiences that transcend the individual's immediate concerns.

Other differences in the two theorists include: (1) Freud viewed libido as the basis of the pleasure principle in humans, Jung observed this energy as one that was able to communicate itself to any field of activity — power, hunger, hatred, religion, or sexuality — without ever being a specific instinct; (2) Freud saw throughout human behavior the dynamics of search for pleasure be it through food, drink or sex, while Jung saw only a "will to live" that through the individual sought to preserve the entire species; (3) Freud found in his patients a damaged reality, Jung discovered instead that life energy had been channeled into a myth-making or fantasy creative process; and finally (4) Freud anchored his ideas in biology — the workings of the body and the mind, but Jung found the roots for his observations in the spirit of his subjects.

ADVANCED PLACEMENT EXAMINATION IN
PSYCHOLOGY

Test 3

ADVANCED PLACEMENT
PSYCHOLOGY TEST 3
SECTION I

TIME: 70 Minutes
100 Questions

DIRECTIONS: Choose the best answer for each question and mark the letter of your selection on the corresponding answer sheet.

---

1. The manifest content of dreams refers to the

    (A) symbolic content.

    (B) actual meaning of the dream.

    (C) literal content as experienced by the dreamer.

    (D) psychoanalytic interpretations of content.

    (E) sexual content.

2. The thalamus serves which of the following functions?

    (A) relay center for sensory impulses

    (B) relay center from spinal cord to cerebrum

    (C) regulates external expression of emotion

    (D) all of the above

    (E) none of the above

3. Which of the following effects does adrenalin have on the human body?

    (A) constriction of the pupils   (B) increased rate of digestion

    (C) accelerated heartbeat   (D) increased hormone production

    (E) decreased hormone production

4. Which of the following plays an important role in the regulation of respiration?

   (A) pons   (B) hypothalamus

   (C) thalamus   (D) forebrain

   (E) midbrain

5. Which of the following constitute monocular depth cues?

   (A) relative size   (B) linear perspective

   (C) interposition   (D) all of the above

   (E) none of the above

6. Responses on the Rorschach Inkblot Test are evaluated in terms of

   (A) locations.   (B) determinants.

   (C) content.   (D) all of the above

   (E) none of the above

7. The first stage of ego development is considered to be

   (A) id, ego, superego conflicts.

   (B) primary identification with the mother.

   (C) autonomous ego functions.

   (D) ego introjects.

   (E) ego boundary settings.

8. Distributions with extreme values at one end are said to be

   (A) positively skewed.   (B) negatively skewed.

   (C) skewed.   (D) histograms.

   (E) measures of noncentral tendency.

9. Which of the following is not a symptom type of melancholic features of depression?

   (A) increased appetite or weight gain   (B) loss of pleasure in all or almost all activities

   (C) early morning awakening   (D) excessive or inappropriate guilt

   (E) depression regularly worse in the morning

10. According to Adler's theory of personality, the Oedipus Complex involves

    (A) strivings to escape the father.

    (B) strivings to become superior to the father.

    (C) strivings to become superior to the mother.

    (D) mainly a sexual phenomenon.

    (E) an expression of latent sexuality.

11. The "conscience" is the part of the superego that

    (A) mediates with the id.   (B) punishes.

    (C) gratifies.   (D) controls the ego.

    (E) contains the sexual urges.

12. Which of the following represents a measure and method of analyzing perceptual thresholds?

    (A) Method of Limits   (B) Method of Average Error

    (C) frequency method   (D) all of the above

    (E) none of the above

13. Anima, according to Jung, is

    (A) a male's unconscious feminine characteristics.

    (B) the developmental phase of midlife.

    (C) the dark side of the personal unconscious.

    (D) a female's unconscious male characteristics.

    (E) the developmental phase of late life.

14. In the technique of shaping behavior, which form of reinforcement is used?

    (A) differential reinforcement (B) positive reinforcement

    (C) neutral acknowledgment   (D) negative reinforcement

    (E) punishment procedures

15. Freud developed the concept of Eros, which is the

    (A) death instinct.

    (B) life instinct.

    (C) third developmental stage.

    (D) sex instinct.   (E) regressive potential.

16. The Milgram experiments on social power figures indicate that

    (A) the use of reward and punishment increases compliance.

    (B) pressure from an authority figure in the situation increases compliance.

    (C) social pressure increases compliance.

    (D) justification increases compliance.

    (E) lack of justification increases compliance.

17. Any procedural variable which can cause a subset of the population to be nonrepresentative of the population is a

    (A) sample error.   (B) sample bias.

    (C) population error.   (D) sample shift.

    (E) population bias.

18. Psychologists and educators have come to realize that creativity and intelligence are

    (A) synonymous.   (B) not synonymous.

    (C) negatively correlated. (D) appear as bimodal functions.

    (E) both measured by I.Q. tests.

19. In Karen Horney's psychoanalytic theory, the fundamental concept is

    (A) basic anxiety.   (B) need to love.

    (C) self-actualization.   (D) need to be loved.

    (E) libidinal instincts.

20. According to Piaget, a child capable of hypothetical thinking is in which developmental stage?

    (A) sensorimotor stage   (B) preoperational stage

    (C) intuitive preoperational stage

    (D) concrete operations stage

    (E) formal operations stage

21. According to Piaget's theory of cognitive development, middle childhood is characterized by

    (A) hypothetical reasoning.   (B) deductive thinking.

    (C) concrete operations.   (D) egocentric thinking.

    (E) INRC binary grouping.

22. The California Psychological Inventory differs from the Minnesota Multiphasic Personality Inventory in that it is used

    (A) on more clinically-deviant groups.

    (B) with children.

    (C) with adolescents.

    (D) on less clinically-deviant groups.

    (E) none of the above

23. Of the following, which is not true of self-report personality measures?

    (A) Subjects rate simple behavioral statements as true or false.

    (B) The test measures usually have extensive norms.

    (C) Subjects are given little freedom in responding.

    (D) Most of the measures provide accurate behavioral prediction.

    (E) The Q-sort is a common technique.

24. Given a sample of data that is homogeneous, you can expect the standard deviation to be

    (A) large.   (B) small.

    (C) above 0.05.   (D) small if the sample size is small.

    (E) large if the sample size is large.

25. The Rorschach and TAT tests are types of _____ tests.

    (A) aptitude   (B) projective

    (C) sociogram   (D) developmental

    (E) objective

26. Word association tests and sentence completion tests are examples of

    (A) verbal techniques.   (B) objective tests.

    (C) subjective tests.   (D) projective techniques.

    (E) verbal projective tests.

27. Ninety-eight percent of the people who take a standardized intelligence test have scores which fall between

    (A) 85 – 115.   (B) 55 – 145.

    (C) 70 – 130.   (D) 100 – 150.

    (E) none of the above

28. Another name for the successive method of approximation is

    (A) reinforcement.   (B) shaping.

    (C) fixed reinforcement.   (D) chaining.

    (E) operant conditioning.

29. Hermann Ebbinghaus is best known for his historical work in

    (A) neuroanatomy.

    (B) sensory processes.

    (C) visual perception of patterns.

    (D) learning and memory performance.

    (E) visical attention processes.

30. Identify the diagnostic category which is not appropriately grouped with the others.

    (A) obsessive-compulsive disorder

    (B) social phobia

    (C) posttraumatic stress disorder

    (D) conversion disorder   (E) panic disorder

31. The Rotter Incomplete Sentence Blank is a (an)

    (A) objective testing technique.

    (B) intelligence test.

    (C) internality/externality assessment scale.

    (D) projective test.   (E) literary competence exam.

32. According to psychoanalytic thinking, the personality structure consists of

    (A) habits.   (B) drives.

    (C) self.   (D) id, ego, and superego.

    (E) consciousness.

33. The sympathetic and parasympathic nervous systems constitute the

    (A) autonomic nervous system.

    (B) central nervous system.

    (C) peripheral nervous system.

    (D) somatic nervous system.

    (E) antagonistic nervous system.

34. The "white matter" of the central nervous system is actually

    (A) nerve fiber pathways.   (B) cell bodies.

    (C) cell centers.   (D) cortical tissue.

    (E) cerebral tissue.

35. Which of the following is present in the synaptic vesicles?

    (A) action potential   (B) neurotransmitters

    (C) Na^+ (D) synaptic inhibitors

    (E) K^+

36. Which of the following has direct control over the function of the pituitary gland?

    (A) pons   (B) cerebral cortex

    (C) hypothalamus   (D) midbrain

    (E) cerebellum

37. Which stimulus cue(s) are not involved in depth perception?

    (A) light and shadow   (B) color intensity

    (C) relative position   (D) linear perspective

    (E) texture-density gradient

38. The wavelength of green is

    (A) greater than yellow but less than blue.

    (B) greater than either yellow or blue.

    (C) the same wavelength as yellow.

    (D) greater than blue but less than yellow.

    (E) greater than red.

39. Physical sounds from our environment are translated into electrical messages in the

    (A) spiral geniculate.   (B) trapezoid body.

    (C) cochlea.   (D) spiral ganglion.

    (E) eustachian tube.

40. The proportion of total variation in a population that is due to genetic variation is

    (A) phenotype.   (B) genotype.

    (C) heritability.   (D) absolute heritability.

    (E) relative heritability.

41. Freud pointed out that an important influence upon behavior is

    (A) unconscious dissonance. (B) level of aspiration.

    (C) cognitive dissonance.   (D) unconscious motivation.

    (E) none of the above

42. Echoic memory refers to

    (A) visual perception.   (B) eidetic perception.

    (C) verbal codes.   (D) auditory perception.

    (E) enactive codes.

43. Which of the following reinforcement schedules has the lowest yield of performance?

    (A) fixed-ratio schedule   (B) variable-ratio schedule

    (C) fixed-internal schedule   (D) variable-internal schedule

    (E) systematic-internal schedule

44. During stage 4 sleep, which brain wave pattern predominates?

    (A) beta waves   (B) sleep spindles

    (C) alpha waves   (D) irregular wave patterns

    (E) delta waves

45. Which of the following "needs" did Carl Rogers place special emphasis on?

    (A) need for social support   (B) need for positive regard

    (C) need for self-regard   (D) (A) and (B)

    (E) (B) and (C)

46. Which part of the eye inverts the image of objects?

    (A) fovea   (B) cornea

    (C) lens   (D) retina

    (E) blind spot

47. According to the DSM IV, dissociative identity disorder is a _____ disorder.

    (A) somatoform   (B) conduct

    (C) personality   (D) psychotic

    (E) dissociative

48. According to Erikson's developmental theory, the maturity stage deals with which of the following crises?

    (A) initiative vs. guilt   (B) identity crisis

    (C) autonomy vs. doubt   (D) intimacy vs. isolation

    (E) integrity vs. despair

49. What is the main disadvantage of cross-cultural tests?

   (A) reliability problems

   (B) We compare people of different cultures.

   (C) Predictive and diagnostic values are lost.

   (D) none of the above

   (E) all of the above

50. Which of the following is true of Short-Term Memory (STM)?

   (A) It has a storage capacity of ten items.

   (B) It does not require rehearsals.

   (C) STM is highly susceptible to interference.

   (D) Information always travels from STM to Long-Term Memory.

   (E) It is a permanent record of experience.

51. According to Freud, the main function of dreams is

   (A) release of the ego.   (B) sexual instinct release.

   (C) unconscious urges.   (D) to balance psychic forces.

   (E) wish fulfillment.

52. In psychology, measurement devices must be

   (A) reliable.   (B) valid.

   (C) conclusive.   (D) (A) and (B)

   (E) (B) and (C)

53. Prominent among monocular depth cues is

   (A) accommodation.   (B) texture-density gradient.

   (C) retinal disparity.   (D) retinal polarity.

   (E) mono-polarity.

54. Deindividuation refers to

    (A) antisocial acts.

    (B) disinhibition.

    (C) anonymity in a group situation.

    (D) aggression.   (E) group aggression.

55. Which of the following describes attributes of color?

    (A) hue   (B) brightness

    (C) saturation   (D) (A) and (B)

    (E) all of the above

56. Which of the following variables should be taken into account when a psychological test is to be administered?

    (A) tester's rapport with subjects

    (B) the subject's amount of anxiety

    (C) the subject's understanding of test directions

    (D) (A) and (C) only

    (E) all of the above

57. According to Kohlberg's theory of moral development, the morality of self-accepted principles is characterized by

    (A) a focus on good and bad behavior.

    (B) premoral behavior.

    (C) an understanding of individual rights, ideals, and principles.

    (D) important peer and social relations.

    (E) none of the above

58. With reference to short-term memory, rehearsal

    (A) assists in the transfer of information from short-term to long-term memory.

    (B) allows material to remain in short-term memory indefinitely.

    (C) is not primarily an acoustic phenomenon.

    (D) (A) and (B)   (E) (B) and (C)

59. A psychological theoretician in the process of developing a theory would be most interested in test measures in terms of their

    (A) construct validity.   (B) face validity.

    (C) predictive validity.   (D) concurrent validity.

    (E) theoretical validity.

60. Which of the following statements does not describe a feature of classical conditioning?

    (A) Behavior affected is usually experienced as involuntary.

    (B) Unconditioned and conditioned stimuli are presented to the organism.

    (C) In the absence of key stimuli the behavior does not occur.

    (D) Reinforcement and punishment are produced by the organism's behavior.

    (E) The unconditioned stimulus occurs without regard to the organism's behavior.

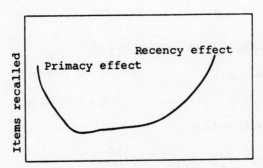

61. The above diagram depicts which of the following choices?

    (A) learning curve   (B) threshold effect

    (C) serial position curve   (D) memory curve

    (E) none of the above

62. The most difficult conflicts to resolve are

    (A) approach-approach.   (B) double approach-avoidance.

    (C) avoidance-avoidance.   (D) double avoidance-approach

    (E) approach-avoidance.

63. A test that measures what a person has already learned in prior training is a (an)

    (A) aptitude test.   (B) objective test.

    (C) experimental test.   (D) intelligence test.

    (E) achievement test.

64. A person is completely unresponsive, stares blankly into space, and never moves. He or she is showing symptoms related to

    (A) paranoia.   (B) schizoaffective disorder.

    (C) catatonic schizophrenia. (D) primary hypersomnia.

    (E) schizotypal personality disorder.

QUESTIONS 65-66 refer to the following paragraph:

In a particular personality test a subject is given a group of self-referential statements and is asked to sort them into piles based on whether the statement is highly characteristic or very uncharacteristic of his personality. It is expected that the sorting will approximate a normal distribution—most of the statements will be considered fairly neutral in terms of the subject's personality.

65. This method of testing is known as a (an)

    (A) t-test.   (B) Q-technique.

    (C) MMPI.   (D) aptitude test.

    (E) projective test.

66. Self-reports have been criticized because

    (A) they have low reliability.

    (B) the subject can deceive the researcher.

    (C) they have low validity.

    (D) both (A) and (B)   (E) all of the above

A researcher has tested a new drug for reducing anxiety on a sample of 100 people. After a treatment period of two weeks, 70 people reported feeling much less anxious and certain physiological tests showed them to be less anxious. The researcher now wants to claim that the drug is effective.

67. In order for this researcher's results to be valid he must have

    (A) chosen a random sample.

    (B) had a placebo group.

    (C) used the double-blind group.

    (D) both (A) and (B)   (E) all of the above

68. According to psychoanalytic theory, when an unpleasant or threatening thought or idea is not permitted into awareness, it is due to

    (A) repression.   (B) projection.

    (C) displacement.   (D) reaction formation.

    (E) compensation.

69. The "Oedipus Complex" occurs during which stage of psychosexual development?

    (A) oral   (B) genital

    (C) anal   (D) phallic

    (E) latency

70. During a child's development, if the amount of frustration and anxiety becomes too great concerning movement to the next stage, development may come to a halt. The individual is said to become

    (A) dependent.   (B) passive.

    (C) fixated.   (D) regressive.

    (E) repressed.

71. Allport proposed a number of essential requirements for a theory of human motivation. Which of the following choices is not a requirement?

    (A) The theory must acknowledge the contemporaneity of motives.

    (B) The theory must account for the ego in motivational acts.

    (C) The theory must be pluralistic, allowing for many types of motivation.

    (D) The theory must invest cognitive processes with dynamic force.

    (E) The theory must recognize that each individual can have a unique set of motives.

72. Learning not to respond to stimuli in some form or another occurs in

    (A) habituation.

    (B) extinction.

    (C) systematic desensitization.

    (D) all of the above   (E) none of the above

QUESTIONS 73-74 refer to the following paragraph:

In a learning experiment subjects were presented with a list of words paired with cues. Some words were paired with strong cues and others with weak cues. After presentation they were given a cued recall test in which some of the cues were the same as before, but others did not match the original cues. The results, of course, were best for those words presented with a strong cue and retrieved with the same strong cue. Recall was found to be superior for words rehearsed and retrieved with the same weak cue rather than when rehearsed with a weak cue and retrieved with a strong cue.

73. The results of this experiment demonstrate the principle of

    (A) paired-associate learning.

    (B) parallel processing.

    (C) encoding specificity.

    (D) reconstructive memory.

    (E) nonspecific transfer.

74. This principle implies that

    (A) items are stored in memory the way they are first perceived.

    (B) memory is context dependent.

    (C) the uniqueness of the link between retrieval cues and the information to be recalled is a major factor in recall ability.

    (D) both (A) and (B)   (E) all of the above

An early experiment by Kohler (1926), investigating the mentality of chimpanzees, involved placing a banana outside the cage beyond the ape's reach and giving him several short, hollow sticks which would have to be pushed together in order to reach the banana. The brightest ape in the experiment tried at first to get the banana with one stick, then he pushed the stick out as far as possible with a second stick without success. Eventually, he saw that the sticks could be connected to form a longer stick, thus perceiving a completely new relationship between the sticks.

75. According to Kohler, problem solving involves

    (A) restructuring the perceptual field.

    (B) insight.

    (C) a long process of trial-and-error.

    (D) both (A) and (B)   (E) all of the above

76. In Piaget's theory of child development, object permanence occurs at the end of the _____ stage.

    (A) sensorimotor   (B) preoperational

    (C) formal operational   (D) concrete operational

    (E) intuitive preoperational

77. According to Adler, the central core of personality functioning is a (an)

    (A) denial of neurotic needs.

    (B) compensatory behavior due to neurotic needs.

    (C) perceived sense of inferiority for which the person attempts to compensate.

    (D) actualizing self.

    (E) autonomous functioning ego.

78. Because the _____ seeks to gratify its desires without delay, it operates on the _____ .

    (A) ego, pleasure principle   (B) id, pleasure principle

    (C) id, reality principle   (D) ego, reality principle

    (E) superego, punishment principle

79. According to Piaget, the child's basic developmental process includes

    (A) assimilation.   (B) schemas.

    (C) accommodation.   (D) (A) and (B)

    (E) all of the above

80. In Allport's theory of motivation, functional autonomy is a principle that refers to

    (A) activities being able to sustain themselves without biological reinforcement.

    (B) the uniqueness of human motivations.

    (C) a self-sustaining ego.

    (D) (A) and (C)

    (E) none of the above

81. The personality test that is used mainly as a diagnostic instrument to differentiate between normal people and those with psychiatric problems is the

    (A) 16 Personality Factors Test.

    (B) TAT.   (C) MMPI.

    (D) Q-technique.   (E) CPI.

82. Which is the most consistent measure of central tendency?

    (A) mean   (B) mode

    (C) median   (D) variance

    (E) standard distribution

83. Which of the following factors would not affect the reliability of a test?

    (A) test length   (B) test-retest interval

    (C) guessing   (D) content of questions

    (E) variation within a test situation

84. Bandura's research on aggressive behavior mostly focused on aggression as

    (A) an innate, inherited trait.

    (B) a result of modeling.

    (C) an instinctual drive common to most everyone.

    (D) unrelated to rewards and punishments

    (E) both (B) and (D)

85. Which one of these psychologists thinks that aggression is an inborn tendency in all animals, including man?

    (A) Freud   (B) Lorenz

    (C) Bandura   (D) Ross

    (E) both (A) and (B)

QUESTIONS 86-87: Choose the item that does not belong with the others.

86. (A) Antisocial Personality Disorder

    (B) Passive-Aggressive Personality Disorder

    (C) Borderline Personality Disorder

    (D) Narcissistic Personality Disorder

    (E) Histrionic Personality Disorder

87. (A) TAT   (B) Rorschach Test

    (C) word association test   (D) MMPI

    (E) Draw-a-Person Test

QUESTIONS 88-89 refer to the following paragraph:

It has been found that a cut through the hindbrain near the locus impairs REM sleep. Descending fibers from the caudal locus coeruleus extend into the spinal cord where they inhibit motor neurons. After damage to this area in the brain of a cat, the cat can still have REM sleep, but the muscles do not relax. The locus coeruleus also releases what are called FTG neurons which are in the reticular formation of the pons. These neurons produce rapid eye movements and desynchronization of the EEG. Just prior to REM sleep, certain inhibiting cells of the locus coeruleus decrease their activity and remove inhibition from the FTG cells.

88. REM sleep is also known as

    (A) paradoxical sleep.   (B) inactive sleep.

    (C) desynchronized sleep.   (D) both (A) and (C)

    (E) all of the above

89. The reticular formation of the brain

    (A) has definite boundaries.

    (B) is critical for wakefulness and alertness.

    (C) can only be activated by certain stimuli.

    (D) is important for conveying precise information.

    (E) all of the above

90. The function of the vestibular organs is to provide

    (A) auditory conduction to the brain.

    (B) visual conduction to the brain.

    (C) a kinesthetic response.

    (D) electrical transmission to receptor cells.

    (E) a sense of balance.

91. Conscience and morality are conceptually defined within the Freudian theory as the

    (A) conscious.   (B) id.

    (C) preconscious.   (D) ego.

    (E) superego.

92. Which theorist believes that all neurotic needs can be reduced to one or another of three categories: toward people, away from people, and against people?

    (A) Rogers   (B) Erikson

    (C) Sullivan   (D) Horney

    (E) Fromm

93. Who among the following was particularly interested in the effect of birth order on personality?

    (A) Rogers   (B) Adler

    (C) Fromm   (D) Sullivan

    (E) Sheldon

Nine rats run through a maze. The time each rat took to traverse the maze is recorded and these times are listed below.

1 min.	1.5 min.	1 min.
2.5 min.	2 min.	0.9 min.
3 min.	1.25 min.	30 min.

94. What is the median of these observations?

    (A) 1.25   (B) 2.0

    (C) 1.5   (D) 1.0

    (E) 4.79

QUESTIONS 95-96 are based on the following information:

CS (tone)

CR (eye-blink)

UCS (air puff)

95. The conditioned response is elicited by the

    (A) unconditioned stimulus before and after conditioning.

    (B) previously neutral stimulus after conditioning.

    (C) unconditioned stimulus only after conditioning.

    (D) both (A) and (B)   (E) both (B) and (C)

96. Classical conditioning

    (A) results in behaviors which operate on the environment to produce an effect.

    (B) is the most significant kind of learning.

    (C) involves reward and punishment.

    (D) always involves two stimuli presented simultaneously.

    (E) none of the above

97. Which of the following is not a controlling factor of conformity?

    (A) whether or not the opinion of the majority is unanimous

    (B) self-esteem of the subjects

    (C) the desire to give the correct answer

    (D) whether or not the group consists of people similar to the subject

    (E) all of the above are controlling factors

98. Social psychologists study _____ , while sociologists study _____ .

    (A) groups, individuals

    (B) group norms, national norms

    (C) individuals, groups

    (D) abnormal people, normal people

    (E) introverts, extroverts

99. Behavior deliberately intended to injure or destroy is the psychological definition of

    (A) sociopathy.   (B) hostility.

    (C) frustration.   (D) instinct.

    (E) aggression.

100. Which of the following is a technique used in psychoanalysis?

    (A) client-centered therapy   (B) systematic desensitization

    (C) dream analysis   (D) implosion therapy

    (E) modeling

ADVANCED PLACEMENT PSYCHOLOGY TEST 3
SECTION II

TIME: 50 Minutes
             2 Essays

DIRECTIONS: In this portion of the test, you will write on both essay questions. We suggest you allow slightly under 25 minutes per essay. Read the question carefully, and then write a response in essay form.

Essay 1: How would Maslow differentiate between an individual who was motivated by lower needs and one who was motivated by self-actualization needs?

Essay 2: Trace the path that visual information takes on its way to the brain. Begin with the retinal receptor cells.

TEST 3

ANSWER KEY

1.	(C)	26.	(E)	51.	(E)	76.	(A)
2.	(D)	27.	(C)	52.	(D)	77.	(C)
3.	(C)	28.	(B)	53.	(B)	78.	(B)
4.	(A)	29.	(D)	54.	(C)	79.	(E)
5.	(D)	30.	(D)	55.	(E)	80.	(A)
6.	(D)	31.	(D)	56.	(E)	81.	(C)
7.	(B)	32.	(D)	57.	(C)	82.	(A)
8.	(C)	33.	(A)	58.	(D)	83.	(D)
9.	(A)	34.	(A)	59.	(A)	84.	(B)
10.	(B)	35.	(B)	60.	(D)	85.	(E)
11.	(B)	36.	(C)	61.	(C)	86.	(B)
12.	(D)	37.	(B)	62.	(B)	87.	(D)
13.	(A)	38.	(D)	63.	(E)	88.	(D)
14.	(A)	39.	(C)	64.	(C)	89.	(B)
15.	(B)	40.	(C)	65.	(B)	90.	(E)
16.	(B)	41.	(D)	66.	(D)	91.	(E)
17.	(B)	42.	(D)	67.	(E)	92.	(D)
18.	(B)	43.	(C)	68.	(A)	93.	(B)
19.	(A)	44.	(E)	69.	(D)	94.	(C)
20.	(E)	45.	(E)	70.	(C)	95.	(D)
21.	(C)	46.	(C)	71.	(B)	96.	(E)
22.	(D)	47.	(E)	72.	(D)	97.	(C)
23.	(D)	48.	(E)	73.	(C)	98.	(C)
24.	(B)	49.	(C)	74.	(E)	99.	(E)
25.	(B)	50.	(C)	75.	(D)	100.	(C)

DETAILED EXPLANATIONS
OF ANSWERS

AP PSYCHOLOGY TEST 3
SECTION I

1. **(C)** Because of the disguised nature of wish fulfillment in dreams, Freud distinguished between the manifest content and latent content of dreams. The manifest content refers to the literal content of the dream as experienced by the dreamer. It is the conscious manifestation of the hidden, symbolic desires and fears in the unconscious.

2. **(D)** The thalamus serves a number of functions. It serves as a relay center for sensory impulses. Fibers from the spinal cord and parts of the brain synapse here with other neurons going to the various sensory areas of the cerebrum. The thalamus seems to regulate and coordinate the external signs of emotion. The thalamus is in the forebrain, located on top of the hypothalamus.

3. **(C)** Adrenalin is a hormone which stimulates the sympathetic nervous system. One of the many resulting effects of adrenalin on the body is the stimulation of the heart. When stimulated, the sympathetic branch to the muscles of the heart causes the heart to beat more rapidly and vigorously. Thus, adrenalin has the effect of accelerating and strengthening the heartbeat.

4. **(A)** The pons is an area of the hindbrain containing a large number of nerve fibers which pass through it and make connections between the two hemispheres of the cerebellum, thus coordinating muscle movements on the two sides of the body. It is also especially important in aiding the regulation of breathing.

5.   **(D)**   All of the choices are monocular depth cues, meaning that they all convey information about space through one eye only. Relative size involves figures becoming smaller as they are seen at a greater and greater distance. Due to linear perspective, lines that would be parallel on the ground converge on the picture plane. Interposition is when one figure interrupts the outline of another and a strong depth cue is produced, indicating the relative positions.

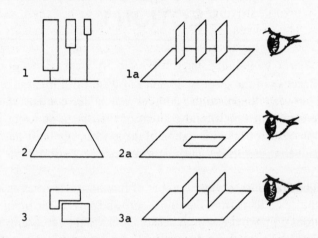

6.   **(D)**   In the Rorschach Inkblot Test, there are three different aspects to each response: location, determinant, and content. Location refers to the area of the blot that the subject responds to. The determinant refers to the characteristic of the blot that determined the subject's response (form, color, and movement). The content category refers to what was seen in the blot: human or animal, male or female, etc. The examiner tabulates the total number of responses and the total in each of the three categories.

7.   **(B)**   Primary identification with the mother occurs during the first few weeks of life. At first it is thought that the infant cannot distinguish itself from its mother. During this stage, the infant's level of differentiation between himself and the mother, and himself and the environment, increases. This early identification is a necessary part of the child's ego development according to psychoanalytic theory.

8.   **(C)**   A skewed distribution is a nonsymmetrical frequency distribution. A distribution can be skewed at either end, in the direction of the longer tail.

Positively Skewed   Negatively Skewed

The positively and negatively skewed distributions are specific forms of the skewed distribution.

9. **(A)**   A person with melancholic features of depression may have significant anorexia or weight loss, anhedonia, early morning awakening, worse depression in the morning, and excessive guilt. Weight gain or increased appetite is found in atypical depression.

10. **(B)**   Adler differed with Freud concerning the purpose of the Oedipus Complex. Instead of being a purely sexual phenomenon, the Oedipal conflicts were seen by Adler to involve strivings to become superior to the father, and to compete with the father. This relates to Adler's larger theory of personality, which was concerned with overcoming a perceived sense of inferiority for which the individual strives to compensate by gaining superiority in many areas of functioning.

11. **(B)**   The superego develops from the ages of 18 months to six years. It is often described as having two divisions. One is the "conscience," which consists of the child's internalized rules. This is the part of the superego which mentally punishes, based on the known internalized rules of what is right and wrong. The other division of the superego is the "ego ideal." This division represents strivings and goals highly regarded by the parents.

12. **(D)**   In order to reliably measure and analyze perceptual thresholds, statistical methods were developed. There are three basic methods used for this purpose, which are the Method of Limits, the Method of Average Error, and the frequency method. They are alike in that they all present (for comparison) a constant Standard stimulus (St), and a variable Comparison stimulus (Co).

13. **(A)**   The projected image of the female throughout history in man's unconscious is the "anima." This internalized image is based on his real experiences with women, particularly his mother or sisters, and the collective experience of men throughout history. The anima determines a man's relationship to women throughout his life. The anima helps a man compensate for his otherwise one-sided view of his interactions with and perceptions of others.

14. **(A)**   The shaping of a new behavior involves the reinforcement of acts similar to the desired one (an approximation). The method involves differential reinforcement, which means that the same act is not continually reinforced. During each successive trial, reinforcement is given only if the subject engages in an act of behavior that more closely resembles the desired behavior. As the training or shaping proceeds, closer and closer approximations are required for reinforcement.

15. **(B)**   Freud defined two instincts in man, one of which is Eros. Eros is the life instinct or the will to live, which includes the libidinal urges. Eros competes with Thanatos, the death instinct, once an individual is fully developed. It is the life-giving urges of Eros that are most intimately connected with the child's development.

16. **(B)**   In his studies on the nature of obedience, Stanley Milgram discovered

that the average middle-class American male would, under the direction of a legitimate power and authority figure, administer severe shocks to other individuals in an experimental setting. This somewhat alarming finding demonstrated the extent to which ordinary people will comply with orders from a legitimate source of social power and authority, even to the point of committing cruel and harmful actions toward their fellow man.

17. **(B)** A sample bias is any procedural variable which causes the sample to be unrepresentative of the population. A sample bias often yields inaccurate predictions about the population under study. Hence, it reduces the statistical power of the analysis on this population.

18. **(B)** Specialists in the fields of psychology and education have come to recognize that creativity and intelligence are not synonymous. Creativity is certainly not measurable by standard I.Q. tests. Creativity is influenced by many non-intellectual, temperamental characteristics, such as a receptive attitude toward novel ideas, specific perceptual tendencies, and ideational fluency.

19. **(A)** The fundamental concept in Karen Horney's psychoanalytic theory is basic anxiety. This is experienced in childhood as a feeling of isolation and helplessness in a potentially hostile world. The anxiety results from parental attitudes toward the child which may take the form of dominance, lack of affection, lack of protective behavior, and many other negative affect states. Horney considers anxiety to be a learned response, not an innate response.

20. **(E)** The stage of formal operations is the final step in Piaget's system of cognitive development. It begins at about age 11 when the child starts to free himself from the period of concrete operations. He can now imagine hypothetical states and he realizes that there are many possible solutions to a problem. Thinking becomes increasingly propositional, logical, and idealistic.

21. **(C)** In Piaget's theory, an operation is a thought. Thought refers to the mental representation of something that is not immediately perceived. During this period of concrete operations, the child is capable of invoking a mental representation or image of an object or event. This representation is linked to a mental image of the "concrete" perceptual experience. It must exist in the physical sense and not be hypothetical.

22. **(D)** The California Psychological Inventory (CPI), as developed by Gough (1957), is an objective personality inventory developed for use with less clinically deviant groups of subjects. Most of the CPI was developed using the method of contrasted groups and internal consistency analysis. Some of the representative scales are: Self-control, Responsibility, Flexibility, Achievement via Independence, Tolerance, and Intellectual Efficiency. The items measure minor forms of maladjustment.

23. **(D)**   Personality tests usually have a limited range of responses or are designed with true/false choices. They may assess a wide range of personality characteristics. Objective personality tests are generally structured with well-documented norms of responding. The Q-sort is one of the techniques used with self-report referential tests. While these tests are well structured and documented, they may not be accurate predictors of future behavior.

24. **(B)**   The standard deviation is a measure of the variability or spread of scores in a group. If the grouping sample is homogeneous, there would be little variation among the subjects; therefore, the standard deviation should be small. The standard deviation is expressed as the square root of the average of the squared deviations from the mean of the group.

25. **(B)**   Projective tests allow the subject to freely associate the stimuli presented. It is assumed that the responses are expressions (projections) of unconscious desires, conflicts, and impulses. Another basic assumption of projective methods is that the production of responses depends largely upon personality factors. The Rorschach test uses inkblots as the stimuli to project experiences while the TAT uses pictures of ambiguous situations between people as the test stimuli. Despite the difference in test stimuli, both the Rorschach and TAT use projective methods to assess personality.

26. **(E)**   Both the word association test and the sentence completion test are referred to as verbal projective tests because both stimulus materials and responses are verbal in nature. The administration of these two tests presupposes a minimum reading level and thorough familiarity with the language in which the test was developed. Both measures permit an almost unlimited variety of responding. Due to the limitations of these tests, they should not be administered to children, illiterates, and people from foreign cultures.

27. **(C)**   A "normal" I.Q. is considered to be about 100, and 99 percent of the people who take intelligence tests fall in the range between 55 and 145. A person who scores below 70 is considered to be mentally retarded.

28. **(B)**   The successive method of approximation involves the reinforcement of acts similar to the desired one (an approximation). The method uses differential reinforcement for behaviors that are successively closer to the desired behavior. The shaping of responses is the teaching of behavior by reinforcing successively closer approximations of the desired behavior until the desired behavior is attained. Hence, both are, by definition, the same behavioral technique.

29. **(D)**   Hermann Ebbinghaus, as a young German philosopher, was the first to examine learning and memory scientifically. His experiments in the late 1800s attempted to give an empirical basis for the study of human learning. Ebbinghaus measured learning difficulty by presenting a subject with a series of items to learn

and counting the number of presentations necessary to learn the material and recall it. He measured memory by requiring subjects to relearn material they knew but had forgotten. He recorded the number of times something had to be rehearsed before perfect recitation of the material occurred.

30. **(D)** Social phobia, PTSD, panic disorder, and OCD are all classified as anxiety disorders. Conversion disorder is a somatoform disorder.

31. **(D)** The Rotter Incomplete Sentence Blank is a verbal projective technique. The sentence completion test permits an almost unlimited variety of responses. This test consists of 40 sentence stems which require completion to such items as: What worries one...; My mother...; My ambition.... The responses are rated on a 7-point scale of adjustment/maladjustment. Some argue that this test is more objectively scored than other such verbal projective tests.

32. **(D)** The personality structure consists of id, ego, and superego. According to Freud, the id is the most fundamental component of personality and is composed of drives, needs, and instinctual impulses. It is unable to tolerate tension, is obedient only to the pleasure principle and is in constant conflict with the superego. The superego develops out of the ego during childhood. It contains values, morals and basic attitudes as learned from parents and society. The ego mediates between the id and superego. The ego is sometimes called the executive agency of the personality because it controls actions and decides how needs should be satisfied.

33. **(A)** The autonomic nervous system is divided into two parts, both structurally and functionally. One part is called the sympathetic nervous system and the other is known as the parasympathetic nervous system. These two branches act antagonistically to each other. If one system stimulates an effector, the other would inhibit its action. The basis for homeostatic regulation by the autonomic system lies in the fact that the sympathetic and parasympathetic system each send a branch to the same organ, causing double innervation.

34. **(A)** The "white matter" of the central nervous system is actually the nerve fiber pathways. The white matter consists mainly of axons. The axons are surrounded by a fatty, white covering called the myelin sheath, hence their nickname, white matter.

35. **(B)** Synaptic vesicles are small, sac-like structures located at the axon of the neuron. They contain neurotransmitters, which are chemicals that permit unidirectional transmission of an action potential from one neuron to another. Acetylcholine and noradrenaline are two types of neurotransmitters.

36. **(C)** The hypothalamus, located under the thalamus, is a collection of nuclei concerned with many important homeostatic regulations. Electrical stimulation of

certain cells in the hypothalamus produces sensations of hunger, thirst, pain, pleasure, or sexual drive. The hypothalamus is also important for its influence on the pituitary gland, which is functionally under its control. Cells of the hypothalamus synthesize chemical factors that modulate the release of hormones produced and stored in the pituitary.

37.   **(B)**   Color intensity is not a stimulus cue involved in the perception of depth. The other choices are all factors involved in depth perception.

38.   **(D)**   Within the color spectrum, blue is perceived at 470–475 nanometers wavelength, green at 495–535 nanometers, yellow at 575–580 nanometers, and red is perceived at 595–770 nanometers wavelength. Hence, with reference to the question, the wavelength of green is greater than blue but less than yellow or red.

39.   **(C)**   Physical sounds from the environment in the form of waves are translated into electrical messages in the cochlea. The cochlea contains special hair cells which are bent as part of a chain reaction due to the vibrations of the ossicles, namely the stapes, which push against the oval window on the cochlea. As these hairs are bent, an electrical event called a generator potential occurs. This potential stimulates nearby nerve cells. The activated nerve cells then carry an electrical message about the original sound wave vibrations along to the brain.

40.   **(C)**   This choice is correct by definition. Heritability is defined as the proportion of the total variation in a population that is due to genetic variation. Since heritability is dependent on a ratio of genetic to nongenetic variation, its value is affected by both factors. Heritability can be increased by either an increase in genetic variation or by a decrease in nongenetic or environmental variation.

41.   **(D)**   Freud's theory of motivational processes represents only a limited segment of his life work, but it is a segment on which much of his other work is built. Freud believed that behavior was motivated largely by unconscious instincts. These instincts were collectively referred to as the "id." The id unconsciously motivates behavior by giving rise to tensions, which the person is motivated to satisfy and reduce.

42.   **(D)**   Echoic memory deals with information taken in through auditory perception. Because auditory perception takes place over a period of time, some kind of memory must preserve it long enough for speech processing to occur. The medium for the temporary storage of auditory information is the echoic memory. The maximum duration of echoic memory has been difficult to determine. This transitory memory decays gradually, and its duration has varied inversely with the difficulty of the task that was used to measure it. Estimates of its duration range from one to 10 seconds.

43.   **(C)**   In a fixed-interval schedule, reinforcement occurs after a fixed period of time. No matter how much work is done, reinforcement is given after a set period

of time. This schedule has the lowest yield in terms of performance. However, just before reinforcement time, activity increases.

44.   **(E)**   During stage-four sleep, delta waves predominate. Delta waves are very slow, occurring about once every second. During this stage of sleep, the sleeper is virtually immobile and not easily woken. Stage four sleep is the deepest stage of sleep with no REM activity; therefore, no dreaming occurs during this sleep stage.

45.   **(E)**   In his theory of motivation, Carl Rogers places special emphasis on two needs: the need for positive regard and the need for self-regard. Both are learned needs. Positive regard refers to the positive assessment an individual receives from other people; the need for positive regard develops in infancy as a result of the love and care a baby receives. The need for self-regard is established as a result of receiving positive regard from others. These two needs are not always in congruence and can, therefore, interfere with the actualizing tendency.

46.   **(C)**   The lens is a transparent tissue that focuses the image by changing shape—thickening for near objects and thinning for distant ones. This process is called accommodation. Like the cornea, the lens is curved in shape. It bends, inverts, and focuses light rays onto the retina.

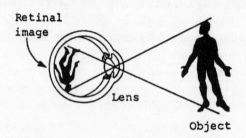

47.   **(E)**   Dissociative identity disorder, formerly known as multiple personality disorder, is the presence of separate and different personalities within the same individual. The individual personalities in this disorder are generally quite discrepant and usually the primary personality remains unaware of the secondary personality. Individuals with this disorder frequently report having experienced severe physical and sexual abuses, especially during childhood.

48.   **(E)**   The eighth and final stage of Erikson's scheme is maturity. The basic crisis during this stage is ego integrity vs. disgust and despair. A sense of integrity develops if the individual, having looked back on his life, believes that it has been meaningful and relatively successful. He feels good about his past and is prepared to live the rest of his life in peace. A feeling of disgust, however, may arise if the individual sees his life as meaningless, wasted, and generally unsuccessful.

49. **(C)** The disadvantage of cross-cultural tests is that the predictive and diagnostic value of the intelligence test is lost. There is little gained by administering culture-fair tests if they do not provide useful information concerning the culturally relevant knowledge and abilities of a student. Cross-cultural tests often miss this relevant information and, therefore, have little meaningful predictive value.

50. **(C)** STM is highly susceptible to interference. For instance, when a person begins dialing a telephone number but is interrupted, the number may be forgotten or dialed incorrectly. Interference can disrupt STM because there is no rehearsal time after a response. Information may also be interrupted because the interfering activity could also enter STM and cause it to reach its capacity for stored items. In either case, displacement of old, unrehearsed items will occur.

51. **(E)** To Freud, dreams represented attempts at wish fulfillment. He reasoned that the dream is a hallucinatory state that structures events not as they would be in reality, but as the dreamer wishes them to be. When unconscious desires conflict with conscious restraints, it is necessary for the dreamwork to disguise the meaning of the dream in order to express the wish.

52. **(D)** Measuring devices must have two characteristics. First, they must be reliable. This means that an individual's score or rating should not vary with repeated testings. For example, an intelligence test which yields highly different scores each time the subject takes the test is useless. Second, a measuring device must be valid. This means that it should measure what it was designed to measure. An I.Q. test, for example, would not yield an accurate measure of anxiety, but it should be an accurate measure of intelligence.

53. **(B)** The texture-density gradient is a monocular depth cue. A gradient is the rate at which some property changes uniformly from one part of the area portrayed to another. The texture gradient of this impression becomes denser as it becomes more distant. This effect is achieved on a pictorial plane by drawing the horizontal parallel lines closer and closer together as greater distance is portrayed.

54. **(C)** Deindividuation is a state in which a person feels a lessened sense of personal identity and responsibility. It is a state likely to be experienced by a person in a large group or crowd situation.

55. **(E)** Hue, brightness, and saturation are all attributes of color. The wavelength of the light determines which "hue" we will perceive. When a single wavelength of light is perceived, the hue appears pure or "saturated." As the intensity of the light increases, the light will appear brighter. These three factors interact to determine the actual color we see.

56. **(E)** Many variables must be taken into account when a test is administered. The subject's understanding of the test, test directions, examiner's rapport, subject's level of anxiety concerning the test, personality type of examiner, and the subject's experience with practice tests are all important variables to consider before the actual test administration. If such variables are not taken into account, there is likely to be systematic bias in the test samples, which will interfere with the factors that the test is specifically trying to examine.

57. **(C)** The third and highest level of morality according to Kohlberg's scheme is called the morality of self-accepted principles. This level initiates the beginning of the individual's moral standards. The child arrives at an understanding of individual rights, ideals, and principles. He can see beyond the literal interpretation of rules and laws. This level of morality is characteristic of the adolescent.

58. **(D)** Rehearsal appears to serve two main functions. The first is to allow material to remain in short-term memory indefinitely. The second appears to be assisting in the transfer of information from short-term to long-term memory. The limited capacities of short-term memory affect the amount of information that can be successfully rehearsed. It is a relatively small amount of material that can be remembered and kept alive through rehearsal.

59. **(A)** When a test is designed to measure a theoretical idea or construct, its validity is judged by the extent to which it conforms to the requirements of the theory. Unlike predictive validity and concurrent validity, construct validity is a matter of logical analysis, not correlation.

60. **(D)** Choice (D) is a characteristic of operant conditioning. It is not charac- teristic of classical conditioning. Classical conditioning is the process of substituting a conditioned stimulus for an unconditioned stimulus to evoke an innate, involuntary or previously-learned response. This procedure involves pairing the conditioned stimulus with the unconditioned stimulus repeatedly. Eventually, the conditioned stimulus alone will elicit or evoke the behavior. The presence of either the CS or the UCS is needed for the behavior to occur.

61. **(C)** The diagram depicts a serial position curve which always has this characteristic shape. Psychologists suggest that the curve is due to a primacy-recency effect. A primacy effect occurs when the items at the beginning of the list are the most easily remembered. A recency effect occurs when items near the end of the list are remembered well. When both effects occur, it is called a primacy-recency effect. It is believed that the accuracy of recalling the last few items in a list is a result of the short-term memory store, and that recall of early items which subjects had been able to rehearse, reflects the contribution of long-term memory.

62. **(B)** A double approach-avoidance conflict is one in which the individual is caught between two goals, both of which have positive and negative qualities. In this type of conflict, the two alternatives are usually similar. These conflicts are usually compli-

cated and involve complex social factors which produce a great deal of frustration.

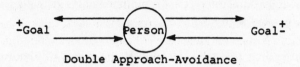

$^+_-$Goal ⟵⟶ Person ⟶⟵ Goal$^+_-$

Double Approach-Avoidance

63. **(E)** A test that measures primarily what a person has already learned in prior training (a uniform prior experience) is an achievement test. Achievement tests are usually administered after training in order to evaluate what the individual has gained through training. An example of a uniform prior experience is a geometry class; the New York State Regents Examination in geometry is an achievement test given to all who have undergone the uniform prior experience of taking a geometry class in a New York State public high school.

64. **(C)** Disturbances in motor functions are the most obvious symptoms of catatonic schizophrenia. A catatonic schizophrenic sometimes alternates between immobility and wild excitement, but the two types can also predominate. The immobile state is more common and is characterized by physical rigidity, muteness, and unresponsiveness. Despite the severity of its symptoms, catatonia is more likely than other forms of schizophrenia to "cure itself" without treatment.

65. **(B)** The Q-technique is an objective personality test which elicits a person's own analysis of his personality. In the Q-sort, used by Carl Rogers, the subject is asked to sort statements into a specified number of piles based on whether they are characteristic of his personality or not.

66. **(D)** Self-reports, such as the Beck Depression Inventory, have low reliability because it is expected that the subjects may try to present their condition either better or worse than it really is. The subjects may give distorted pictures of themselves in order to "defend" themselves. They may also base their decisions on social desirability.

67. **(E)** In a true experiment, the sample should be chosen randomly and divided into groups by random assignment. It is necessary in drug research to have an experimental group and a control group in order to be able to measure the effects of the drug. The double-blind technique assures that neither the experimenter nor the subject can affect the results, because neither knows which person is in which group.

68. **(A)** Repression is a major defense mechanism in psychoanalytic theory. Repression describes the mechanism whereby an unpleasant or threatening thought or idea is not permitted into awareness. Repression occurs when an individual experiences a painful event and tries to forget it. He represses the experience by burying it in his unconscious mind. The unconscious mind is replete with repressed feelings toward painful experiences.

69. **(D)** The "Oedipus Complex" occurs during the phallic stage of psycho-sexual development. It is considered a substage. The Oedipus Complex occurs due to the boy's growing sexual interest in his mother and his growing jealousy and fear of castration associated with his father.

70. **(C)** According to Freud, fixation is the result of abnormal personality development. In his scheme of personality development, consisting of progressive stages, Freud stated that there is a certain amount of frustration and anxiety as the person passes from one stage to the next. If the amount of frustration and anxiety over the next stage is too great, development will halt, and the person becomes fixated at one stage. A very dependent child is an example of an early fixation preventing him from becoming independent.

71. **(B)** This choice is not a requirement for Allport's motivational theory. Allport did not like to use the term ego because he did not want to be involved in the confusion of hypothesizing the existence of an agent inside man's head that organizes and controls the personality. He preferred to think in terms of a number of ego functions that he called propriate functions.

72. **(D)** Habituation, extinction, and systematic desensitization are all varia-tions on the applications of learning theory. All three contain the essential compo-nent of learning not to respond to stimuli. Habituation involves a decreased response to a stimulus because it has become familiar. Extinction involves learning not to respond to a specific stimulus that was previously learned and responded to. Systematic desensitization involves reconditioning so that a previously learned aversive stimulus is no longer responded to with fear.

73. **(C)** The encoding specificity principle states that recall is highly dependent on the congruity between encoding and retrieval cues. Thus, even though a strong cue is better than a weak cue by itself, it is not effective at retrieval if the word was encoded with a weak cue. The uniqueness of the encoding leads to better recall.

74. **(E)** According to the encoding specificity principle, items are stored in memory the way they are first perceived. Uniqueness of the connection made between the word and the cue is very important, as is the context in which the item was presented.

75. **(D)** As a Gestalt theorist, Kohler held that problem solving involves restructuring the perceptual field. This can only be accomplished when the subject can view the task as a whole. He believed that true problem solving requires insight and realistic thinking.

76. **(A)** In the Piagetian theory of child development, object permanence occurs at the end of the sensorimotor stage. This is a critical achievement of this early period of life. Object permanence is the awareness that objects exist outside of the

child's own sensory experiences and motor manipulations and that they endure even when he neither sees them nor moves them around.

77. **(C)**   According to Adler, the central core of personality functioning is a subjectively perceived sense of inferiority for which an individual strives to compensate by gaining superiority. Because of this, an individual's life-meaning could not be fully comprehended without knowledge of the goal toward which he or she was striving. Furthermore, Adler felt that the normal, healthy individual was motivated by a goal that was related to his fellow man.

78. **(B)**   The pleasure principle is a concept originated by Freud. It is the idea that man strives to avoid pain and seek pleasure. It is on this principle that the id operates, seeking immediate gratification. The id is the most fundamental component of personality, comprising drives, needs and instinctual impulses. The id is unable to tolerate tension or to compromise and, therefore, is obedient only to the pleasure principle.

79. **(E)**   According to Piaget's theory of child development, the infant at birth has very basic schemas, such as sucking reflexes, as well as the ability to assimilate and accommodate to his environment. These later produce more complex schemas. Assimilation is the taking in of information. It eventually results in the accommodation of information. Accommodation is the adaptive modification of the child's cognitive structures in order to deal with new experiences. A schema is an organized pattern of behavior.

80. **(A)**   Allport's requirements for a theory of motivation are met by his concept of functional autonomy. The principle of functional autonomy states that a given activity or form of behavior may become an end or goal in itself, in spite of the fact that it was originally engaged for some other reason. Activities are capable of sustaining themselves without biological reinforcement. An example of this principle is Allport's explanation for the reason a man would continue to hunt animals even though he does not need them for food. Allport maintains that the man hunts simply because he likes to hunt.

81. **(C)**   The MMPI (Minnesota Multiphasic Personality Inventory) is the most widely used personality test. It consists of 550 self-report "true/false" questions. Normal people answer these questions differently than psychiatric patients. Although sometimes used to assess individual differences among those with normal personalities, it is mostly used to distinguish between normal people and those with psychiatric problems.

82. **(A)**   In comparison with other measures of central tendency, the mean is the most consistent measure. If you take large independent sets of data and analyze the measures of central tendency, the mean varies less from data set to set than do other measures of central tendency. Therefore, the mean is more consistent as a measure

over many data sets and is the most commonly used of all the measures of central tendency.

83. **(D)**   The actual content of the questions in a test should not affect the reliability of the test as long as the questions remain the same over testing periods. If questions change, the content changes and essentially, you have a different test with different reliability measures. The five factors that do affect reliability are: test length, test-retest interval, variability of scores, guessing, and variation within a test situation.

84. **(B)**   Most psychologists today believe that aggression is a learned behavior. Bandura, a social learning theorist, studied the effects of modeling on aggression. Modeling is simply a process whereby a person learns a new behavior by watching another person engage in it. He found that children exposed to aggressive models (either live, filmed or cartoon) were significantly more likely to demonstrate aggressive behavior than those not exposed to aggressive models. He also found that reward contingencies played a very important role in the effectiveness of model learning.

85. **(E)**   Freud originally introduced this idea in his psychoanalytic theory in the 1930s. Today this approach to aggressive behavior has been most supported by the work of Lorenz. Lorenz is an ethologist—that is, one who studies the behavior of animals in their natural habitat. He believes that because humans use their intelligence to aggress, they have never developed natural controls on aggression against their own species.

86. **(B)**   Antisocial, Borderline, Narcissistic and Histrionic Personality Disorders are all classified as Cluster B personality disorders. In the DSM IV, Passive Aggressive Personality Disorder is not an official diagnosis. People with personality disorders usually are able to meet the demands of life, and usually do not seek therapeutic treatment.

87. **(D)**   The MMPI is an objective personality test which consists of 550 statements to which the subject is to answer "true," "false," or "cannot say" with respect to himself. The TAT, Rorschach, word-association, and Draw-a-Person tests are projective personality tests which are unstructured and thus demand originality.

88. **(D)**   REM sleep is known as paradoxical sleep because although the EEG pattern resembles wakefulness, the person is more difficult to awaken than in any other stage. The EEG is desynchronized, thus the term desynchronized sleep. It is also known as active sleep.

89. **(B)**   The reticular formation is critical for wakefulness and alertness. The input and output of the reticular formation are diffuse. The area appears more irregular and disorderly than most of the rest of the brain. Any strong stimulation

activates the system and thus diffusely activates the entire cerebral cortex.

90. **(E)** Our vestibular organs provide us with a sense of balance. They do this through information about the movements and position of the head. There are two groups of vestibular organs. These are the semicircular canals and the otolith organs, both located in the inner ear. The three semicircular canals are fluid filled and respond to the changes in rate of motion of the head. The otolith organs are small stone-like crystals which respond to the actual position of one's head.

91. **(E)** Morality and conscience are conceptually defined as the superego functions. The superego represents the taboos and mores or rules of the society in which the child lives. It may encompass religious rules as well. The process by which the child learns cultural norms and identifies with them is called socialization. Hence, the development of the superego represents the socialization functions in the child.

92. **(D)** Karen Horney postulated 10 different neurotic needs which could all be reduced to three categories of neurotic styles. They are: 1) a movement toward people, indicating a need for love; 2) a movement away from people, indicating a need for independence; and 3) a movement against people, indicating a need for power.

93. **(B)** Of the theorists in the neo-Freudian movement, it was Adler who placed the emphasis on the relationship between personality and birth order. He believed that the oldest, middle, and youngest children have very different social experiences resulting in different personality formations. The eldest child is believed to feel "dethroned" upon the birth of a sibling. This leads to lifelong feelings of insecurity and hostility. The middle child is believed to be very ambitious and have a tendency for jealousy. The youngest child is most likely to be spoiled and to have a lifelong behavior problem.

94. **(C)** When the times are arranged in order from lowest to highest, the median, which is the middle number in an array, turns out to be 1.5 (0.9, 1.0, 1.0, 1.25, 1.5, 2.0, 2.5, 3.0, 30.0).

95. **(D)** Classical conditioning involves the repeated pairing of some conditioned stimulus with the unconditioned stimulus. After a while, the conditioned stimulus, when presented alone, will elicit the unconditioned response. Thus, the conditioned response is basically the same as the unconditioned response. It is elicited by the unconditioned stimulus before and after conditioning, and by the previously neutral stimulus after conditioning.

96. **(E)** Classical conditioning is the learning of a response to a particular stimulus which previously could not elicit that response. It does not involve reward and punishment as does discrimination learning, and it does not result in behaviors

which produce an effect on the environment as does operant conditioning. The two stimuli are not always presented simultaneously. The most significant kind of learning for human beings is verbal learning.

97. **(C)**   Controlling factors of conformity include whether or not the opinion of the majority is unanimous, whether or not the group consists of the subjects' friends or of experts or peers, and the self-esteem of the subjects. The desire to give the correct answer is not a factor since subjects will choose an obviously incorrect answer so as to avoid group rejection.

98. **(C)**   Social psychologists study how the individual is affected by the group. They would be interested in how peer pressure influences the individual. Sociologists, on the other hand, are interested in group behavior.

99. **(E)**   Aggression is defined as behavior intended to hurt living things for purposes other than survival, or the destruction of property. Instrumental aggression refers to cases where aggression is socially sanctioned, such as a fireman breaking down a door.

100. **(C)**   In psychoanalysis, all problems stem from unresolved childhood conflicts and subconscious influences. Dreams are an avenue for the subconscious to manifest itself on the conscious mind. Choice (A) is the humanistic approach. The other choices are from the behavioral approach to therapy.

SECTION II

Here are examples of good essay answers:

Essay 1:

Maslow's Hierarchy of Needs theory proposes five motivational levels that direct human behavior in a hierarchical manner. The most basic needs are physiological, these are followed by safety and security needs, love and belonging, self-esteem and finally, self-actualization needs. As one need is satisfied, the next in the hierarchy becomes the important motivating factor. According to Maslow, there is a marked difference between the behavior patterns of people motivated by lower needs (deficiency-oriented) and those motivated by self-actualization needs (growth-oriented). The deficiency-oriented person can be contrasted to the growth-oriented individual on a number of different behavior characteristics.

The person who is still motivated to satisfy lower needs is characterized by a tendency to be self-centered and concerned with his own needs, to reject his own impulses, to seek goals that are common to many others, to look for gratifications that are relatively short-term and temporary, to seek gratification that results in tension-reduction, to behave mainly on the basis of external cues, and to view others in terms of how they can satisfy his needs.

On the other hand, the growth-oriented person is likely to be more concerned with the nature of the world at large and other people than with himself, to be accepting of his impulses, to attain goals that are individualistic and unique to him, to be attracted to gratifications that lead to permanent and long-term change, to behave from internal rather than external cues, and to view people for what they are, not as potential subjects he can utilize to satisfy his needs.

This picture of the self-actualizing individual may be partly responsible for the increasing number of mental health therapists who have adopted Maslow's theory or some variant of it as a goal model for their patients. Self-actualizing behavior is clearly that of an optimally developed individual. Before Maslow's conceptualization of the term through his study of exceptional individuals, the literature was scarce in its descriptions of healthy behavior and heavy in its concentration of pathological tendencies. It was Maslow who formally introduced to psychology the model of a healthy, optimally functioning individual.

That so many have adopted his theoretical stance is evidence of the need that existed for the work he has done.

Essay 2:   Visual information, first received by the retina's receptor cells, passes through a number of different cells and undergoes a number of transformations before it reaches the brain. First, the information passes through the cell layers of the retina. That is, it is passed through the bipolar and ganglion cell layers. From the ganglion cells, visual information is carried by the optic nerve into the central nervous system.

About halfway to the brain, the optic nerve reaches an intersection called the optic chiasm (from the Greek letter chi, χ). Here, some fibers from our left eye cross over to proceed to the right side of the brain, and vice versa. Some fibers continue up along the side from which they originate.

Once past the optic chiasm, nerve fibers carrying visual information are called optic tracts. Information from the optic tract is carried to the visual center of the thalamus. This center is called the lateral geniculate body. Finally, the lateral geniculate body relays the information to the visual cortex for final processing.

ADVANCED PLACEMENT EXAMINATION IN
PSYCHOLOGY

Answer Sheets
& Writing Grids

Advanced Placement Examination in
PSYCHOLOGY — Test 1

1. Ⓐ Ⓑ Ⓒ Ⓓ Ⓔ
2. Ⓐ Ⓑ Ⓒ Ⓓ Ⓔ
3. Ⓐ Ⓑ Ⓒ Ⓓ Ⓔ
4. Ⓐ Ⓑ Ⓒ Ⓓ Ⓔ
5. Ⓐ Ⓑ Ⓒ Ⓓ Ⓔ
6. Ⓐ Ⓑ Ⓒ Ⓓ Ⓔ
7. Ⓐ Ⓑ Ⓒ Ⓓ Ⓔ
8. Ⓐ Ⓑ Ⓒ Ⓓ Ⓔ
9. Ⓐ Ⓑ Ⓒ Ⓓ Ⓔ
10. Ⓐ Ⓑ Ⓒ Ⓓ Ⓔ
11. Ⓐ Ⓑ Ⓒ Ⓓ Ⓔ
12. Ⓐ Ⓑ Ⓒ Ⓓ Ⓔ
13. Ⓐ Ⓑ Ⓒ Ⓓ Ⓔ
14. Ⓐ Ⓑ Ⓒ Ⓓ Ⓔ
15. Ⓐ Ⓑ Ⓒ Ⓓ Ⓔ
16. Ⓐ Ⓑ Ⓒ Ⓓ Ⓔ
17. Ⓐ Ⓑ Ⓒ Ⓓ Ⓔ
18. Ⓐ Ⓑ Ⓒ Ⓓ Ⓔ
19. Ⓐ Ⓑ Ⓒ Ⓓ Ⓔ
20. Ⓐ Ⓑ Ⓒ Ⓓ Ⓔ
21. Ⓐ Ⓑ Ⓒ Ⓓ Ⓔ
22. Ⓐ Ⓑ Ⓒ Ⓓ Ⓔ
23. Ⓐ Ⓑ Ⓒ Ⓓ Ⓔ
24. Ⓐ Ⓑ Ⓒ Ⓓ Ⓔ
25. Ⓐ Ⓑ Ⓒ Ⓓ Ⓔ
26. Ⓐ Ⓑ Ⓒ Ⓓ Ⓔ
27. Ⓐ Ⓑ Ⓒ Ⓓ Ⓔ
28. Ⓐ Ⓑ Ⓒ Ⓓ Ⓔ
29. Ⓐ Ⓑ Ⓒ Ⓓ Ⓔ
30. Ⓐ Ⓑ Ⓒ Ⓓ Ⓔ
31. Ⓐ Ⓑ Ⓒ Ⓓ Ⓔ
32. Ⓐ Ⓑ Ⓒ Ⓓ Ⓔ
33. Ⓐ Ⓑ Ⓒ Ⓓ Ⓔ

34. Ⓐ Ⓑ Ⓒ Ⓓ Ⓔ
35. Ⓐ Ⓑ Ⓒ Ⓓ Ⓔ
36. Ⓐ Ⓑ Ⓒ Ⓓ Ⓔ
37. Ⓐ Ⓑ Ⓒ Ⓓ Ⓔ
38. Ⓐ Ⓑ Ⓒ Ⓓ Ⓔ
39. Ⓐ Ⓑ Ⓒ Ⓓ Ⓔ
40. Ⓐ Ⓑ Ⓒ Ⓓ Ⓔ
41. Ⓐ Ⓑ Ⓒ Ⓓ Ⓔ
42. Ⓐ Ⓑ Ⓒ Ⓓ Ⓔ
43. Ⓐ Ⓑ Ⓒ Ⓓ Ⓔ
44. Ⓐ Ⓑ Ⓒ Ⓓ Ⓔ
45. Ⓐ Ⓑ Ⓒ Ⓓ Ⓔ
46. Ⓐ Ⓑ Ⓒ Ⓓ Ⓔ
47. Ⓐ Ⓑ Ⓒ Ⓓ Ⓔ
48. Ⓐ Ⓑ Ⓒ Ⓓ Ⓔ
49. Ⓐ Ⓑ Ⓒ Ⓓ Ⓔ
50. Ⓐ Ⓑ Ⓒ Ⓓ Ⓔ
51. Ⓐ Ⓑ Ⓒ Ⓓ Ⓔ
52. Ⓐ Ⓑ Ⓒ Ⓓ Ⓔ
53. Ⓐ Ⓑ Ⓒ Ⓓ Ⓔ
54. Ⓐ Ⓑ Ⓒ Ⓓ Ⓔ
55. Ⓐ Ⓑ Ⓒ Ⓓ Ⓔ
56. Ⓐ Ⓑ Ⓒ Ⓓ Ⓔ
57. Ⓐ Ⓑ Ⓒ Ⓓ Ⓔ
58. Ⓐ Ⓑ Ⓒ Ⓓ Ⓔ
59. Ⓐ Ⓑ Ⓒ Ⓓ Ⓔ
60. Ⓐ Ⓑ Ⓒ Ⓓ Ⓔ
61. Ⓐ Ⓑ Ⓒ Ⓓ Ⓔ
62. Ⓐ Ⓑ Ⓒ Ⓓ Ⓔ
63. Ⓐ Ⓑ Ⓒ Ⓓ Ⓔ
64. Ⓐ Ⓑ Ⓒ Ⓓ Ⓔ
65. Ⓐ Ⓑ Ⓒ Ⓓ Ⓔ
66. Ⓐ Ⓑ Ⓒ Ⓓ Ⓔ
67. Ⓐ Ⓑ Ⓒ Ⓓ Ⓔ

68. Ⓐ Ⓑ Ⓒ Ⓓ Ⓔ
69. Ⓐ Ⓑ Ⓒ Ⓓ Ⓔ
70. Ⓐ Ⓑ Ⓒ Ⓓ Ⓔ
71. Ⓐ Ⓑ Ⓒ Ⓓ Ⓔ
72. Ⓐ Ⓑ Ⓒ Ⓓ Ⓔ
73. Ⓐ Ⓑ Ⓒ Ⓓ Ⓔ
74. Ⓐ Ⓑ Ⓒ Ⓓ Ⓔ
75. Ⓐ Ⓑ Ⓒ Ⓓ Ⓔ
76. Ⓐ Ⓑ Ⓒ Ⓓ Ⓔ
77. Ⓐ Ⓑ Ⓒ Ⓓ Ⓔ
78. Ⓐ Ⓑ Ⓒ Ⓓ Ⓔ
79. Ⓐ Ⓑ Ⓒ Ⓓ Ⓔ
80. Ⓐ Ⓑ Ⓒ Ⓓ Ⓔ
81. Ⓐ Ⓑ Ⓒ Ⓓ Ⓔ
82. Ⓐ Ⓑ Ⓒ Ⓓ Ⓔ
83. Ⓐ Ⓑ Ⓒ Ⓓ Ⓔ
84. Ⓐ Ⓑ Ⓒ Ⓓ Ⓔ
85. Ⓐ Ⓑ Ⓒ Ⓓ Ⓔ
86. Ⓐ Ⓑ Ⓒ Ⓓ Ⓔ
87. Ⓐ Ⓑ Ⓒ Ⓓ Ⓔ
88. Ⓐ Ⓑ Ⓒ Ⓓ Ⓔ
89. Ⓐ Ⓑ Ⓒ Ⓓ Ⓔ
90. Ⓐ Ⓑ Ⓒ Ⓓ Ⓔ
91. Ⓐ Ⓑ Ⓒ Ⓓ Ⓔ
92. Ⓐ Ⓑ Ⓒ Ⓓ Ⓔ
93. Ⓐ Ⓑ Ⓒ Ⓓ Ⓔ
94. Ⓐ Ⓑ Ⓒ Ⓓ Ⓔ
95. Ⓐ Ⓑ Ⓒ Ⓓ Ⓔ
96. Ⓐ Ⓑ Ⓒ Ⓓ Ⓔ
97. Ⓐ Ⓑ Ⓒ Ⓓ Ⓔ
98. Ⓐ Ⓑ Ⓒ Ⓓ Ⓔ
99. Ⓐ Ⓑ Ⓒ Ⓓ Ⓔ
100. Ⓐ Ⓑ Ⓒ Ⓓ Ⓔ

AP PSYCHOLOGY TEST 1 – ESSAY 1

AP PSYCHOLOGY TEST 1 – ESSAY 2

Advanced Placement Examination in
PSYCHOLOGY — Test 2

1. Ⓐ Ⓑ Ⓒ Ⓓ Ⓔ
2. Ⓐ Ⓑ Ⓒ Ⓓ Ⓔ
3. Ⓐ Ⓑ Ⓒ Ⓓ Ⓔ
4. Ⓐ Ⓑ Ⓒ Ⓓ Ⓔ
5. Ⓐ Ⓑ Ⓒ Ⓓ Ⓔ
6. Ⓐ Ⓑ Ⓒ Ⓓ Ⓔ
7. Ⓐ Ⓑ Ⓒ Ⓓ Ⓔ
8. Ⓐ Ⓑ Ⓒ Ⓓ Ⓔ
9. Ⓐ Ⓑ Ⓒ Ⓓ Ⓔ
10. Ⓐ Ⓑ Ⓒ Ⓓ Ⓔ
11. Ⓐ Ⓑ Ⓒ Ⓓ Ⓔ
12. Ⓐ Ⓑ Ⓒ Ⓓ Ⓔ
13. Ⓐ Ⓑ Ⓒ Ⓓ Ⓔ
14. Ⓐ Ⓑ Ⓒ Ⓓ Ⓔ
15. Ⓐ Ⓑ Ⓒ Ⓓ Ⓔ
16. Ⓐ Ⓑ Ⓒ Ⓓ Ⓔ
17. Ⓐ Ⓑ Ⓒ Ⓓ Ⓔ
18. Ⓐ Ⓑ Ⓒ Ⓓ Ⓔ
19. Ⓐ Ⓑ Ⓒ Ⓓ Ⓔ
20. Ⓐ Ⓑ Ⓒ Ⓓ Ⓔ
21. Ⓐ Ⓑ Ⓒ Ⓓ Ⓔ
22. Ⓐ Ⓑ Ⓒ Ⓓ Ⓔ
23. Ⓐ Ⓑ Ⓒ Ⓓ Ⓔ
24. Ⓐ Ⓑ Ⓒ Ⓓ Ⓔ
25. Ⓐ Ⓑ Ⓒ Ⓓ Ⓔ
26. Ⓐ Ⓑ Ⓒ Ⓓ Ⓔ
27. Ⓐ Ⓑ Ⓒ Ⓓ Ⓔ
28. Ⓐ Ⓑ Ⓒ Ⓓ Ⓔ
29. Ⓐ Ⓑ Ⓒ Ⓓ Ⓔ
30. Ⓐ Ⓑ Ⓒ Ⓓ Ⓔ
31. Ⓐ Ⓑ Ⓒ Ⓓ Ⓔ
32. Ⓐ Ⓑ Ⓒ Ⓓ Ⓔ
33. Ⓐ Ⓑ Ⓒ Ⓓ Ⓔ

34. Ⓐ Ⓑ Ⓒ Ⓓ Ⓔ
35. Ⓐ Ⓑ Ⓒ Ⓓ Ⓔ
36. Ⓐ Ⓑ Ⓒ Ⓓ Ⓔ
37. Ⓐ Ⓑ Ⓒ Ⓓ Ⓔ
38. Ⓐ Ⓑ Ⓒ Ⓓ Ⓔ
39. Ⓐ Ⓑ Ⓒ Ⓓ Ⓔ
40. Ⓐ Ⓑ Ⓒ Ⓓ Ⓔ
41. Ⓐ Ⓑ Ⓒ Ⓓ Ⓔ
42. Ⓐ Ⓑ Ⓒ Ⓓ Ⓔ
43. Ⓐ Ⓑ Ⓒ Ⓓ Ⓔ
44. Ⓐ Ⓑ Ⓒ Ⓓ Ⓔ
45. Ⓐ Ⓑ Ⓒ Ⓓ Ⓔ
46. Ⓐ Ⓑ Ⓒ Ⓓ Ⓔ
47. Ⓐ Ⓑ Ⓒ Ⓓ Ⓔ
48. Ⓐ Ⓑ Ⓒ Ⓓ Ⓔ
49. Ⓐ Ⓑ Ⓒ Ⓓ Ⓔ
50. Ⓐ Ⓑ Ⓒ Ⓓ Ⓔ
51. Ⓐ Ⓑ Ⓒ Ⓓ Ⓔ
52. Ⓐ Ⓑ Ⓒ Ⓓ Ⓔ
53. Ⓐ Ⓑ Ⓒ Ⓓ Ⓔ
54. Ⓐ Ⓑ Ⓒ Ⓓ Ⓔ
55. Ⓐ Ⓑ Ⓒ Ⓓ Ⓔ
56. Ⓐ Ⓑ Ⓒ Ⓓ Ⓔ
57. Ⓐ Ⓑ Ⓒ Ⓓ Ⓔ
58. Ⓐ Ⓑ Ⓒ Ⓓ Ⓔ
59. Ⓐ Ⓑ Ⓒ Ⓓ Ⓔ
60. Ⓐ Ⓑ Ⓒ Ⓓ Ⓔ
61. Ⓐ Ⓑ Ⓒ Ⓓ Ⓔ
62. Ⓐ Ⓑ Ⓒ Ⓓ Ⓔ
63. Ⓐ Ⓑ Ⓒ Ⓓ Ⓔ
64. Ⓐ Ⓑ Ⓒ Ⓓ Ⓔ
65. Ⓐ Ⓑ Ⓒ Ⓓ Ⓔ
66. Ⓐ Ⓑ Ⓒ Ⓓ Ⓔ
67. Ⓐ Ⓑ Ⓒ Ⓓ Ⓔ

68. Ⓐ Ⓑ Ⓒ Ⓓ Ⓔ
69. Ⓐ Ⓑ Ⓒ Ⓓ Ⓔ
70. Ⓐ Ⓑ Ⓒ Ⓓ Ⓔ
71. Ⓐ Ⓑ Ⓒ Ⓓ Ⓔ
72. Ⓐ Ⓑ Ⓒ Ⓓ Ⓔ
73. Ⓐ Ⓑ Ⓒ Ⓓ Ⓔ
74. Ⓐ Ⓑ Ⓒ Ⓓ Ⓔ
75. Ⓐ Ⓑ Ⓒ Ⓓ Ⓔ
76. Ⓐ Ⓑ Ⓒ Ⓓ Ⓔ
77. Ⓐ Ⓑ Ⓒ Ⓓ Ⓔ
78. Ⓐ Ⓑ Ⓒ Ⓓ Ⓔ
79. Ⓐ Ⓑ Ⓒ Ⓓ Ⓔ
80. Ⓐ Ⓑ Ⓒ Ⓓ Ⓔ
81. Ⓐ Ⓑ Ⓒ Ⓓ Ⓔ
82. Ⓐ Ⓑ Ⓒ Ⓓ Ⓔ
83. Ⓐ Ⓑ Ⓒ Ⓓ Ⓔ
84. Ⓐ Ⓑ Ⓒ Ⓓ Ⓔ
85. Ⓐ Ⓑ Ⓒ Ⓓ Ⓔ
86. Ⓐ Ⓑ Ⓒ Ⓓ Ⓔ
87. Ⓐ Ⓑ Ⓒ Ⓓ Ⓔ
88. Ⓐ Ⓑ Ⓒ Ⓓ Ⓔ
89. Ⓐ Ⓑ Ⓒ Ⓓ Ⓔ
90. Ⓐ Ⓑ Ⓒ Ⓓ Ⓔ
91. Ⓐ Ⓑ Ⓒ Ⓓ Ⓔ
92. Ⓐ Ⓑ Ⓒ Ⓓ Ⓔ
93. Ⓐ Ⓑ Ⓒ Ⓓ Ⓔ
94. Ⓐ Ⓑ Ⓒ Ⓓ Ⓔ
95. Ⓐ Ⓑ Ⓒ Ⓓ Ⓔ
96. Ⓐ Ⓑ Ⓒ Ⓓ Ⓔ
97. Ⓐ Ⓑ Ⓒ Ⓓ Ⓔ
98. Ⓐ Ⓑ Ⓒ Ⓓ Ⓔ
99. Ⓐ Ⓑ Ⓒ Ⓓ Ⓔ
100. Ⓐ Ⓑ Ⓒ Ⓓ Ⓔ

AP PSYCHOLOGY TEST 2 – ESSAY 1

AP PSYCHOLOGY TEST 2 – ESSAY 2

Advanced Placement Examination in
PSYCHOLOGY — Test 3

1. Ⓐ Ⓑ Ⓒ Ⓓ Ⓔ
2. Ⓐ Ⓑ Ⓒ Ⓓ Ⓔ
3. Ⓐ Ⓑ Ⓒ Ⓓ Ⓔ
4. Ⓐ Ⓑ Ⓒ Ⓓ Ⓔ
5. Ⓐ Ⓑ Ⓒ Ⓓ Ⓔ
6. Ⓐ Ⓑ Ⓒ Ⓓ Ⓔ
7. Ⓐ Ⓑ Ⓒ Ⓓ Ⓔ
8. Ⓐ Ⓑ Ⓒ Ⓓ Ⓔ
9. Ⓐ Ⓑ Ⓒ Ⓓ Ⓔ
10. Ⓐ Ⓑ Ⓒ Ⓓ Ⓔ
11. Ⓐ Ⓑ Ⓒ Ⓓ Ⓔ
12. Ⓐ Ⓑ Ⓒ Ⓓ Ⓔ
13. Ⓐ Ⓑ Ⓒ Ⓓ Ⓔ
14. Ⓐ Ⓑ Ⓒ Ⓓ Ⓔ
15. Ⓐ Ⓑ Ⓒ Ⓓ Ⓔ
16. Ⓐ Ⓑ Ⓒ Ⓓ Ⓔ
17. Ⓐ Ⓑ Ⓒ Ⓓ Ⓔ
18. Ⓐ Ⓑ Ⓒ Ⓓ Ⓔ
19. Ⓐ Ⓑ Ⓒ Ⓓ Ⓔ
20. Ⓐ Ⓑ Ⓒ Ⓓ Ⓔ
21. Ⓐ Ⓑ Ⓒ Ⓓ Ⓔ
22. Ⓐ Ⓑ Ⓒ Ⓓ Ⓔ
23. Ⓐ Ⓑ Ⓒ Ⓓ Ⓔ
24. Ⓐ Ⓑ Ⓒ Ⓓ Ⓔ
25. Ⓐ Ⓑ Ⓒ Ⓓ Ⓔ
26. Ⓐ Ⓑ Ⓒ Ⓓ Ⓔ
27. Ⓐ Ⓑ Ⓒ Ⓓ Ⓔ
28. Ⓐ Ⓑ Ⓒ Ⓓ Ⓔ
29. Ⓐ Ⓑ Ⓒ Ⓓ Ⓔ
30. Ⓐ Ⓑ Ⓒ Ⓓ Ⓔ
31. Ⓐ Ⓑ Ⓒ Ⓓ Ⓔ
32. Ⓐ Ⓑ Ⓒ Ⓓ Ⓔ
33. Ⓐ Ⓑ Ⓒ Ⓓ Ⓔ

34. Ⓐ Ⓑ Ⓒ Ⓓ Ⓔ
35. Ⓐ Ⓑ Ⓒ Ⓓ Ⓔ
36. Ⓐ Ⓑ Ⓒ Ⓓ Ⓔ
37. Ⓐ Ⓑ Ⓒ Ⓓ Ⓔ
38. Ⓐ Ⓑ Ⓒ Ⓓ Ⓔ
39. Ⓐ Ⓑ Ⓒ Ⓓ Ⓔ
40. Ⓐ Ⓑ Ⓒ Ⓓ Ⓔ
41. Ⓐ Ⓑ Ⓒ Ⓓ Ⓔ
42. Ⓐ Ⓑ Ⓒ Ⓓ Ⓔ
43. Ⓐ Ⓑ Ⓒ Ⓓ Ⓔ
44. Ⓐ Ⓑ Ⓒ Ⓓ Ⓔ
45. Ⓐ Ⓑ Ⓒ Ⓓ Ⓔ
46. Ⓐ Ⓑ Ⓒ Ⓓ Ⓔ
47. Ⓐ Ⓑ Ⓒ Ⓓ Ⓔ
48. Ⓐ Ⓑ Ⓒ Ⓓ Ⓔ
49. Ⓐ Ⓑ Ⓒ Ⓓ Ⓔ
50. Ⓐ Ⓑ Ⓒ Ⓓ Ⓔ
51. Ⓐ Ⓑ Ⓒ Ⓓ Ⓔ
52. Ⓐ Ⓑ Ⓒ Ⓓ Ⓔ
53. Ⓐ Ⓑ Ⓒ Ⓓ Ⓔ
54. Ⓐ Ⓑ Ⓒ Ⓓ Ⓔ
55. Ⓐ Ⓑ Ⓒ Ⓓ Ⓔ
56. Ⓐ Ⓑ Ⓒ Ⓓ Ⓔ
57. Ⓐ Ⓑ Ⓒ Ⓓ Ⓔ
58. Ⓐ Ⓑ Ⓒ Ⓓ Ⓔ
59. Ⓐ Ⓑ Ⓒ Ⓓ Ⓔ
60. Ⓐ Ⓑ Ⓒ Ⓓ Ⓔ
61. Ⓐ Ⓑ Ⓒ Ⓓ Ⓔ
62. Ⓐ Ⓑ Ⓒ Ⓓ Ⓔ
63. Ⓐ Ⓑ Ⓒ Ⓓ Ⓔ
64. Ⓐ Ⓑ Ⓒ Ⓓ Ⓔ
65. Ⓐ Ⓑ Ⓒ Ⓓ Ⓔ
66. Ⓐ Ⓑ Ⓒ Ⓓ Ⓔ
67. Ⓐ Ⓑ Ⓒ Ⓓ Ⓔ

68. Ⓐ Ⓑ Ⓒ Ⓓ Ⓔ
69. Ⓐ Ⓑ Ⓒ Ⓓ Ⓔ
70. Ⓐ Ⓑ Ⓒ Ⓓ Ⓔ
71. Ⓐ Ⓑ Ⓒ Ⓓ Ⓔ
72. Ⓐ Ⓑ Ⓒ Ⓓ Ⓔ
73. Ⓐ Ⓑ Ⓒ Ⓓ Ⓔ
74. Ⓐ Ⓑ Ⓒ Ⓓ Ⓔ
75. Ⓐ Ⓑ Ⓒ Ⓓ Ⓔ
76. Ⓐ Ⓑ Ⓒ Ⓓ Ⓔ
77. Ⓐ Ⓑ Ⓒ Ⓓ Ⓔ
78. Ⓐ Ⓑ Ⓒ Ⓓ Ⓔ
79. Ⓐ Ⓑ Ⓒ Ⓓ Ⓔ
80. Ⓐ Ⓑ Ⓒ Ⓓ Ⓔ
81. Ⓐ Ⓑ Ⓒ Ⓓ Ⓔ
82. Ⓐ Ⓑ Ⓒ Ⓓ Ⓔ
83. Ⓐ Ⓑ Ⓒ Ⓓ Ⓔ
84. Ⓐ Ⓑ Ⓒ Ⓓ Ⓔ
85. Ⓐ Ⓑ Ⓒ Ⓓ Ⓔ
86. Ⓐ Ⓑ Ⓒ Ⓓ Ⓔ
87. Ⓐ Ⓑ Ⓒ Ⓓ Ⓔ
88. Ⓐ Ⓑ Ⓒ Ⓓ Ⓔ
89. Ⓐ Ⓑ Ⓒ Ⓓ Ⓔ
90. Ⓐ Ⓑ Ⓒ Ⓓ Ⓔ
91. Ⓐ Ⓑ Ⓒ Ⓓ Ⓔ
92. Ⓐ Ⓑ Ⓒ Ⓓ Ⓔ
93. Ⓐ Ⓑ Ⓒ Ⓓ Ⓔ
94. Ⓐ Ⓑ Ⓒ Ⓓ Ⓔ
95. Ⓐ Ⓑ Ⓒ Ⓓ Ⓔ
96. Ⓐ Ⓑ Ⓒ Ⓓ Ⓔ
97. Ⓐ Ⓑ Ⓒ Ⓓ Ⓔ
98. Ⓐ Ⓑ Ⓒ Ⓓ Ⓔ
99. Ⓐ Ⓑ Ⓒ Ⓓ Ⓔ
100. Ⓐ Ⓑ Ⓒ Ⓓ Ⓔ

AP PSYCHOLOGY TEST 3 – ESSAY 1

AP PSYCHOLOGY TEST 3 – ESSAY 2

REA's Test Prep Books Are The Best!

(a sample of the <u>hundreds of letters</u> REA receives each year)

" I am writing to congratulate you on preparing an exceptional study guide. In five years of teaching this course I have never encountered a more thorough, comprehensive, concise and realistic preparation for this examination. "
Teacher, Davie, FL

" I have found your publications, *The Best Test Preparation...*, to be exactly that. "
Teacher, Aptos, CA

" I used your *CLEP Introductory Sociology* book and rank it 99% — thank you! "
Student, Jerusalem, Israel

" Your *GMAT* book greatly helped me on the test. Thank you. "
Student, Oxford, OH

" I recently got the *French SAT II* Exam book from REA. I congratulate you on first-rate French practice tests."
Instructor, Los Angeles, CA

" Your *AP English Literature and Composition* book is most impressive."
Student, Montgomery, AL

" The REA *LSAT* Test Preparation guide is a winner! "
Instructor, Spartanburg, SC

(more on front page)